AFTER PROGRESS

AFTER PROGRESS

FINDING THE
OLD WAY FORWARD

ANTHONY O' HEAR

BLOOMSBURY

For my family, Tricia, Natasha, Jacob and Thea,
hope but not progress.

Facing page copyright © The Estate of Evelyn Waugh, 1946.
Reprinted by permission of The Peters Fraser and Dunlop Group Ltd
on behalf of The Estate of Evelyn Waugh.

Published by Bloomsbury Publishing, New York and London.
Distributed to the trade by St. Martin's Press

A CIP catalogue record for this book
is available from the Library of Congress

ISBN 1-58234-040-4

First published in the U.K. by Bloomsbury Publishing Plc 1999
First U.S. Edition 2000
10 9 8 7 6 5 4 3 2 1

Typeset by Hewer Text Ltd, Scotland
Printed in the United States of America by
R.R. Donnelley & Sons Company,
Harrisonburg, Virginia

'What I was going to suggest was – I wonder if you will consider taking some other subject as well as the classics? History, for example, preferably economic history?'

'No, headmaster.'

'But, you know, there may be something of a crisis ahead.'

'Yes, headmaster.'

'Then what do you intend to do?'

'If you approve, headmaster, I will stay here as long as any boy wants to read the classics. I think it would be very wicked indeed to do anything to fit a boy for the modern world.'

'It's a short-sighted view, Scott-King.'

'There, headmaster, with all respect, I differ from you profoundly. I think it is the most long-sighted view it is possible to take.'

(Evelyn Waugh, *Scott-King's Modern Europe*)

Contents

Preface

This book has been written to mark the passing of the second millennium. It is not a celebration of the start of a new millennium. That, indeed, is part of its point. The book is as much about what we have lost at the end of the second thousand years of Christianity as about anything we might have gained. More precisely, it is about how the gains of the past two or three centuries, particularly in the fields of science and democratic politics – which I do not deny are gains in various ways – have, almost inevitably it seems, brought about deep and significant losses. As will emerge, these losses have arisen particularly in the areas once thought of as allied to religion, or close to it, such as art, education, morality and philosophy.

It is not surprising that our national and international celebrations of the millennium are marked by a hesitancy, even an embarrassment about just what it is we are celebrating. Publicly we do not know whether religious themes should play any part in what we will be doing on 1 January 2000. Although it is not written from the standpoint of any dogmatic religion, my book is an attempt to understand and explain this embarrassment. But I hope also to draw positive lessons from our unease and uncertainty. For at the end of the day, the half-light of my pessimism regarding the present is tinged with the dawn of a future optimism. There is still enough in human life and experience to afford grounds for real hope, providing only we rid ourselves of the illusions to which we and our leaders are cripplingly and unthinkingly subject.

In developing this theme I will be drawing on the work of many thinkers, philosophical, political and religious, from classical Greek times to the present day. In some ways, then, this book could serve as an introduction to their thought, or even as a reminder of ideas and truths we once knew, but have collectively preferred to forget.

I make no apology for referring to thinkers of the past or for discussing their ideas in analysing our predicament, as it is at the start of the twenty-first century. It is the thought of Plato and Aristotle, of St Augustine and other thinkers of the Christian tradition, of Bacon and Newton, of Diderot and Voltaire, of Rousseau and Kant, of Burke and Herder, of de Tocqueville and Nietzsche, of Marx, Darwin and Freud, and of their critics and opponents that has made us what we are. If we want to understand our present state, we have to confront the ideas of these and other thinkers of the remote or recent past, and take a stand on them, one way or another. Otherwise we will be simply fumbling in the thickets of the present, unable to see the wood for the trees. I hope that this book will give its readers the perspective necessary to locate themselves in the map of where we are today. Then at least we will have a sense of where we should be going and why we should seek salvation in one place rather than another.

The original idea for the book grew out of a seminar I gave at the joint St Paul's Schools study day in May 1998 on the theme of progress. Even today, even among the young, even (yet more remarkable) in institutions of education, oases of civilization still exist. Another fruitful discussion was with pupils and staff of Wellington College in March 1999, and yet another at about the same time at St Paul's Girls' School. Naturally I have discussed the themes of the book with many people over many years, including Roger Scruton, the late Peter Fuller, David

Matthews, Norman Barry, John Haldane, Bryan Appleyard, Melanie Phillips, Chris Woodhead, George Walden, Richard Addis, Digby Anderson, Roger Fellows, Roger Hausheer, John Gray, and Kenneth Minogue. None will agree with all I have written, and some with very little, but at a time when universities are dominated by academic narrowness, political dogmatism and crass managerialism, one is very grateful for friends of intellectual breadth and generosity.

During the course of the book, I have things to say about the influence of the state on our lives, the extent of its power and the operation of its bureaucracies. While this is not a matter of an intellectual debt in the conventional sense, I should record that my conclusions come from direct experience of politics and bureaucracy. Over seven years I was on three key national educational quangoes in Britain, those overseeing teacher training, the national curriculum and school examinations. I also had direct access to government ministers, including two secretaries of state, and to the Prime Minister's policy unit. I was thus able to observe the workings of government at first hand, and to see for myself how, time and again, policies were altered and distorted by civil servants and lobbyists, how governmental agencies are subject to ideological capture and also to domination by providers of services rather than those who the services are supposed to be for. I also saw how initiatives supposed to decrease the power of the state almost invariably ended up putting more power into the hands of state bureaucracies and those who work in them. This book is not directly about these experiences, but what I learned from them gives substance and backing to my conclusions about moral, social and political trends in advanced democratic societies such as ours.

September 1999

Introduction:
Progress and Its Discontents

As we stand on the brink of the third millennium, the human race may feel justified in a certain complacency. There are far more people on earth than there have ever been. The vast majority of them are better fed, better housed, better clothed and better educated than all but the richest and most powerful in previous generations. Technological and scientific developments have been phenomenal. Alongside the material, there have also been political and ethical advances: equality, democracy and human rights are now part of a worldwide agenda. More, the ideological and religious wars and persecutions that disfigured much of the first twenty centuries since the birth of Christ seem in 1999 largely to have run their course. In much of the world, and certainly in its most prosperous parts, relatively minor differences notwithstanding, we are all basically liberal, fundamentally pacific and reasonably affluent.

But my aim in this book is not to indulge complacency, nor is it to foster millennial celebration or self-congratulation. I do not know whether, in the year 1999, we are on the brink of anything remarkable or worthy of comparison with the achievements of earlier ages. In the fields that interest me most, and some of which seem to me to matter most – religion, education, art, music, literature – it is pretty clear that we are not.

My theme is not progress, but loss. More particularly it is the loss that comes with progress, especially with the sort of progress characteristic of the past few centuries in the West. And here is a scandalous thought. Could it be that the type of material and political progress on which we pride ourselves is actually the cause of spiritual and aesthetic decline?

And not only spiritual and aesthetic decline. There is no evidence that increasing affluence and an increasing insistence on democracy and human rights produce a corresponding growth in individual contentment or happiness. Maybe the opposite is true. People in Britain and the United States, two of the most advanced and affluent societies the world has known, are taking increasingly to psychotherapy and other kinds of treatment to assuage their sense of personal failure and inadequacy (and this although there is no hard evidence that most types of psychological procedure help in these circumstances).

Some, not all of them therapists, would applaud this trend. They argue that it demonstrates that people nowadays have higher expectations of life, are less easily satisfied and less readily fobbed off with illusions than were people in earlier times. None the less the combination of widespread affluence, widespread unhappiness and the absence of self-esteem we hear so much about ought to worry us. Could the root cause of our discontents be lack of inner resources, rather than higher expectations of life? Is there not an abject failure of the plenty we enjoy to supply that lack? Might the therapies to which so many of us run actually contribute to the ills they claim to cure by promoting lopsided ideas of human fulfilment? Could it also be that the notions of human rights and equality, which are so prominent a feature of our modern consciousness, fail to prepare people for the fundamental fact that not all are equal, that not all can achieve equally, that they leave us unable to cope with what is inevitably the condition of each of us in one or more respects?

Of course, not everyone will accept that we are in a time of spiritual and aesthetic decline. During the course of this book I will defend the claim that we are, in such a way that I hope even those who disagree with it will come to understand what might be meant by talking in these terms, and why what has happened might be thought of as decline. A hint, though, of what is meant might be given by comparing the vacuity and incoherence of Britain's £750 million Millennium Dome project with the plenitude and integrity of a medieval Gothic cathedral: on the one hand, an empty canopy with no clear reasoning about what should go in it, and uncertainty as to whether it has any religious content at all; on the other hand a structure containing every aspect of the medieval world, all unified architecturally and symbolically in the service of an overarching and inspiring vision. We might also consider how it is that Britain, the nation which produced Constable and Turner, Henry Moore and Graham Sutherland, should in the late 1990s choose as officially representative of its 'cool' and 'flourishing' artistic scene animal corpses, images of human excrement and videotapes of bodily orifices.

More generally, we need to consider the implication of the view – accepted without question in so many fields today – that (as a sign on an American building site had it) we should be 'knocking down yesterday to build tomorrow'. What about today, one feels like asking. In any case, where do our identity, our values and our knowledge come from but yesterday? And how can we be so certain about the worth of tomorrow if we are starting from nowhere? One of the most telling and frightening images of recent times is the cover of Bill Gates's book: a picture of Gates himself, and behind him an empty road in a trackless, featureless desert.

Political slate-cleaning in the Leninist mode is no longer in fashion, but the progressivist cast of mind that inspired and underlay it is very much alive and well, all the more dangerous for the way it is accepted without question in so many fields, as if it were nothing more than a harmless cliché. Is Gates the gateway to the future? And what sort of future would it be, without tradition, meaning or human resonance?

It is no part of the argument of this book that affluence is a bad thing or that population levels should be pegged back to those of earlier centuries. Environmentalists who advocate population reduction should explain just how they would achieve this goal – and it is hard not to sympathize with non-Europeans who feel that insistence on population control ill becomes members of nations who after centuries of exponential growth appear rather late in the day to have grown weary and unfruitful. Nor is it suggested that democracy and human rights are in themselves undesirable. Correctly interpreted, they are not. They have been used to correct many injustices and abuses. Further, once in place, there is no nonviolent or unrepressive way of removing them. Like the science and the critical rationality with which they and material affluence have been closely associated historically and conceptually, they are here to stay.

The point is rather that in the journey over the last few centuries to where we are now, there has been loss as well as gain, and that the loss and the gain are inextricably intertwined. We are free to welcome the rise of democracy, of science and of rationality. We can call these things progress, if we like. But it is not progress all the way. We need also to consider what we have lost on the journey, whether that loss was inevitable, and how many of our most cherished assumptions we need to jettison if we are to repair the loss. That, anyway, is the story I want to tell. In telling it I will consider first how we arrived at where we are today. I will then look at some of those thinkers from the past who would have suspected the very idea of progress, let alone what we might consider progress. For if we are to make any headway intellectually and spiritually as we enter the third millennium, the first notion we have to deconstruct is that of progress itself, and the first illusion that of the soaraway future.

We need to ask why it is that, despite all our progress, so many of us are unhappy today. Is it because of our progress? The examination of philosophers and thinkers of the past on which we are about to embark may seem to some a strange way to examine our current predicament. But it has to be done if we are to understand ourselves. For it is the ideas expressed and articulated by the thinkers we are about to examine that have made us what we are today. And if we want to find ways out of our morass, might not the best hope be to look at some of those who did not accept what have come to be the clichés of today's discourse of progress?

I

Images of Enlightenment

It is commonplace these days to attack what is called 'scientific rationality' and to pour scorn on Enlightenment values. All manner of post-modernists, feminists, deconstructionists and new age thinkers do so. But they tend to do so partially and uncritically, retaining the Enlightenment's most potent image.

It is not just that the critics accept the bits of science and technology on which they rely while in their rhetoric rejecting the bits they find offensive. More profoundly, we are all in some measure in thrall to the notion that we can become enlightened if only we purge ourselves of the prejudices of the past. In our time this assumption is so pervasive that we easily overlook that it is only comparatively recently in the history of human thought that progress has come to be seen as systematic forgetfulness of the past. Indeed, as we will see, for the two thousand years following Plato it was just as characteristic of Western thought to regard the future with foreboding, and to see the hope for civilization as lying in the recovery of what had been lost: renaissance or revival, rather than the clean sheet of scientific progress; 'these fragments I have shored against my ruins' rather than the rubble clearing of enlightenment progressivism.

All this, of course, is metaphor, on the one side or the other. Further, in contrast to pagan notions of decline and of the need to recover what had been lost, the Judaeo-Christian tradition furnishes us with strong images of hope for the future, of the ideal being in the future. The Messiah, the Last Judgement, heaven itself, all embody radical critiques of the present and of the past along with the promise of things infinitely better to come. In that sense, the scientific Enlightenment and its associated political and ethical visions can reasonably be seen as secular versions of old religion. Unfortunately, in these secular reworkings, truths central to the old religions have been systematically distorted and falsified, truths which, in these enlightened days, most of us are reluctant to admit.

Francis Bacon: The Shattering of the Idols

One of the earliest and most forceful proponents of Enlightenment rationality and of forgetfulness in the service of progress was the English statesman and philosopher Francis Bacon. In his *Novum Organum* of 1620, Bacon expresses much of what in the years to come was to be seen as commonplace. Providing it was pursued systematically, and with rigour and objectivity, modern science would isolate the true causes of things.

By contrast, medieval science had been dominated by the philosophy of Aristotle and the dogmas of the Church. As a result it had been little more than an amalgam of haphazard and unreliable information and sheer superstition. The medieval scientist, according to Bacon, 'did not consult experience, as he should have done for the purpose of framing his decisions and axioms, but having first determined the question according to his will, he then resorts to experience, and bending her into conformity with his placets, leads her about like a captive in a procession'.

This is to get things exactly the wrong way round. If we want to command nature, we must begin by obeying her, by patient, systematic and unprejudiced observation. Then and only then will we understand the true causes of things. Then for the first time will we be able to manipulate nature in a systematic way for our benefit, which is what science is really for. In the Baconian scheme of things, the overall aim of science was indeed and in his words 'the relief of man's estate'.

Science's aim, then, was not to glorify God, or even to glorify man. Nor was it to achieve wisdom or, Faust-like, to probe the mysteries of the universe. It was to relieve man's estate. Thus, as early as 1620, we find the philosophy that today prefers kidney machines to symphony orchestras, and would turn ancient churches into 'community centres', selling their works of art to provide crèches and set up mother-and-toddler groups. We find already in Bacon the obsessive harping on happiness in a material sense, which makes our life today so mediocre in so many ways, which forgets that what is really worthwhile can be achieved only through struggle and suffering, that there are aims in life higher than the elimination of pain and the cultivation of pleasure.

And in relieving man's estate, what is sought is primarily the lowest common denominator: the promotion of pleasure and the reduction of pain, that which we all share and which, as Jeremy Bentham was to make explicit two hundred years later, we also share with animals. So, as a result of ever-increasing democratic inclusiveness, animals as well as the whole of the human race become part of the moral community, and this despite the obvious fact that there is no way animals can recognize duties of their own or play a genuine part in any moral community. Nevertheless, at the end of the twentieth century the relief of man's estate is subject to the proviso, shouted with ever-increasing stridency, that it should not be at the expense of the estates of other sentient beings, logical enough if all that counts morally are pleasure and pain, but otherwise destructive and disastrous.

Bacon's methods were as reductionist and as levelling as his aims. The key idea was fundamentally negative: the destruction of the 'idols' that held our minds captive. These were the idols of the tribe, illusions foisted on us by the limitations of our perceptions; the idols of the cave, the various prejudices and biases individuals bring to their enquiries; the idols of the marketplace, confusions due to human language; and the idols of the theatre, philosophical systems and theories that obstruct the unprejudiced observation of nature.

What scientists had to do was to 'lay their notions by and begin to familiarize themselves with facts'. We must 'begin anew from the very foundations, unless we would revolve for ever in a circle with mean and contemptible progress'. Above all, we must not assume any correspondence between our minds and the natural world. Such an assumption had been the undoing of medieval science, a fatal proneness to assume that the natural order of things would conform immediately to our ideas of how it should be: 'all depends on keeping the eye steadily fixed upon the facts of nature and receiving the images simply as they are. For God forbid that we should give out a dream of our own imagining for a pattern of the world.'

The true scientist is he or she who is prepared to 'try the whole thing anew on a better plan, and to commence a total reconstruction of sciences, arts, and all human knowledge raised upon the proper foundations'. In his utopian text *The New Atlantis*, Bacon envisages a whole society run by scientists. Living in a kind of priestly community, they study and interpret nature, using their discoveries to 'produce great and marvellous works for the benefit of mankind'.

In *The New Atlantis*, the scientists are in effect the rulers. They decide what of their discoveries shall be communicated to the public at large. It is their discoveries that determine what will count as the relief of man's estate, and what shall be done. Through what they discover we can do, they define the direction of society and human life. It is on their foundations that the reconstruction of science, the arts and humanity itself is based. And this is to be done in conscious rejection of ancient wisdom and prejudice, a state of affairs close to realization in 1999. In 1999 scientific developments, particularly in the fields of genetics and medicine, are laying to waste ancient conceptions of the sacredness of life and of human life. Science is pushing the development of our systems of value, and not vice versa. At a deep level, science is not value-free, but itself determines the erosion of value, by what it makes possible and by what it seems to be telling us about ourselves.

In Bacon we find the characteristic Enlightenment stress on science, and on the scientific method as essentially the absence of prejudice and presupposition. What, indeed, is enlightenment (*Aufklärung*) but allowing light to shine in dark corners? What are prejudices but shadows falling across what would otherwise be clear? Like some of his contemporaries and many of his successors, Bacon had a vivid sense of himself as a pioneer. He was striking out anew after centuries of obfuscation by dogmatic and repressive authorities, by the encrustations of age, and by the sheer laziness and complacency of custom, language and tradition. Bacon wrote, 'What happiness it would be to throw myself into the river Lethe, to erase completely from my soul all knowledge, all art, all poetry; what happiness it would be to reach the opposite shore, naked like the first man.'

Notwithstanding his own evocative use of classical allusion, Bacon campaigned against the foundation of Charterhouse School on the grounds that its curriculum was to be based on the ancient classics. Renaissance ideals were in another world from that foreshadowed by Bacon.

By the 1990s Bacon's wishes in respect of classical learning had been granted. In Britain, these days, examinations in Latin and what is called classical civilization are taken by less than 3 per cent of sixteen-year-olds, while ancient Greek is practically non-existent in schools. At A level, out of 750,000 papers taken annually by our brightest eighteen-year-olds, olds, barely 7,000 are in classical subjects. The fastest growing disciplines, if that is the correct term, are media studies and sports science, while governmental efforts concentrate on getting pupils to study business and technical subjects.

But it is not just in education that we are living in a Baconian world. The idea of scientific enlightenment has penetrated deep into the mentality of the twentieth century, so much so that many of its presuppositions are taken for granted by many who would see themselves as critics of our actual practice of science. During the course of the book, we will see over and over again the way scientific developments and theories have affected our most precious insights and beliefs. Science does not and cannot leave everything else as it is. In its very pretension to complete unprejudiced objectivity, it dismisses everything that does not fit into its framework as mere superstition. It is here that, if we have a care for the human world, we must begin to resist the imperialism of science, its claim to be able to tell us everything about the world and what we are.

Bacon himself made no contribution to science. There were also ways in which his philosophy of science would actually have impeded scientific progress, had anyone actually followed it. For example, it was not philosophical presuppositions that held up medieval science. In so far as it was actually held up, it was the wrong philosophical presuppositions. Bacon's actual scientific contemporaries – Kepler, Brahe, Galileo and Descartes – were very influenced by philosophy, as was Newton later, and indeed Bacon himself, in his case by the philosophical presupposition that progress might be achieved by abandoning presuppositions altogether.

But in the seventeenth century the ideology of mental slate-cleaning and rational investigation *de novo* was immensely powerful. It seemed to reflect what was actually happening at the time. For the sixteenth and seventieth centuries were a period of astonishing scientific advance. In astronomy and physics there were Copernicus, Galileo and Kepler; in mathematics, Descartes and Pascal; in medicine and biology, Vesalius, Harvey and van Leeuwenhoek; in chemistry, Boyle and Hooke. The key to the advance appeared to be observation, observation and more observation – dissection, the telescope and the microscope. And there was Newton.

Newton's World Machine

It was above all Newton's achievement on which the Enlightenment thinking of the eighteenth century rested, and the model to which thinking and research in areas way beyond physics and astronomy were to aspire. What Newton did was to show that the vast majority of movements throughout the universe could be explained in terms of three simple mathematical laws. These laws governed the operation of forces, which for Newton famously included the force of gravity as well as the action by contact of billiard balls and the like.

In Newton's words the laws are:

1. Every body continues in its state of rest, or of uniform motion in a right (that is, straight) line, unless it is compelled to change that state by forces impressed upon it.

2. The change of motion is proportional to the motive force impressed; and is made in the direction of the right line in which that force is impressed.

3. To every action there is always opposed an equal reaction; or the mutual action of two bodies upon each other is always equal, and is directed to contrary parts.

In fact, pre-Einstein it was generally believed that the behaviour of every particle of every body, in the heavens, on earth and in the microscopic realm, could be explained and predicted with complete accuracy and precision on Newtonian principles. It was a staggering and audacious achievement, and hardly surprising that it came to dominate men's minds for centuries.

For what Newton was telling us was that, despite all surface differences, billiard balls, farmers' carts, the tides and winds, the rotation of the planets and everything else, even the falling of a leaf, operated on the same principles. Moreover, they were pre-ordained or determined to operate as they did. Further, Newton showed that for the purposes of scientific explanation the appearances of things – their colour, feel, taste, sound and smell – could be ignored. These so-called secondary qualities, the features of things so prominent in our perception of the world, could be reduced to and explained in terms of the Newtonian movements of colourless, tasteless, soundless and textureless particles. Colour, for example, was produced by colourless particles, moving at great speed hitting our retinal surfaces and causing colour sensations in our brains. Similarly sound, as in a bell or musical instrument, is, in Newton's words, nothing but a 'trembling motion propagated in the air' that we perceive as sound.

Newton's own theories did not directly cover chemical reactions or biological processes. But the assumption was that such things would before long be brought within the ambit of Newtonian principles. After all, had not Newton shown – in the face of centuries of tradition and dogma and mystical nonsense to the contrary – that what went on in the heavens was, in principle, no different from what went on down here on earth? And had he not shown that things like colour and sound could be reduced to more basic properties, so why not reactions in chemistry and life itself?

In Newton's own phrase, all these things were revealed by 'experimental philosophy', that is, simply inferred from the patient and systematic analysis of phenomena. '*Hypotheses non fingo*', he said, 'I do not invent hypotheses.' But his non-hypotheses disenchanted the world. They deprived it not just of the secondary qualities that dominate our perception of it: the Newtonian world was also regular, predictable and determined as a piece of clockwork. Contained within the New-tonian universe was the dream (or the nightmare) of the superhuman Intelligence of the mathematician Laplace.

Laplace, who lived from 1749 to 1827, did much to iron out problems in the Newtonian system. He showed, for example, that the movements of the planets were entirely consistent with Newton's laws and required no divine interventions to explain them. He went on to dream of a superhuman Intelligence who, armed with knowledge of Newton's laws and of the state of the universe at just one particular time, would thereby be able to know everything about every other state of the universe. To such an Intelligence, 'nothing would be uncertain, and the future, as the past, would be present to its eyes'. The nightmare of total determinism, of the complete absence of freedom and chance in the world, was upon us.

Laplace's Intelligence was superhuman only in its detailed knowledge of all the states of the universe at a given time. As Laplace put it, 'the human mind offers, in the perfection which it has been able to give to astronomy, a feeble idea of this Intelligence'. Feeble it might be, but as Newton's science was applied in increasing detail and depth, we humans appeared to be approaching the condition of the Intelligence to an ever greater degree. Laplace's Intelligence might have been the limiting case of the Newtonian scientist, but it was a limit to which we were getting ever closer.

Newton himself did not attempt to extend his methods or his theories into the human realm. Nor was he a materialist or an atheist. In fact, he dabbled in alchemy, in biblical theology and appears to have been inspired by an almost mystical belief in the godhead expressing himself in the universe he con-structed on strictly mathematical principles and in which he had to intervene to maintain its stability.

But those thinkers of subsequent centuries most influenced by Newton's achievements did not share his inhibitions or restraints. Laplace showed that the solar system could get on perfectly well on Newtonian principles without any help from God. More radically, it became clear that if human beings were also part of the material world described by Newton, then surely human nature must be explicable in terms similar to the other types of things in that world. As material beings, our behaviour and activity must be as predictable and determined as the other types of object that fell under the Newtonian laws. Human freedom, then, was an illusion, and would be seen to be once the science of human behaviour was worked out.

And so, increasingly, was God. Once Newtonian science had finally and completely triumphed, there would be no need of God to explain any particular event anywhere in the universe. Newton's laws would be enough. God was, at most, some remote, increasingly withdrawn and distant entity that put the whole process in motion in the beginning; at best a hypothesis of which, for all practical purposes, one had no need, because God impinges on us in no way at all. As Laplace put it when questioned on the subject of the divinity by Napoleon, 'Sire, je n'ai pas eu besoin de cette hypothèse', a position virtually indistinguishable from atheism.

Enlightenment Optimism: Science, Reason and Society

All these consequences of the Newtonian world-view were drawn by the so-called Enlightenment thinkers of the eight-eenth century. Men like Voltaire and Diderot, Condillac and Condorcet, d'Alembert and Helvetius, La Mettrie and Holbach were writers, encyclopedists and philosophers (and not philo-sophers of the first rank), rather than scientists. But in their writings they defined the spirit of their age, and to a consider-able degree of ours. They drew the conclusions that followed or that seemed to follow from the new science of the seventeenth century and its successes. They applied its lessons to the whole of experience, including human experience.

There were, of course, many differences between the various thinkers of the Enlightenment. Voltaire, for example, held a high-minded belief in a remote and distant God as first cause of the universe, whereas Diderot was an atheist; Voltaire consorted with rulers, whereas Diderot attacked benevolent despotism, and d'Alembert was a republican. But what united them all was a spirit, a drive and an optimism, all based on the sense that after centuries of intellectual and political stagnation, by analogy with the success of Newton in the physical world, human reason was about to usher in an era of unprecedented harmony and light.

For Voltaire, enlightenment was above all a matter of removing the obstacles that stood in the way of intellectual and human progress: censorship, the Church, the nobility, the *ancien régime* – all vested interests conspiring to keep men in ignorance and submission. '*Écrasez l'infâme*' was his watchword; crush the infamy, get rid of religious dogmatism, superstition and fanaticism, for 'those who can make you believe absurdities can make you commit atrocities'. The aim of any society and its laws ought to be the happiness and freedom of its individual citizens. History is mankind's progressive struggle for rational culture, and in the eighteenth century we are well on the way to removing the obstacles to progress.

Voltaire shared with all Enlightenment thinkers a strong sense that the religion and philosophy of the past had diminished mankind. For what, in the West, did that religion say? It said that men were as children before their Heavenly Father, and errant children to boot. Not only was God totally superior to man, and man totally dependent on God. Not only would man achieve happiness only when he humbled himself before God and obeyed God's plans. Not only were our fate and our destiny not in our own hands. Above all this, man was in a state of sin and congenital weakness. Man could do nothing without the continual intervention of divine grace, a grace bestowed according to principles of God's own choosing, on terms largely obscure to human reason or our sense of justice.

Not only did the need to submit to a divine order outside us and to the whims of an apparently capricious God find little resonance in the world order revealed by modern science. Its already unbelievable precepts became doubly incredible when one looked at the custodians of the true faith and their natural allies and supporters: the corrupt and shifty Catholic Church and the absolute monarchs of Catholic Christendom. In Christianity as actually practised, Voltaire found persecution, dissension, fanaticism, infamous morals and absurd doctrines upheld by atrocity, all commonplace thoughts these days, but radical enough in the eighteenth century. Exaggerated as Voltaire's message was when he announced it, he at least had the excuse that he was saying something new and striking; in addition he had not had our century's experience of the persecutions and atrocities of explicitly humanistic and anti-religious tyrannies.

Compared to the cruelty and belittling of human reason Voltaire found in Roman Catholicism, he and his followers saw something immensely liberating in the calm and rational empiricism espoused by Bacon and developed by Locke and the thinkers of the British-scientific tradition. From the premise that all our beliefs and dogmas must be tested in the experience of individuals honestly and without prejudice seeking the truth, both political liberalism and scientific rationalism seemed to follow. For Voltaire, as for Locke, the elevation of mankind to intellectual and political adulthood seemed to be imminent. And Voltaire praised Locke above all for his attempts to analyse the human mind scientifically, without prejudice and through patient observation of its workings, just as Newton had ana-lysed nature. In contrast to the mystical outpourings on the soul, which emanated from metaphysicians of previous ages, Locke was the first to bring empirical principles to the study of the history and development of the mind in the same spirit as 'an excellent anatomist unfolds the mechanisms of the human body'.

If it was Voltaire above all who provided the rhetoric for the politics and anti-religious tenor of the Enlightenment, the underlying ideology was ineluctably materialist, atheist and scientific. For the encyclopedist Diderot, the philosophers Holbach and La Mettrie, and the mathematician Condorcet, the human mind and society were to be analysed and explained scientifically, just as physical bodies were being taken apart and reduced by Newtonian physics. Social and psychological science would reveal the springs of human activity to be fundamentally the search for pleasure and the avoidance of pain. With this knowledge we would be able to free ourselves from the shackles of instinct, passion, prejudice and oppressive and mendacious traditions, making us out to be things we were not. Once we understood how men and societies were formed and the basis on which they operated, we would be able to construct a new world order in which the freedom and desires of myriad individuals would be harmonized in a realm of universal peace and order.

For were not all men equal in their possession of reason, and also in their basic need to seek pleasure and avoid pain? Was it not simply the operation of prejudice, dogmatism and self-serving superstitions that were preventing mankind from realizing its true destiny? In Condorcet's terms the destiny of humanity was to re-establish 'the rights and dignity of its nature', by founding an 'Elysium which reason knows how to create'. In this Elysium, the crime and injustice that 'still sully the earth' will be vanquished once and for all, along with greed and fear, envy and want. Hence the liberty, equality and fraternity of the French Revolution.

But already, even in the first flush of Enlightenment optimism, cracks could be discerned. The very revolution Condorcet had welcomed was forcing him to flee for his life in 1793, even as he was writing his inspiring words about the Elysium of science and reason. His death in a Jacobin prison in 1794 was just one of the multitude of revolutionary crimes, injustices and cruelties which before the end of the eighteenth century made the despised *ancien régime* look like a paradise of light and harmony.

But the difficulties with the Enlightenment project did not arise solely from the practicalities of its political implementation, though these should never be underestimated. In typically bullish style in his encyclopedia article on eclecticism, Diderot had been insistent that the true philosopher would 'trample underfoot prejudice, tradition, venerability, universal assent, authority – in a word, everything that overawes the crowd'. He will dare to think for himself and admit nothing 'save on the testimony of his own reason and experience'. In the same spirit, Condorcet had written in his significantly entitled 'Sketch of a Historical Picture of the Progress of the Human Spirit', published posthumously in 1795:

> It is at last permitted to proclaim loudly the right so long unrecognized, of submitting all opinions to examination by our own reason. We must, in other words, use the only instrument which has been given to us to seize the truth. Every individual comes to learn, with a sort of pride, that nature has not destined him to have to rely in belief on the say-so of another.

But what if the reasoning and experiences of different people come up with different and conflicting conclusions? Whose proud reason is to hold sway? And what did equality of reason amount to in practice? Was everyone, however able or stupid, however liberated in thought or unthinkingly attached to old prejudices, to have an equal voice? Are we, as idealists of all stripes are constantly urging, to submit all policies to popular referenda? Unhappily, as is now all too clear, any such extension of consumer values into the political realm is likely to come up with very poor results from the point of view of the Enlightenment, in favour of capital punishment, nationalism, punitive treatment of those incapable of doing a day's work and all kinds of similarly atavistic values. Are those who favour such things any less proud, any less using their reason than their enlightened opponents? (That is probably what would be said, but it seems to indicate a degree of arrogance rather beyond Condorcet's pride.)

And what if it were not possible to harmonize everyone's pleasures and pains? Or some people had incorrigibly evil wills and perverse desires? And if pleasure and pain are the true and the only mainsprings of human action, what becomes of our higher goals and aspirations, including the much-vaunted quest for reason itself? And finally, and most problematic of all, if we are scientifically explicable – in the end no different from the particles and planets of the Newtonian system and just like them determined to act as they do by laws and forces over which they have no control – what becomes of freedom, morality and human dignity?

Not a lot, according to La Mettrie:

When I do good or evil; when I am virtuous in the morning, vicious in the evening, it is my blood that is the cause of it . . . Nevertheless, I persist in believing I have made a choice; I congratulate myself on my liberty . . . What fools we are! Fools all the more unhappy, for that we reproach ourselves ceaselessly for having done what it was not in our power not to do.

Enlightenment optimism thus irretrievably shatters under the weight of its own contradictions. Reason is identified with science. Negatively this amounts to the destruction of religion, an idle hypothesis in the Newtonian scheme. In one sense, and particularly at the outset, this is invigorating and liberating. Mankind will take control of its own destiny, free from irrationalism, prejudice and superstition. Unfortunately, though, the model of man that science and reason reveal is reductionist, dark and unflattering.

The quasi-Newtonian forces determining human action are pleasure and pain. Just as in Newtonian science the secondary qualities of colour, feel, sound, taste and smell are shown to be mere appearance, so in the new scientific psychology all our airs and graces are no more than vehicles for the satisfaction of pleasure and the avoidance of pain. Holbach made the connection between Newtonian physics and moral psychology explicit:

> Self-preservation is the common goal towards which all energies, forces, and human faculties seem continuously directed. Scientists have named this tendency or direction gravitation to a centre. Newton calls it the force of inertia, moralists have called it in man self-love . . . the tendency to preserve oneself . . . the love of well-being and pleasure.

And again, in the words of La Mettrie:

> The soul is an empty symbol of which one has no conception, and which a sound mind could employ only in order to denote that which thinks in us. Given the least principle of movement, animate bodies will possess all they need in order to move, sense, think, repeat and behave, in a word, all they want of the physical; and of the mental, too, which depends thereon.

The nemesis of the Enlightenment is to be found in the theories of Marx, Darwin and Freud, all essentially Enlightenment figures, all rationalists to their fingertips, but who reveal, or purport to reveal, the subterfuges to which this psychological inertia will go to keep what La Mettrie and Holbach called the human machine in a state of internal balance. Ultimately the mind is just the brain, part of the physical body, in particular states, serving the aims of the rest of the physical body. What it – as the rest of the body – does, is as unfree and determined by factors outside its control as is the behaviour of any other bit of nature.

As we shall see, for all the talk of fraternity, brotherhood and harmony, morality can hardly survive once it is accepted that pleasure and pain are the only determinants of human activity. For where within the Newtonian universe and the pleasure-pain psychology is any room for 'ought'? We just have these pleasures and pains. We are forced to act on their imperatives. They are what they are. Beyond what they are, there is no good or evil, no sense that one pleasure is better than another, or some vicious or insupportable. The criminal and the pervert are not to be blamed or punished, but at most pitied and reformed, their desires brought into conformity with the rest of society.

The problem, then, with a Frederick West or a Peter Sutcliffe or a Mary Bell is not an evil will, but bad upbringing and an unhygienic mix of emotions. They need diagnosis and cure, not punishment and reproach. Not that this line of thought increases individual freedom. On the contrary, by denying choice at the moral level, it actually licenses the compulsory incarceration of people deemed possible or potential psychopaths, who are deemed to have no control over what they do or feel until 'cured' by drugs or behavioural therapy – a measure actually being introduced by Jack Straw, the British Home Secretary in 1999.

With telling symbolism, one of the few prisoners of the

ancien régime actually in the Bastille in July 1789 was the Marquis de Sade. Was de Sade not, in a perverse sense, a true child of the Enlightenment? Not just in the relentlessly mechanistic way he treated human behaviour, but rather more in his pretension to be a scientist of human nature, bringing a shameless honesty to bear on our passions. And what, anyway, from the point of view of the pleasure–pain psychology is so wrong with the practices he describes?

As de Sade himself put it:

> Nothing is forbidden us by nature . . . [Laws], those popular restraints, reflect nothing sacred, nothing legitimate in the eyes of philosophy, whose flame dispels all errors and leaves in the eyes of the wise man only the aspirations of nature; she has never imposed limits upon us, nor has she dictated us laws.

De Sade is right. There is, in fact, no room within Enlightenment philosophy and psychology for any condemnation. We are natural beings, subject to natural forces, as unfree and constrained as any other part of nature. In a true democracy of passion and taste, supported by its scientific claims, the Enlightenment in a sense liberates and legitimates de Sade. It is, after all, as would be said in a later idiom, just a matter of whatever turns you on.

But it is not just morality that Enlightenment rationality subverts. There is also rationality itself. For if we are just bits of the Newtonian world-machine, caused to act by Newtonian forces themselves blind and unresponsive to anything but the laws of physics, how can we be said to be free in our thoughts? How can we actually judge according to the canons of truth and in the light of reason, if − in reality − all we do is determined by forces that know nothing of truth or reason, those same forces that, equally non-rationally, determine the winds, the tides, falling stones and all the rest of nature? And if

24

all we do is determined by our body's need to gain pleasure and avoid pain, won't any purportedly rational activity simply be a cloak for more self-interested and less rational purposes?

As we will see, these questions will take on more dramatic pertinence as we examine the development of rationalism in the nineteenth and twentieth centuries. But the general shape of the story is already clear. Enlightenment rationality promised to free mankind from irrational and ignoble domination by corrupt and ignorant authorities, particularly those of a religious nature. But the chosen means of liberation – Newtonian science and its extension into the human realm – revealed human nature itself to be determined through and through by non-rational forces. The ennobling of man through reason, then, turns out in practice to destroy the basis of his self-respect. While science has certainly been the agent of the material progress on which our current optimism and Utopianism depends, it has been at the same time the agent that has brought us and our pretensions down. If Francis Bacon (the other Francis Bacon) is the quintessential painter of the late twentieth century, in his cruel and merciless exposure of everything dignified about our humanity, all he is doing is pushing to its logical conclusion a tendency that seemed, when it began, to be ushering in humanity's most optimistic moment.

David had seemed to be the quintessential painter of the Enlightenment, with his images of noble and rational Romans defying sentiment in the name of reason: Brutus receiving the bodies of his own sons, whom he had condemned to death for treachery, the Horatii swearing their patriotic oath unto death. But this was an illusion. What the Enlightenment actually unleashed was a quite different vision of human nature, that captured by Bacon with his screaming popes and hurried, loveless couplings under naked lightbulbs: human beings as raw, febrile creatures, driven alternately by lust, by fear and by violence.

2

The Counter-Enlightenment

The contrasts are easy to state. If the Enlightenment stressed reason, the Counter-enlightenment stressed feeling. If the Enlightenment stressed science and modern civilization, the Counter-Enlightenment stressed nature and the primitive life. It looked within, into our hearts, where the Enlightenment sought objectivity. Further, the Counter-Enlightenment emphasized the diversity of human society, and questioned the very notion of progress that saw modern societies as better than ancient or primitive ones.

Human nature was not universal, it was particular and historical: different peoples had their own cultures and norms, and they could not be compared or judged except prejudicially – from the point of one society or the other. And where the Enlightenment sought to found social institutions on human reason and human choices, the Counter-Enlightenment looked for religious foundations for society and morality. Finally, where the Enlightenment would submit all old beliefs to the test by contemporary scientific reason, the Counter-Enlightenment saw virtue in habits and beliefs just because they were old, because they had stood the test of time, because they embodied ancient and not necessarily immediately discernible wisdom.

However, despite the overt contrasts, apart from the elevation of old prejudice as a good and the quest for divine foundations, Counter-Enlightenment themes have become very much part of our modern condition, in some cases joining seamlessly with Enlightenment ideas. Nowhere is this more true than with the stress on subjectivity and on the naturalness and innocence of desire, which we first find in the thought of Rousseau.

Rousseau

Today, many of us place a higher value on what is natural than on what has been produced artificially or technologically, even as surrounded by high-tech gadgets and supports we take for granted. We yearn, somewhat fruitlessly, for a return to a simple life in harmony with nature – a fact well known to advertisers and the Body Shop; we decry consumerism and competition as eroding community and fraternity, and we see the happiness and organic development of the individual child as the keys to a humane style of education. All these attitudes, almost articles of faith for so many in the 1990s, have their roots in the writings and influence of Jean-Jacques Rousseau, the one-time associate and later the scourge of the advocates of the French Enlightenment.

Way before his time, Rousseau was master of the sound-bite: 'Everywhere man is born free; everywhere he is in chains'; 'God makes all things good, man meddles with them, and they become evil'; 'Let us lay it down as an incontrovertible rule that the first impulses of nature are always right'; 'You are undone if you once forget that the fruits of the earth belong to us all and the earth itself to no one.' So, there is no original sin in the human heart. We should advocate freedom rather than re-straint; we should cultivate the innocence of nature and the purity of the human heart against the wickedness of human institutions; we should see property and what we call culture as originating in depravity. Rousseau elaborated his theories of human nature, politics and education in the 1750s and 1760s.

Revolutionary as they may have been then, such thoughts are almost commonplace at the end of the twentieth century. But if man is born free and the human heart pure, where did wickedness, oppression and servitude come from?

Rousseau's answer, unconvincing as it is in the final analysis, has a powerful resonance still. So long as we are simply attempting to preserve our own existence and satisfy our own natural physical and psychological needs (food, shelter, sex), so long as we look good within, all is good. It is when we start making odious comparisons without, with other people, that the problems start. Vanity and the consequent treadmill of competition is what corrupts us, and it corrupts us endlessly and hopelessly. For, luvvie-like, the desire for praise and reassurance from others is insatiable, once we come to rely on it. And it leads us not just to attempt to keep up with our neighbours in a material sense.

It leads also to the more pernicious extravagances of high culture: useless and harmful scientific research, scholarship and learning that improve none morally or mentally, and ever more ornate and decadent productions in the arts. In Rousseau's view, none of these useless and ultimately harmful activities of 'high' culture would occur, were men – and women – not motivated by the sort of self-regarding vanity that fuels productions such as *Vogue* and *Vanity Fair*, and with which high culture has more than a passing similarity.

What we need to do is to eschew extravagance, ostentation and cleverness, and return to the peasant-like simplicity of manner and taste. Rousseau practised what he preached by writing music of an almost ostentatious plainness and, it might be said, tedium. As he himself put it, 'the world of reality has its bounds, the world of the imagination is boundless; as we cannot enlarge the one, let us restrict the other'. 'We should, therefore, desire mediocrity in all things, even in beauty.'

What is unconvincing about all this is the obvious point that the drives for competition and for the self-esteem that derives from competition are as deep-rooted in our nature as any of our other drives, as are plenty of negative desires and emotions. There is no human society without competition, display and fiercely guarded differences of rank. But Rousseau's aim is always to elevate the natural at the expense of the artificial, and to do this he has implausibly to put our negativity on the side of the artificial.

There is in Rousseau more than a touch of the plea for kidney machines, rather than symphony orchestras, to say nothing of an advocacy of rural simplicity as against urban sophistication. Like those who today reject selection in education, he implies that what all cannot share, none should aspire to. Notions of the superiority of one person to another are anathema to him, not just because of his dislike of the vanity that inspires thoughts of superiority, nor simply because of the restless and destructive competition it fuels. There is also his notion of the general will: the belief that I can rediscover my true, innocent and original self and what I really want when I sink my selfish and idiosyncratic ambitions in projects and goals that all can share and on which all can agree. I and all my rights are given to the whole community. In doing this I do what both virtue and universal reason demand. On this point Rousseau was as rationalistic and universalistic as any Enlightenment figure, and in working out the demands of universal reason, fraternity will emerge from the ensuing democracy, based on an equality of need and power.

There are, to be sure, aspects of Rousseau that are profoundly anti-Enlightenment, notably, his dislike of science and urban culture and his esteem for simple peasantry and their local clergy. But at a deeper level Rousseau is very Enlightenment, very modern. The 'noble' savage, whom Rousseau was the first to extol and to compare favourably with the modern bourgeois city dweller, and the general will through which men could retrieve something of the innocence of the life of nature, fit in very well with the moral psychology of the Enlightenment.

We have our desires, given to us by nature. In themselves, they are good (or at any rate, not evil). So no original sin. What brings about evil are despotism, tyrannies, moralities and bad social arrangements generally. These and the consequent evils can be eliminated by better, more rational, more democratic arrangements, which will allow the personalities of the citizens to flourish, in democratic communities in which the will of all happily coincides with the will of each, rather than by the arbitrary prejudices, deceits or artificial power-systems. Similarly, in his educational views, Rousseau's focus on the child, and his or her psychology and growth, fits very well with the Enlightenment conceptions of all social activities as, at root, a matter of applying the results of psychological knowledge. Rousseau initiates the trend in education to see teaching in terms of applied child psychology, rather than initiation into traditional forms of learning and culture – many of which Rousseau disliked.

Further, for Rousseau and the standard Enlightenment view, what amounts to progress in a social sense is a harmonious and unified flourishing of natural human subjectivity freed from prejudice, superstition and exploitation. If in Rousseau there is greater emphasis on nature, sentiment and subjectivity (though with a balancing stress as community), this is still to draw on themes already present in writers such as Diderot and Holbach. Further, developing his theory of the general will (in which individual desires and projects are merged in common), Rousseau is only devising and describing actual mechanisms for promoting social harmony where the earlier Enlightenment figures had rather optimistically left matters not a little under-described.

In practice, Rousseau's theory of sentiment has too often degenerated into a Diana-like cultivation of sentimentality without the counter-balancing Roman-style stoicism that Rousseau himself admired; his child-centred approach to education has led to a systematic erosion of the authority of the teacher and of the value of what is taught, and his idea of the general will has led disastrously easily to tyranny and the suppression of individuals and their wills, starting in the French Revolution itself. That was the first of many occasions on which individual will – and persons – were crushed on the wheel of the general will. Perhaps these things could and should have been foreseen even while Rousseau was alive.

Whether or not this is so, all these notions continue to play their part in our conception of progress, more than two hundred years later, and we have done little to resolve their difficulties. That is to say, our yearning for natural simplicity is not reconciled with our technological addictions; our infatuation with our inner feelings threatens social and familial stability at every turn, as stability requires the repression of feeling. Nor have we achieved any genuine reconciliation of individual desire and idiosyncrasy with collective aims and policies; consequently we oscillate between collectivist tyranny or at least bossiness and market anarchy, even – as in Britain's 'Third Way' of 1999 – in the same country at the same time.

Herder and the Particularity of Culture

The Enlightenment was based on straightforward scientific optimism. Human society was moving forward in the same sort of way as human knowledge. In science we had got rid of illusion and superstition. In morality and politics an age of reason was dawning. It would be liberal and enlightened, with institutions and customs based on scientific knowledge about man and society, rather than on the arbitrary whims of the powerful or the fantasies of priests and old women.

This view was not only optimistic and hopeful: for those

who held it, it was extremely flattering, for where the future was being formed was where those who held the view were living, writing and thinking. They were the future. It was their vision of man and society that had history and reason on its side. Indeed, in the most extreme versions of Enlightenment progressivism (Hegel's), history was reason (or Reason) moving towards its end point (of something like constitutional monarchy, guaranteeing individual freedom and reason, or a secular liberal democracy).

Whether in mild or extravagant form, this type of progressivism implicitly contrasted the rational present (or near future) in Europe with the past in general and with what was going on at the time outside Europe. The contrast was generally unfavourable to what was not the European present. The odd Voltairean nod in the direction of ancient China and the almost universal acclaim for classical Greece aside, other places and times were primitive and endarkened to a greater or lesser degree, enslaved as they were to superstition, ignorance and oppression.

We have already seen that Rousseau did not regard the bourgeois type represented by the intellectuals and scientists of the Enlightenment as the goal to which all humanity was striving, consciously or otherwise. But a far more radical and, in the end, damaging criticism of Enlightenment progressivism is to be found in the writings of J. G. Herder (1744–1803). In Herder we find a line of thought, which, right through to our own day, has proved obstinately resilient and influential. (And not just because it may seem attractive to non-whites and non-Europeans: its most tenacious hold is in the minds of the university-educated young of the affluent West.)

Herder rejected the belief that reality, including human reality, was organized in terms of timeless universal and objective laws discoverable by science. In what in retrospect seems the first flowering of what is known today as multi-culturalism, he insisted on the uniqueness of historical periods and events. Indeed, it is because of Herder's influence, diffused through a thousand lessons and textbooks, that every well-meaning young person of our time is 'non-judgemental' in moral and cultural matters – except, of course, where someone else claims some kind of authority or superiority for 'Western' values. (The fact that non-judgementalism is, *par excellence*, a 'Western' value, which would not be intelligible in any other context, is usually, and conveniently, overlooked.)

Crucially, Herder denied that the methods of the natural sciences can be applied to human history and human society. In human affairs, each age, each period, each nation had its own particular character, in terms of which it and its inhabitants had to be understood. Herder's historical relativism went deep. It did not extend simply to the description of a society: it extended to the evaluation of its activities, customs and morals. We do not have to get inside the mentality of other peoples simply to describe their activities adequately. We can judge those activities fairly only to the extent that we share their values. If, as Voltaire and Diderot did, we condemn the Middle Ages for being priest-ridden and intellectually craven, we are simply imposing our self-styled 'rational', 'enlightened' values on them. Doubtless they could reply that Voltaire and Diderot were blasphemous, hubristic and shallow, and condemn them with as much right as they themselves are condemned for being irrational and unenlightened. What we have are different ages, different spirits. There is no neutral or objective ground from which to evaluate one or the other. And in looking at human history there is never an escape from evaluation.

Against the Enlightenment faith in the unity of mankind and in progress, Herder stressed the plurality of societies and their differences, arguing that it was impossible to talk of historical progress in any uncontested way. According to Herder, each of us is what we are because of the group to which we belong and the history we share with others of our people. Our identities depend on our particular language and our culture.

Further, activities and self-expression are valuable to the degree to which they reveal the unique personality of the individual and that of the group to which he or she belongs and from which he or she derives his or her identity. He stressed the organic nature and growth of human societies, rejecting centralization, bureaucracy and, above all, imperialism. In the ironically entitled *Letters on the Advancement of Mankind* (1783–7), Herder asked his reader to 'name a land where Europeans have entered without defiling themselves for ever before defenceless, trusting mankind . . . Our part of the earth should not be called the wisest, but the most arrogant, aggressive, money-minded . . . What it has given [the colonies] is not civilization but the destruction of the rudiments of their own cultures . . .'

Hence it has deprived the colonized of their identity, nature and inheritance. Interestingly the young Goethe met Herder and as a result wrote in 1772 an article on German architecture, which is shot through with Herderian resonance. It takes the form of an address to Magister Ervinus (Erwin von Steinbach), the architect of Strasbourg cathedral.

Goethe praises Steinbach's Gothic against the classical architecture of the eighteenth century, which was pre-eminently the international style of the day. He comments on how an Italian would describe the cathedral as in 'niggling taste', a Frenchman would call it puerile while triumphantly snapping open his snuffbox '*à la Grecque*', while he himself set out as the 'sworn enemy of the confused caprices of Gothic ornament'. However, when he arrived in Strasbourg, he was overwhelmed by its naturalness. He came to thank God that 'this is German architecture, our architecture. For the Italian has none he can call his own, still less the Frenchman.' The German Gothic is a characteristic art, as such the only true art 'unaware of all foreign elements and whether it be born of savagery or of a cultivated sensibility, it is a living whole'. Among different nations there are countless different degrees of characteristic art. At Strasbourg we have an example of the 'deepest feeling for truth and beauty of proportion, brought about by the strong rugged German soul on the narrow, gloomy priest–ridden stage of the *medii aevi*'.

While Goethe later modified his views on 'characteristic' art in favour of a generous cosmopolitanism, what he said in 1772 of Strasbourg would be echoed by aestheticians and cultural critics right down to our own time, particularly, but not exclusively, when dealing with the productions of primitive peoples. Herder and Goethe are indeed right in drawing attention to the influence of culture, its variability and the distinctiveness of different cultures, which make direct comparisons and simplistic talk of progress problematic in all sorts of ways. If Herder had done no more than this, there would be few who would dissent. But Herder's relativism was deep. It follows from his views that there is nothing universal in human nature, there are no grounds on which we can objectively say that female circumcision or child slavery is wrong, as opposed to just part of the culture of some alien folk.

That even today, and despite Enlightenment influence, many would profess themselves unhappy to condemn such practices, providing they can be shown to be deep-rooted in a society, demonstrates the extent to which Herderian ideas have taken root in twentieth-century egalitarianism of culture. However, this position is in the end unsustainable. While Herder himself was notably pacific and opposed to violence, hierarchies and the state itself, not all cultures are so benign. What happens if one culture declares its vocation to reign supreme over others? The very imperialism Herder himself deplored could be an integral part of the self-image of a particular nation, and the relativism Herder espoused would afford him no logical space to object.

This, of course, was no merely theoretical possibility. Within a few years of Herder's death, Fichte was delivering his 'Speeches to the German People', in which the German nation was proclaimed, the Favoritvolk, with consequences only played out in the middle years of our century. Arguably much of nineteenth- and twentieth-century history can be seen in terms of a life and death struggle between the universalism of the Enlightenment and the nationalism of the Counter-Enlightenment. But if 'modernity' *circa* 1999 would pronounce in favour of the Enlightenment, against nationalism and in favour of the federal super-state, that is not to say that supra-nationalism is right, possible or even desirable.

After all, as de Maistre put it in his attack on the talk of 'man' in the French Revolution, while he has seen a Frenchman, an Italian and a Persian, what he has never seen is a man, pure and simple. Not only do our identities derive from our traditions and localities, but we have so far devised no sense of belonging or community that is not based on units considerably smaller, more unified and more focused than humanity in general. The un-resolved difficulty is to show how one can recognize the particularity of culture without lapsing into a relativism that deprives us of any ability to criticize repugnant cultures and customs; or, from the other point of view, to formulate a universalism about human nature that does not simply obliterate the important differences between peoples and thereby trample roughshod over histories and traditions quite justifiably vener-ated by those who belong to them. And, even if the veneration is not justifiable, as we see in the Ireland in our own day, it is no use for politicians 'this side of the water' simply to think that by talking 'good sense' one can get warring tribes to lay down their centuries-old hostility, particularly if the politicians in question have not taken the trouble to understand the relevant history.

Even modernizers, though, betray uneasiness at times. Thus the same people advocate both the breaking up of the United Kingdom into separate national statelets *and* Euro-federalism. It seems that in 1999 many of us are pulled by both Enlightenment and Counter-Enlightenment here without really seeing the tension, let alone being able to resolve it.

In one crucial and important respect, however, Herder and the Enlightenment philosophers are united as thinkers of the modern age. With cataclysmic consequences in the twentieth century, both Enlightenment universalists and romantic nationalists look for salvation in the works of man, the reason of enlightened individuals in the one case, the historical experience and development of the particular nation in the other. In other words, both are humanisms, in the essential sense of that term: whatever invocation there is of some transcendent power in the writings of either universalists or nationalists, all the work of evaluatory legitimation and inspiration is being done by us here below.

Burke and de Maistre: Prejudice Defended

If Rousseau can be accommodated, albeit uneasily, within the broad sweep of Enlightenment thought, and Herder and his followers be seen as attending to issues that arise directly within Enlightenment ideology, Burke and de Maistre, the great conservative critics of the French Revolution, represent the wholesale rejection of everything the Enlightenment stands for. Perhaps this is the reason why, while both Rousseau and Herder have contributed key elements to the tapestry of modern thought, Burke and de Maistre stand resolutely apart from everything that constitutes modernity.

Burke and de Maistre were reactionaries in the strict sense of the word. That is to say, they presented positive views only when and in so far as they were responding to events – in both cases those of the French Revolution (though it is worth recalling that Burke's astonishingly prescient *Reflections on the Revolution in France* actually appeared in 1790, some time before either the regicide or the Terror, both of which he foresaw). What they saw in the Revolution convinced both that it was far easier to destroy than to build, that there was a wisdom in human affairs inaccessible to contemporary reason, and, above all, that human society could not function peacefully without transcendent authority. This would make Burke, de Maistre and all their followers deeply suspicious of notions of social order as founded on any sort of human contract or agreement: what depends on human agreement would be in danger of collapse as soon as the consenting partners changed their minds and ceased to agree.

The social contract is a profoundly modern idea. In essence it is anti-conservative, anti-traditionalist and anti-religious. This may seem strange, for its first major proponent seems to have been Thomas Hobbes, a thinker of the seventeenth century normally regarded as highly authoritarian, and as both pessimistic and conservative. Certainly Hobbes had a far more lively sense of original sin and of human imperfectibility than, say, Rousseau or even Locke, two other historically significant social-contract theorists. For Hobbes, in contrast to Rousseau, life in a state of nature was, in his famous phrase, 'nasty, brutish and short', inevitably a war of all against all in which the weakest would go to the wall and the strong survive only so long as they held off stronger competitors. The only solution to the insecurity and misery of this war of all against all is for all the protagonists to contract to put themselves under a sovereign, whose primary function would be to guarantee civil peace. For this the sovereign would need absolute power and the subjects would have to give him complete obedience. But in one respect it would be conditional obedience, conditional on the sovereign delivering peace. A sovereign presiding over or causing disorder or anarchy could justifiably be removed by the subjects, as breaking his side of the contract.

Much of Hobbes's own political philosophy was anti-Enlightenment: the stress on human wickedness, a mistrust of human reason, arguments in favour of limited government, and an advocacy of state censorship to squash religious dissent and fanaticism, which, as a witness of the seventeenth-century wars of religion, Hobbes abhorred.

But the idea of the social contract was both beguiling and much in accordance with the rationalism, liberalism and anti-authoritarianism of the Enlightenment. On the social-contract view, society is not a divinely constituted and hierarchical order, but the ever-revisable outcome of the decisions of freely judging, freely consenting adults. We could choose our political and social arrangements as they seemed best to us, and revise and reorder them as, from time to time, it seemed fit. And this is how the social contract has come to be interpreted, as it has developed from John Locke, at the time of the Glorious Revolution of 1688, down to John Rawls in our own day, who sees a main function of the state as being to redistribute goods and position so that the only inequalities in society will be those benefiting the worst off.

Rawls justifies this conclusion by means of a thoroughly modern social-contract device. He asks us to imagine what sort of society we would choose to be in if we were in what he calls the 'original position'. In the original position, we are behind a 'veil of ignorance', that is, we know general facts about human nature, but nothing about our own birth, wealth or ability. In such a situation, what sort of society would we choose to be in? Rawls believes that, given we might be badly off in terms of ability and the rest, we would regard as just a society that sought to eliminate inequality as far as possible. However, knowledge of human nature teaches us that people need incentives for long training and effort, and that society, including the worst off, needs skilled surgeons, teachers, administrators, etc. So what we, in the original position, would opt for is a society that redistributed its goods on a basis of equality, except where inequalities were the result of the incentives necessary to promote the well-being of the worst off, through providing skilled doctors and the rest. It is, of course, immensely beguiling to regard society as based on a contract which, as in Rawls's version, and in its own way in Hobbes's, also defines the duties of the rulers. It is flattering to see ourselves not as subjects, subservient to a sovereign endowed with authority derived from a sacred, non-human source, but as citizens freely determining the law of the land, and the constitution itself, which would be constrained by the general principles of the contract.

It is also plausible to identify democracy with the social contract, because if, as in democracy, we can get rid of individual rulers as we wish, can't we equally transform authority itself? Isn't political authority itself a human construction, revisable and dispensable? Plausible, but not clearly necessary. We *could* regard democracy as primarily a process of selecting individual rulers within a broader and pre-existing framework of authority and obedience, rather than the source and origin of political allegiance at its most basic level.

Something like that would have to be held by a follower of Burke, who was also a democrat to any degree. For, on the Burke–de Maistre view, the idea of a social contract as the basis of political authority is deeply incoherent. The incoherence is this: according to social-contract theorists, we see ourselves as moving from a state of nature into civil society by means of an initial contract. We therefore envisage the contract as made and upheld by beings who are not yet in society, and who do not have any of its institutions. But the practice of contracts, and their enforcement, is eminently a social institution. Contracting requires a pre-existing society: therefore it cannot be the foundation of society.

Thus the very idea of non-social animals, savages freeing themselves from the war of all against all, coming together to contract, is nonsense. Such beings could never construct a system depending on the mutual recognition of promises and the enforcement of contracts. On the other hand, creatures who could enter a contract, respecting each other's rights and freedoms, and punishing breaches of obligation in a measured way with due legal process, would already in some sense be in a society, and hence have no need of a primeval contract. They might make changes to the details of social and political arrangements, but the fundamental socio-political bond and the disposition to respect it would have to be already there, written into their hearts or even into the fabric of the universe.

Both Burke and de Maistre are acutely aware of the need for a power and for a corresponding sense of awe beyond any reversible contract. Burke speaks of 'that tribunal of conscience which exists independently of edicts and decrees'. If men have that then, once again, society is to all intents and purposes already there, prior to contract. If not – as perhaps Hobbes was aware – the sovereign will have in the end to rely on terror, as in the French Revolution and in Soviet Russia. But a rule of terror is despotism, Burke goes on to point out, 'Your despots govern by terror. They know that he who fears God fears nothing else; and therefore they eradicate from their mind, through their Voltaire, their Helvetius, and the rest of that infamous gang, that only sort of fear which generates true courage. Their object is, that their fellow citizens may be under the dominion of no awe, but that of the committee of research, and of their lanterne.'

There are both positive and negative aspects to this: positive in that with the limits to permissible human activity inscribed by God and in our consciences, men will have some guarantee of freedom and from interference from despots; negative in that that same sense will invest laws that are just with the degree of awe needed to make most men obey them without the need for police or terror.

In 1999 these, of course, are uncomfortable thoughts. However, we are now more aware than Burke of the lengths to which godless regimes will go to defy all human decency and sensibility, even, as in Nazi Germany, democratically elected regimes, or, as in the case of Soviet Russia, regimes with impeccably liberal constitutions. Burke was right to insist that neither a democratic majority nor the best of constitutions is any guarantee of rights or liberties, a point worth remembering these days when all the talk is of charters and bills of rights. If we do not want simply to feather the nests of lawyers, if we really care about liberty, what we need in men is some sense of right and wrong that is prior to agreements, votes, or conventions, and which, in the view of Burke and de Maistre, can come only from God.

De Maistre, whose criticisms of the social contract I have largely been echoing, held that society is made not by man, weak as he is and his 'reason' a feeble pretence, but by God. Men are not naturally benevolent, co-operative or peaceful. Like other parts of nature, and as history has taught us over and over again and continues to teach us, human beings constantly slaughter each other, given the chance, for the most trivial of reasons. The idea that a peaceful society can be brought about by education and political discussion is as absurd an idea as any ever devised, and dangerous to boot. It is only God's law and our obedience to it that can lift us out of anarchy into a tolerable social existence.

So any attack on the social order amounts, in de Maistre's view, to blasphemy.

Further, rather like those despots Burke criticizes, de Maistre believes that society is held together only by the executioner, 'the terror of human society and the tie that holds it together'. In proposing this view – and in complimenting the Jacobins for the fact that they, unlike the earlier revolutionaries, used terror to enforce a type of order – de Maistre might be thought to be indulging in his considerable penchant for provocation. Burke would not have agreed with him.

For, central to Burke's view, is that over and above its divine foundation, the main defence the state provides against anarchy and the war of all against all is not brute power. Sheer brute power – despotism and terror – is simply an extreme form of the war of all against all; in its abrogation of law and restraint it is actually a form of anarchy. It is not that Burke had any more illusions about human motivation or ability than de Maistre – or Hobbes, for that matter. It is rather that he saw that for a tolerable social life sentiment had to be added to terror and naked power, and also that, inconceivable as this may be to rationalists, local and historical sentiment, pageantry and ritual, even ancient rank and hierarchy, can contribute significantly to human well-being and to a fulfilled life for all in a society.

But how are we to think of the state, its institutions and the values that, in Burke's view, embellish life by giving us allegiances to which we respond? Like de Maistre, Burke believed that 'no great human institution results from delib-eration'. That it could be is a fallacy perpetrated not just by French revolutionaries, but by reformers and legalists of all types, including, of course, those in the European Commission, whose best-laid plans – as in the case of the Common Agricultural Policy – have an uncanny knack of stifling with regulation and interference the very enterprises they are in-tended to liberate. In fact, on the contrary, 'human works are fragile to the degree in which science and reasoning' have been involved in their construction.

As de Maistre put it, 'threads which can be broken by a child at play can nevertheless be joined to form a cable capable of supporting the anchor of a great vessel'. Both in its positive and in its negative aspects this aphorism is entirely Burkean in spirit.

Negatively, seemingly trivial criticisms and changes can undermine great enterprises and institutions. Positively, what binds a great society need not seem onerous to its subjects.

Indeed, for Burke – if not for de Maistre – it must not. For Burke what is vital in a successful constitution are 'the pleasing illusions' that make 'power gentle and obedience liberal', that harmonize 'the different shades of life' and that incorporate 'into politics the sentiments which beautify and soften private society'. Revolutionaries and rationalizers would tear off this 'decent drapery of life', misunderstanding its function and regarding it as mere frippery and ornament, or worse, a cloak for self-interest and inefficiency. But in tearing off that which inspires and beautifies, they expose our 'naked shivering nature', rather in the manner of a Lucian Freud or a Francis Bacon. On the deflationary, rationalist scheme of things:

> a king is but a man; a queen is but a woman: a woman is but an animal; and an animal not of the highest order. All homage paid to the sex in general as such . . . is to be regarded as romance and folly. Regicide and parricide, and sacrilege, are but fictions of superstition . . . The murder of a king, or a queen or a bishop, or a father are only common homicide; and if the people are by any chance, or in any way gainers by it, a sort of homicide much the most pardonable, and into which we ought not to make too severe a scrutiny.

Burke actually wrote this passage before the regicide in France. But no doubt he would have pointed out that the popular gain from it was a tyranny far more oppressive than any inconvenience of the *ancien régime*, a sequence to be repeated, and not as farce, in Russia in 1919. The Burkean – conservative – point would be that the ceremony, ritual and colour, and even the inequalities and injustice, associated with these ancient monarchies actually softened and civilized the subject peoples, *and* their rulers, in ways unintelligible to the rationalist, who could see in it only illusion, oppression and outdated artificiality, but whose removal, far from leading to a rational harmony among those who now saw themselves as citizens or comrades, led to a Hobbesian war of all against all, followed by regimes in which laws would be supported only by their own terror.

To the rationalist, much of what Burke was upholding would appear to be mere prejudice, the maintenance of values, traditions and hierarchies just because they were old, and despite any virtue or reason in them or obvious function they fulfilled (other than the self-serving one of bolstering the status quo). In his obstinate affection for old institutions and practices, Burke would be seen as prejudiced not only by reforming bureaucrats but also by the equally rationalistic business community, intent on sweeping away any ancient relic that seemed to impede the development of trade. Centralist planners and captains of industry would disagree on a lot, but both have been inveterate advocates of the motorway as opposed to the rolling English drunkard's rolling English road – and all that is encapsulated by that notion, which is perhaps why the Labour Party and big business, after decades of misguided antipathy, have in the late 1990s come to realize that they are actually on the same side.

Against the modernizers, political or entrepreneurial, Burke would concur that he was upholding prejudice, but for him, and most scandalous of all to the modern mind, this would not be taken as a criticism. Quite the contrary. For Burke, prejudice is a far more reliable source of wisdom than reason, particularly the arrogant reason insensitive to past ways of doing things or not schooled in actual experience, which 'reason' tends to be: 'We are afraid to put men to live and trade each on his own private stock of reason; because we suggest that this stock in each man is small, and that individuals would do better to avail themselves of the general bank and capital of the nations, and of ages.'

Burke argues that old prejudices should be cherished both because they are prejudices and because they are old. Prejudices act as a useful rule-of-thumb in situations where unguided decision-making on first principles is uncertain and unreliable. They can also become habitual, rendering a man's virtue his habit. Further, if examined sympathetically, most prejudices will be found to embody a deposit of wisdom, hewn from age and experience, and which is all too likely to elude us if we rely solely on our present stock of wisdom.

Burke's attitude to prejudice and tradition, and also to the divine foundation of human society, was the complete antithesis to that of the Enlightenment, and even more so to that of the French Revolution, its political wing, so to speak. To argue in favour of things that had previously been taken for granted, and which were powerful precisely because they had been taken for granted, may have seemed quixotic in 1789. All I can say at this stage is that after two centuries of political, moral and aesthetic slate-cleaning, and starting from scratch on 'rational' or first principles, a Burkean attitude to change, to tradition and to reason itself no longer seems so unreasonable. Nor, after a century of explicitly godless politics in many parts of the world, does his instinct that a benign social order needs to rest on more than human foundations.

At this point, our conclusion must be that while the Rousseauan psychology of feeling has fairly easily become part of modernity's self-image, and Herderian nationalism one of its powerful if bastardized offspring, Burkean-style reflection will inform the deepest and most necessary critique of our pretensions and optimism.

3

Two Hundred Years of the Progress of Reason

When we look at the history of the past two hundred years, for all the qualifications and exceptions that would need to be made, it is possible to discern certain constant threads: the rise and rise of science and technology; consequent disenchantment of the world, including downgrading our perception of it; a stress on individual reason and feeling as the source of judgement and value; the extension of democracy and human rights; and with the erosion of religious perspectives, a sense that our happiness in this life is what really matters morally and spiritually.

All these threads seem to be based on what scientific reason tells us. Progress, then, is what advances scientific reason and its apparent applications in moral, social and political spheres.

Reason, Equality and Human Rights: Immanuel Kant

In considering the Enlightenment, we saw reason mainly in terms of its role in promoting knowledge and removing prejudice, in delivering the truths and theories and in what emerged through its exercise. But there are also powerful moral and political messages that may be and, at the end of the eighteenth century, were drawn from the fact of its possession.

Merely possessing reason is held to entitle rational people to all kinds of rights and privileges.

The French Revolution was supposed to usher in an age of reason. But part of this age of reason was a commitment to equality and to the rights of man. Similarly, the founding fathers of America took the rights to life, liberty and human happiness to be 'self-evident', as being part of our endowment as rational beings. Were these revolutionaries right in forging a connection between reason and equality, between reason and human rights? That they were correct emerges in the thought of the most complex of Enlightenment thinkers, Immanuel Kant, and one who in his complexity brought out some of its inherent contradictions.

Kant believed that there were two aspects to our nature. On the one hand, we were part of the physical world, physical beings, as such wholly subject to Newtonian laws and forces, and our actions explicable through psychological laws; but on the other hand, we were also rational and free, guided not just by forces of nature but capable of acting freely on moral considerations. So we are wholly in the physical world and, therefore, a suitable case for scientific investigations, but at the same time, through our possession of reason and our sense of duty, we are also part of a spiritual 'kingdom of ends' whose inhabitants are capable of acting for purely moral reasons, and free from the demands and constraints of our ordinary physical and psychological makeup.

It is fair to say that Kant did not succeed in explaining to anyone's satisfaction other than his own how we could be both fully part of the physical world and, at the same time, free and part of another realm altogether. Without going into detail it could also be said that the problem Kant is dealing with is the most intractable difficulty posed by the scientific world-view and not satisfactorily resolved even today. While the scientific world-view sees all physical things, including human beings, as subject to physical laws, we know in our own experience that there is more to us than what is given in physical law. We know ourselves to be both self-conscious and free. We know that, in that sense, we are not part of the physical world, at least not part of the physical world as explained by science. But knowing this means that there are bits of the world (us) which will ever evade scientific investigation and explanation.

To deny our subjectivity and our freedom would be to make nonsense of most of our life and our attitudes to each other, which depend on the assumption that when dealing with other people we are dealing with free agents, capable of exercising their freedom for better or worse, and not with scientifically programmed automata. We see this denial, of course, every time some well-meaning cleric or social worker excuses bad or wicked behaviour on the grounds that the person responsible may not really be responsible; blame parents, upbringing, child abuse, bad housing, anything but the guilty party. But this attempt to excuse diminishes even the person in question: we are, in effect, saying that they are not responsible human beings, that they are not in control, that they are just bits of the natural world, pushed around like leaves or bits of inanimate matter. And, in our hearts, and in our dealings with those we live with, and love or hate, we know that this is not true. We know that people are beings of a different order from the natural. We know that we ourselves and those we live with are originators of action and attitude, and to be loved or blamed, pitied or praised accordingly.

It was this that Kant was getting at when he located human beings in a moral and spiritual 'kingdom of ends' as well as in the world of nature. The individual human being, as a member of the kingdom of ends, must be treated as an end in him or herself, respected, valued, praised and, at times, blamed in a way that would make no sense so long as we were dealing merely with trees or stones or even speechless animals.

For those unprepared to limit the extent of science and its explanations on the one hand or to deny the reality of human subjectivity and freedom on the other, there is indeed an impasse – which is actually inherent in much enlightened thought, emphasizing as it does both the omniscience of science, and human rationality and freedom.

Kant, being unprepared to give up either the universal scope of science or human freedom, was unable to escape the impasse, but he did have important and influential things to say about human beings. In one significant respect what he said is quintessentially modern: for Kant, as reasoning rational beings, we are capable of making our own decisions and of deciding on our own rules of action. In his terms we are autonomous. And we are all autonomous. What we should each do in exercising our individual autonomy is to respect the automony of all other similarly constituted beings. We should not do to others what we would not want them to do to us. We are to treat others as ends with their own plans and projects, and not as means to our ends. That, indeed, is for Kant the fundamental principle of morality: to treat others as we would like them to treat us, to treat them as ends.

Kant's working out of this principle is both democratic and egalitarian in spirit and clearly the inspiration for Rawls's original position: it is not in virtue of any specific features of your status, abilities, upbringing or personality that I am to treat you as an end, it is because of your base-level rationality and your ability to frame your own projects and goals, which you and I and everyone else have because we are human beings. From that perspective we are all equal; as ends in ourselves, we must all be heard. But no one more than another, and all because of the same rationality, which we all share.

The logic of the Kantian position is a notion of universal human rights combined with treating differences of birth, upbringing, culture, class, nation and even gender as secondary, dispensable and trivial. In his political writings Kant followed Rousseau in basing political authority on a combination of the general will and a social contract (even though, inconsistently with his philosophical views and with characteristic philosophical timidity, he argues against democracy and excludes the lower orders and women from the 'active' citizenry who would vote and legislate).

What is particularly modern about all this is the upgrading of the abstract, rational individual combined with the downgrading of everything about his or her actual circumstances, abilities and character. He or she becomes the bearer of rights simply by virtue of existence, not by anything he or she is or has done. In earlier times, my life plan would have been given to me largely by my birth and upbringing (my station and, in Bradley's terms, its duties), and fulfilment and happiness would and often did flow from my fulfilling those duties.

But for Kant, as for moderns generally, what counts is the free, rational and equal individual exercising his or her autonomy, and achieving happiness through living life in accordance with his or her decisions and choices. Kant actually defined enlightenment as 'man's emerging from his self-imposed immaturity', immaturity that he defined as the craven and cowardly inability to use one's own understanding without guidance from another. To the contrary: '*Sapere aude!* Have courage to use your own understanding – that is the motto of enlightenment.' Against this ideal, it becomes politically imperative to remove values and institutions that impose purely contingent and rationally unjustifiable allegiances on us, thus hampering autonomy, individuality and independence.

It also became imperative to formulate moral and social systems in which the same duties and rights were accorded to everyone, by virtue of their rationality. And this, too, brought the new Enlightenment rationality into conflict with traditional, hierarchical social set-ups just because they institutionalized historically contingent inequalities, such as privileges of birth. We hear Kantian notes in our current deliberation of the 'indefensible' makeup of the House of Lords, indefensible certainly on Kantian principles, nor can we imagine any social contract, starting society from scratch, ever coming up with such a conception. But, as Nietzsche was later to argue, are those Kantian principles of equality among autonomous beings themselves defensible? In saying, as Kant and his myriad contemporary followers do, that all moral norms and political right should be the same for all human beings, are we not flying in the face of the manifest inequalities of talent, virtue and effort we encounter every day in our dealings with our fellows? Why should some indolent, ignorant layabout have the same political rights and be accorded the same moral respect as a hard-working and responsible doctor or policeman? Does the fine-sounding kingdom of ends not, in fact, privilege the weak and reward the undeserving? Does one really respect human autonomy by shutting one's eyes to morally significant differences, standing and achievement in the name of a formal equality of rights? Maybe upbringing, background and education ought to confer privileges on those who have them to the degree that they are better able to decide and to rule.

That, following the progressive political and social reforms of the past two hundred years, such questions are never seriously entertained is not, of course, proof that they have no sense or pertinence. It is, rather, a testament to the extent that progressivist rationalism is able to marginalize anyone who really does dare to think. And let no one think that the vast majority of those politicians and bureaucrats who campaign or rule in the name of equal rights actually live by the message they preach, or have ever done so. Today's Euro MPs and cabinet ministers, exulting in their privileges and champagne lifestyles, are only doing what rulers have always done, but with this difference: only in the twentieth century have rulers done it in the name of the common man and in defence of his rights and equality.

Utilitarianism

Happiness. If Kant-based theories of rights provide one leg of modern moral sensibility, utilitarianism provides the other, not that the two currents of thought are formally consistent. But no matter, what the free, autonomous modern agent is primarily seeking is happiness. Again, we have a striking transformation. For us in 1999, the aim of life and society is no longer salvation, or honour, conquest, excellence, achievement, or even Kantian moral rationality. It is happiness and, in particular, the greatest happiness for the greatest number.

In considering the Enlightenment, we have already noted the utilitarian strain, the stress on pleasure and pain, the idea that pleasure and pain had somehow been shown scientifically to constitute the springs of human motivation, and the hope that society as a whole could be organized to produce harmonious happiness all round. These ideas were developed and expressed in their classical form by the English philosophers Jeremy Bentham and John Stuart Mill. Bentham was interested in government, above all in schemes for new constitutions, in legal codes and famously, or notoriously, in his model prison, the Panopticon. This was a scientifically designed institution in which the disorder, corruption and waste of the prisons of his time would be replaced by a regime of hard, useful work on the part of the prisoners and of constant vigilance on the part of the warders and the governor, who would himself live in the middle of the prison. He would be able to view what went on elsewhere in it and, because totally surrounded by it, would be the first to suffer from disorder within it.

Bentham's basic premise is that 'nature has placed mankind under the governance of two sovereign masters, pleasure and pain'. So in answer to the question raised by the Kantian philosophy (and largely left unanswered by that philosophy), as to *which* goals we should choose freely to pursue, Bentham would answer, the pursuit of pleasure and the avoidance of pain. Kant would not have liked the assumption that nature is commanding anything, or that our wills are constrained by sovereign masters. But an amalgam of Kant and utilitarianism is very much part of modernity's inheritance. We are free agents, but what we are free to do is pursue our individual and collective happiness, in accordance with the best scientific knowledge we have about what promotes happiness.

But is there any scientific knowledge here? And could there be a politico-social system which maximized the happiness of everyone? How can we measure such things? Bentham was in no doubt on any of these questions. He advocated that we operate a so-called felicific calculus. By calculating the amount of happiness particular activities would yield, we could then devise a political and legal system that most promoted those activities, to the benefit of all and each.

The most contentious aspect of the felicific calculus was pointed out by Bentham himself. It assumed a single scale of pleasures and pains, on which one could compare the relative merits or happiness produced by, say, poetry and pushpin (a sort of bagatelle). Poetry and pushpin was Bentham's own example. His conclusion was that 'quantity of pleasure being equal, pushpin is as good as poetry', a strikingly democratic and egalitarian sentiment, and one not a million miles from those who prefer kidney machines to symphony orchestras, or from so-called 'culture secretaries' who can see no difference between Keats and Bob Dylan.

Mill was rather more high-minded than Bentham, and a more interesting thinker. Following youthful infatuation with the works of Wordsworth and Coleridge, he agonized over poetry and pushpin, over what he called the higher and lower pleasures. It struck him that, perhaps, the higher pleasures (poetry, philosophy and the like) had built-in costs, so that just as the pleasures they afforded might be higher, so might the agonies and disappointments. Mill was in no doubt about where he stood on the poetry–pushpin issue: 'it is better to be a human being dissatisfied than a pig satisfied; better to be Socrates dissatisfied than a fool satisfied'. And he adds that if the fool or the pig are of a different opinion, 'it is because they only know their own side of the question. The other party to the comparison knows both sides.'

Well, maybe; but it does not follow that the other party would agree. Rousseau, Tolstoy and Wittgenstein, who certainly knew both sides, frequently waxed lyrical on the happiness of the uneducated peasant. In academic life I see many contorted, unfulfilled and bitter individuals, who might well have been happier had they never gone to university in the first place and very likely better human beings too. It would be hard to hold George Eliot's Casaubon up as an example of a good life. Isn't the unreflective and impulsive Ladislaw an altogether healthier and more admirable type?

Mill did not solve his dilemma. Nor did he see that it might have arisen from the nature of utilitarianism itself. The poetry–pushpin problem is not *just* that it is impossible to compare various pleasures and satisfactions on a single scale, 'scientifically' or otherwise. Rather more, it is that there are all sorts of worthwhile goals in human life, which are pursued for their own sake and have nothing to do with pleasure or even happiness. Poetry is one example. Others might be science, philosophy, religion, love of one's family, honour, virtue and music. Happiness or pleasure, if they arise from any of these things, are incidental and are not the reasons the activities are undertaken. There are many values in human life to which the pursuit of happiness is irrelevant and which will, on occasion, be pursued at the expense of happiness. Many of Mill's higher pleasures are of this sort, and many of them bring in their train unhappiness and lack of fulfilment. Does this mean they should not be pursued?

This difficulty with utilitarianism has not prevented it dominating moral thought in both private behaviour and public politics. Again, following the distinction Mill made between public and private activity, almost any 'private' goal is held to be acceptable, providing – as it is said – it is done by consenting adults and harms no one. Whether there are any such activities, which are purely private and which have no effect on the social fabric generally, might well be doubted and has been the basis of criticism of Mill since his own time. And, judging by the almost compulsory pornography on late-night television, to say nothing of the scenes enacted nightly on London's Hampstead Heath and Clapham Common, not a merely theoretical objection: the advocacy of the public–private distinction and the removal of all sexual matters to the private side of the divide has had the profoundest effect on public life and attitudes, not least in the extent of divorce, illegitimacy and abortion, matters, surely, of general and not purely private concern.

Meanwhile, states throughout the world pursue politics to secure the greatest happiness of the greatest number quite irrespective of their effects on individual freedom and responsibility, gradually taking over more and more roles that previously would have been regarded as the province of individuals, families or autonomous institutions, acting outside the orbit of the state. The problem is that, once universal happiness becomes the goal of human activity, as it does under utilitarianism, there is no bar on the extent of the means used to bring it about. Rather, there is a strong sense that it is the duty of those in power to bring it about, so the paternalist and interventionist state grows inexorably, to prevent anyone ever being in danger, to ensure everyone, come what may, has a comfortable, stress-free life.

This, though, has never been fully justified in utilitarian terms. From the fact (if it is a fact) that we operate under the sovereign masters pleasure and pain, why does it follow that it is the duty of each of us to promote the greatest happiness of the greatest number, to promote the happiness of everyone else? Where does all this talk of duty come from? Don't my 'sovereign masters' enjoin simply that I pursue my own pleasure and happiness to the utmost, and let everyone else go hang, as de Sade insisted? One can only conclude that within the utilitarian cast of mind, there is a residual moralism, hard to justify on utilitarian grounds.

Nevertheless the utilitarian mentality fits well with bureaucratic scientism, with the notion that by means of science and political organization a better world will be instigated free from all the old oppressions, fanaticisms, irrationalities and prejudices. It is certainly true that this high-minded paternalist mentality has, in our time, been immensely popular with politicians and civil servants; it is no less true that the sense that it is the duty of administrative and scientific 'experts' to organize the lives of the rest of the population has been as corrosive of traditional values and allegiances as any force in the modern world. After all, if basic questions of human life are to be settled by policy-makers whose terms of reference are scientific and administrative, it is hard to see where considerations such as the sacredness of life or our duty to our ancestors can get a look in.

Political policy-making is bound to be largely problematic. For policy-makers utilitarianism is the perfect philosophy, emphasizing quantity and the broader picture at the expense of tradition, quality and the individual. It gives policy-makers apparently commonsensical criteria on which to operate, which cut across otherwise irreconcilable differences of principle or tradition. Abortion? Euthanasia? Embryo experimentation? These are all areas in which people have profound worries and differences. But, says the utilitarian politician, desperately seeking solutions to practical dilemmas, let us be reasonable. Let us accept that there are hard cases where it would – from the perspective of happiness and human well-being – be *very* unreasonable to outlaw any of these practices. We will allow them at the margins, subject, of course, to stringent regulation and control . . . And in twenty years we move from abortion in only extreme cases to what is virtually abortion on demand, and if attitudes do not change, I predict that in the next millennium we will move to virtually compulsory euthanasia for the terminally ill and also to embryo nurseries for spare parts farms and wholesale genetic experimentation, including doubtless cloning. When guided by utilitarian considerations, the extension of the political into areas such as health, education and welfare is bound to militate against intimations of the sacred, the transcendent and the uniquely individual, which are hardly amenable to broad-brush policies determined on quantitive grounds.

Reason Destructive of Reason

The problems with utilitarianism notwithstanding, Enlightenment reason has continued to dominate thought in all fields over the past two hundred years. In this section, I want to look at the impact reason has had on itself (or rather, should have had, were those who have used reason to denigrate other aspects of human life to have turned their weapons on themselves). More precisely, I want to look at the way scientific approaches have been applied to humanity itself, how we ourselves have fared when our own activity has been treated as, in some way, part of the natural world.

The outcome has not been encouraging for our self-esteem, or for our sense of ourselves as free, rational agents, dignified and at least in part capable of transcending our physical roots.

For all Kant's protestations that we are part of two realms, the physical *and* the moral, scientific inquiry into the human has focused exclusively on humanity as part of the physical world. To put it schematically, what we have been faced with is the following conundrum: (i) rationality urges us to investigate the world scientifically; (ii) the world includes human beings; (iii) we investigate human beings scientifically; (iv) the upshot of this investigation is that far from being rational, free, etc., our behaviour is demonstrated to be substantially determined by non-rational forces; (v) this includes our 'rationality'; (vi) so rationality self-destructs, in the sense that rationality shows us not to be rational. In other words, what from the Enlightenment perspective is the most elevated aspect of our humanity turns out to undermine its own standing and existence. It shows us that we are not, in that respect, elevated after all.

Of course, part of the devil is in the detail, the demonstration of the nature and scope of the non-rational forces in question. We will look particularly at the types of analysis offered by Darwin, Marx and Freud as, historically speaking, these have been the most influential in charting our descent from Voltairean intelligence to mere cog in the world machine. Within a century the noon-day of human optimism had produced a twilight image of man as hidden to himself and moved largely by dark forces outside the illumination of science that he could barely perceive, let alone control.

It is, though, worth bearing in mind that what I have just called a conundrum raises a critical question: if reason shows itself to be non-rational, doubt must attach to the truth of what reason tells us. This includes the proposition that reason itself is non-rational. Should we, therefore, accept the proposition in question, which has now been shown to rest on non-rational grounds? But this is a question Darwinists, Marxists and Freudians rarely ask themselves. They use their arguments to discredit other aspects of our rationality – and humanity, more broadly speaking – but without realizing the implication that their arguments, if valid, would discredit their own investigations as well.

Darwinism

We are now so used to the proposition that man is descended from the apes, and to stories about the opposition to Darwin of religious fundamentalists – and its pretty hasty overthrow in polite circles – that we have still not really assimilated his message. Or its dangers. Maybe the Victorians who opposed Darwin chose the wrong ground on which to fight, and maybe they were vanquished in pretty short order. Maybe 'Soapy Sam' Wilberforce, Bishop of Oxford, was made mincemeat of by T. H. Huxley, Darwin's 'bulldog'. The Bishop is alleged to have asked Huxley if he would rather have been descended from an ape on his grandfather's or his grandmother's side, and Huxley to have replied that he would rather have been descended from an ape than from a bishop misusing his position and introducing ridicule into scientific debate. A good story, but it should not have been used, as it has been so often, to *end* debate on one of the key issues raised by modern science.

The debate actually and misleadingly centred on the *descent* of man. There are indeed many questions about descent and about the plausibility of the evolutionary account, far more than evolutionists like to admit. But these questions were, and remain, beside the main point. The main point is not human origins but human reality as it is now, a point on which the Bishop might have had the better of the argument: he was the son of William Wilberforce, the liberator of the slaves. Bishop Sam was concerned about Darwin's implicit racism, the idea that some races were closer to our ape-ancestors than others. He might also have been concerned about the eugenic potential of Darwinism: the implication that if we have the future of the race at heart, we should ensure that only the better stock breeds. Those who read Darwin's *The Descent of Man* will find ample scope in Darwin's own words for both worries, which follow, quite consistently, from Darwinian principles: how, on Darwinian principles, do we ensure the integrity and advance of the species, except by allowing or even assisting 'the elimination of the unfit'? And aren't parts of the human race less fit, less advanced than others? Of course, I am assuming, unlike many of today's genetic engineers, that we *ought* not to take the Darwinian line on disability, but the problem is to show how we can argue for morality so long as we stay within the Darwinian framework.

Conflation and confusion of the issues began with Darwin himself. So anxious was he to gain acceptance for the thesis that mankind was descended from the apes (or, more accurately, from some proto-apes, from whom both present-day apes and *homo sapiens* are descended) that in *The Descent of Man*, he emphasizes the continuities between human beings and the rest of the animal kingdom. Even more damagingly, he and his followers, right down to the evolutionary psychologists and geneticists of our own day, like to argue that human behaviour is largely explicable in terms of the same processes of natural selection that, according to the theory of evolution, hold sway in the rest of nature.

Natural selection occurs when three conditions are met: (i) there is competition in nature for scarce resources; (ii) parents pass bodily and behavioural characteristics to their offspring through their genes; (iii) there are sometimes small but significant variations between parents and offspring, which are due to slight genetic differences (themselves due either to the mixing of parental genes in sexual reproduction or to random genetic mutations). In these circumstances, though most variants (under (iii)) will be harmful, members of a particular species born luckily with beneficial variations will tend to do better than the rest of the population in the struggle for existence. They will then pass the beneficial variation on to their offspring, who will do the same over generations, until the new variant becomes dominant in the population. Over huge periods of time, lines of small variations from original populations will lead to the branching off of new and separate species from original common ancestors.

For our purposes, the detail of the theory is unimportant. What matters is the idea that the bodily organs and behavioural dispositions currently in members of a given species are present in that species because in the distant past just those organs and dispositions had given their ancestors competitive advantages. In so far as natural selection is true of humanity, this is true of our organs and faculties too. And, as with all other creatures in the natural world, the competitive advantage our attributes serve is the evolutionary one of survival and reproduction of individual members of the species.

This, too, is a key point. Nature, strictly speaking, has no aim; neither does evolution. But what drives nature and evolution on is the instinct of all individual creatures to survive and to reproduce. Once an individual has survived long enough to replicate its genes in as many and varied offspring as possible, who will themselves further propagate the ancestral genes, it has fulfilled its evolutionary role. The process is a process of the propagation of one's genes. Variations and other features of one's life and existence are useful in so far as they contribute to that process. And, by a remorseless symmetry, what does not contribute to reproductive success and, even more, what interferes with it, will be weeded out in the population as a whole: those individuals with features not contributing to their survival and ability to reproduce will tend not to survive and reproduce, so those unhelpful features will not be passed on to or by their offspring, because they will not have any.

Although Darwin did not have our knowledge of genetics,

so did not formulate his theory in terms of the propagation of genes, in all essentials this is his theory. As he put it in his own words, what the 'law of natural selection' states is that in the natural world individuals having 'any advantage, however slight, over others, would have the best chance of surviving and reproducing their kind. On the other hand, any variations in the last degree injurious would be rigidly destroyed.' Conversely, we may add, those aspects of creatures most deeply embedded in their nature or behaviour will be those that have proved in the past most productive in the struggle for life to those individuals who have been able to pass them on to offspring.

But, it will be asked, although some aspects of our activity are easy to see as survival-promoting, do we not also find in human behaviour lots of prominent features irrelevant to individual survival and reproduction, or even hostile to these ends? According to the Darwinian, only apparently so. While Darwin himself was not altogether a consistent Darwinian when he discussed human society and morality, his late twentieth-century successors have been far less inhibited, in part because their knowledge of genetics has supplied the crucial element of the theory lacking to Darwin himself. What they do is engage in a campaign of unmasking human motivation, of showing that beneath apparently selfless or self-sacrificial behaviour, actually my reproductive purposes or those of my genes are being served, even if I do not realize it. Take, for example, our capacity to help people in need or our instinctive feeling of sympathy for someone. These are prominent features of human life in most societies. How could such things be hard-wired into us by evolutionary processes directed only at agents' individual survival? Easy, say the Darwinians, once you see that altruism and sympathy actually benefit the altruist and the sympathizer, for they are just the types who are most likely to attract help and attention when they themselves are in trouble. Conversely, those who do not help out when they can are far less likely to get helped themselves when they need it. Once you see altruism – apparently selfless doing good to others – not in terms of the individual altruistic action, but as part of a pattern of mutual co-operation, selflessness begins to look like a rather clever form of long-term selfishness.

Beneath, then, the smiles of benevolence and the sacrifices of the charitable, there is actually the naked ape in devious pursuit of his or her own benefit. Or, in the language of the 1990s, that of his genes. We are survival machines, not for ourselves, but for our genes, which are directing our bodies and our behaviour. While our bodies die, they will have served their evolutionary functions if they have allowed our genes to propagate themselves in future generations. Beneath the altruistic human being lie his or her selfish genes.

And genetic Darwinism explains not just co-operation in general, but also – which is hard for all kinds of other theorists to account for – the extraordinary and species-wide tendency for human beings to favour and help their own relations, and even to die for them. The explanation is that my blood relations share many of my genes, so in helping them I will be enhancing the survival and propagation chances of my genes. Again, no contradiction between Darwinism and the mother who sacrifices herself so that her children might live. On the contrary, that is exactly what genetically she has been built and programmed to do! In sacrificing herself for her children, she is ensuring the continuation of her genes beyond her death.

From these examples it will be clear that a Darwinian explanation of an aspect of human activity consists in showing how, even despite appearances, that activity might contribute to the well-being of an individual who engages in it. To the extent that we think Darwinism offers a complete account of human activity, we will be saying that, whatever appears to be the case on the surface, at bottom both the motivation and the rationale for what we do is self-interested in the specifically Darwinian sense.

We may think that we are being altruistic, but we are really just storing up credit to be drawn on later. We may think we are pursuing truth for its own sake, but really we are just exercising our mental agility to help us in the struggle for existence. We may think that in painting a beautiful picture we are inspired by thoughts of beauty, but the whole art game is – like the peacock's tail – an elaborate ploy to get more and better mates than our peers.

I do not pretend that the Darwinian accounts are convincing or even remotely plausible. Indeed, in Darwin's own day, Alfred Russel Wallace, the co-discoverer of the theory of evolution, argued that our rationality, our disinterested pursuit of knowledge, our moral and religious sense and our love of beauty could not possibly be explained in terms of survival promotion. He concluded that this must mean that there was more to human nature than evolution could account for and, being religious, looked for the answer in divine intervention. It was this point, rather than the sterile debate about origins and apes, that should have occupied Darwin's original religious opponents. They should have focused on the way crucial and significant aspects of our lives were unDarwinian in nature: that we seek truth, love and beauty and feel bound by the good for their sakes, not for any competitive advantage, and further, that these things are so central to our conceptions of the good life that they cannot – as the Darwinian account would aver – be seen as mere incidental by-products of dispositions that have selective advantage.

Nevertheless, if human beings can be explained scientifically, and if our activity is really dominated by the twin sovereigns of pleasure and pain, a Darwinian-style explanation will be both seductive and powerful. And so, since Darwin's day, it has proved. For all our pretensions and finery, science and reason reveal that ultimately we are nothing more than survival machines, programmed by nature to survive and reproduce. We are descended from apes, and in the end our aims and objectives are the same. Our means may be different and in some ways more complicated, but the difference is only one of quantity, not of type or quality.

In the Darwinian view, even our reason is simply an instrument for survival. It was not given to us to unearth the ultimate truth about things but simply to find our way around the savannah well enough to survive and reproduce. That we have a disinterested power to seek and the ability to find the truth for its own sake is as much of an illusion as our faith that our moral sense is truly altruistic and other-regarding. It may, be like our moral faith, a useful illusion, for purposes of survival and reproduction, in that having the illusion may encourage us to uncover facts that aid survival. But it is an illusion none the less, foisted on us by our genes, that we are really engineered by nature to discover ultimate, universally valid truth. Neither our sense nor evolution in general provides any guarantee that what our investigations reveal is the real truth, as opposed to a set of notions useful for a time in the struggle for existence, which of course, leaves a question over the Darwinian notion itself that we are basically survival machines. Is that real truth or merely a notion useful in the struggle for survival? The Darwinian account, seeing our knowledge, as everything else about us, in terms simply of selective advantage, gives us no scope for deciding.

Marxism

If Darwinism represented one enlightened hammer-blow to human self-esteem, Marxism represented another. For Darwinism, as eventually became clear, we were in effect prisoners

of our genes. Marx would not have agreed with the indivi-
dualistic psychology implicit in Darwinism, or with its lack of
any real sociology. For Marx, in bourgeois society anyway, we
were prisoners of our society and its institutions, which were
themselves to be unmasked as the façade that covered the
runnings of the economic self-interest of the rich and powerful.

Marx, for all his pretensions to scientific knowledge and the
scorn he heaped on merely 'ethical' socialists, was passionate
and impassioned. As all readers of Marx will be aware, much of
his writing is little more than crude, laboured invective, in its
own way as leaden and soul-destroying as the jargon of his
'scientific' and often dishonest analyses of history and capital.
And here there is another link with his eighteenth-century
antecedents: to the scientific analysis of society he adds the
hostility to the society of the time of Rousseau. For Marx
enlightenment entails unmasking *and* judgemental fervour *and*
reconstruction of a better world on rational principles.

Whether or to what extent Marx was a determinist has been
disputed ever since he actually wrote; what is not in dispute is
that he was the author of the doctrine of historical materialism –
that is, 'the mode of production of the material means of
existence' determines and shapes much else in society and
consciousness. Over and and above the distinction between
causally active infrastructure (economics and technology) and
the superstructure it produces (law, politics, morality, education, art and culture), there are the notions of alienation and
false consciousness. In industrial society in particular, men are
alienated – separated from the fruits of their labour (which go
to another) – and suffer from the illusion that how things are is
how they have to be or would be even in a better society.
Marxist 'science' enlightens by making men aware of the
illusions engendered by false consciousness, and in doing so
provides the first step on the road to the revolution necessary to
overthrow the existing forms of oppression and injustice.

So Marx, like Darwin, is an unmasker. He and his methods show the forms of bourgeois society, its law, its politics, its philosophy, its rationality and its culture, to be neither universally valid nor disinterested. They are, in fact, part of the means by which the capitalist system keeps itself in power and reproduces itself, by presenting its cultural forms as universally valid and disinterested, and by getting its victims to pass them on to their children.

This type of sociological–political unmasking has survived the collapse of Marxism proper. It continues to fuel great swathes of contemporary sociology, of political theory, of feminism and, above all, of literary and cultural studies, all of which are largely devoted to showing how all kinds of apparently innocent activities and institutions, from the family through elements of high and low culture right down to language itself are instruments by which those in power keep and maintain their power. This 'hermeneutics of suspicion', which, following Rousseau, Marx sowed in Western thought, has taken deep root in contemporary culture and education.

It is surely one of the more unfortunate legacies of the Enlightenment in that it really does alienate. It makes it impossible for those in its thrall to take at face value the institutions and social and artistic forms of their society and it does this without putting anything in their place. So, to the currently 'enlightened' mind, we are not only Darwinian apes, we are Darwinian apes surrounded by a veneer of mendacious and empty institutions and cultural forms – never mind that those forms are actually the fruit of long experience and contain within themselves the resources for constructive reform of many of the oppressive and unprepossessing aspects of contemporary life.

Like all revolutionaries, Marx believed profoundly that there was a better way of doing things. In his case this better way was to involve systematic planning. Instead of the waste and injustice inherent in capitalist competition, the state would ensure that labour and resources were used most productively and efficiently, so that the real needs of all the people would be met adequately without failure, misery or the unedifying competition and advertising of the free market. Ultimately, the Marxist ideal is of a situation of plenty in which the state has withered away, the division of labour and other social divisions abolished, and every man (and woman, presumably) free to hunt in the morning, fish in the afternoon, rear cattle in the evening and criticize after dinner.

Needless to say, one big factor in the discrediting of Marxism has been the signal failure of centralized state planning to provide even the basic necessities of life, let alone of socialist states to show signs of withering away. But the dream of a better-planned world system has not gone away. It re-emerges with every international crisis of whatever sort. It remains one of the most seductive legacies of the Enlightenment and of Marx. And one of the most powerful forces in its favour is the continuing ability of post- or sub-Marxist intellectuals to engage large numbers of young people in deconstruction of the institutions and values of their own societies.

Freud

Along with Darwin and Marx, the third great Enlightenment unmasker was Freud. Freud's thought is based on the premise that much of our mental life, and much of what is of most importance, is hidden and unconscious. Underlying this belief is a model of the human psyche derived straight from natural science, from hydraulics, in fact. The idea is that our mental and motivational life consists of a system or build-up of pressures (through desires) and their release in one way or another. For psychological health and stability, this system has to be kept in a state of equilibrium. If this is not done smoothly and naturally, through the natural release of desire, particularly sexual desire, then all kinds of problems will manifest themselves in the psychic life of the subject. These are the mental disorders, the neuroses and psychoses, which Freudian practice is designed to relieve, largely persuading the subject (who is now the patient) to become conscious of the repressed events and desires that are causing his or her blockages and problems.

Freud can be seen as an Enlightenment thinker in at least two ways. First, he purported to be giving a scientific account of human behaviour. He actually intended to link his hydraulic model of desire and its release to its supposed physical basis, though this task was never accomplished. Further, the scientific account is one that enlightens by unmasking, showing us what we really are – highly charged, highly sexual beings, subjects even in childhood of an intense and sexual psycho-history. From time to time Freud denied that he wanted to reduce all desire and all motivation to the sexual, but it was the notion that sexual desire is all-pervasive and the driving force beneath apparently non-sexual motivation that captured and continues to capture the imagination.

So did the idea that the repression of sexual instinct can be damaging, both personally and to society as a whole, where repression is the norm. And this is the second way in which Freud is a characteristically Enlightenment thinker: enlightenment about our hidden desires and motivations is supposed to free us from their tyranny. Certainly Freud followed both Diderot and Rousseau in attempting to dispel the shame, secrecy and hypocrisy which, according to them, accompanied purely natural and healthy instincts, and to demystify the attendant taboos and prohibitions. In Rousseauian vein, Freud tells us that 'it is easy for a barbarian to be healthy, [while] for a civilized man the task is hard', because the barbarian is able to give free rein to his appetites, whereas the civilized man is bound by the constraints of society and family life.

At the same time, particularly in his later writings (such as *Civilization and Its Discontents*), he enjoyed posing as a stern moralist: while repression of our basic instincts and their control and sublimation into the forms of civilized life were painful, not to control them at all would be even more painful both for the individuals and for society as a whole. As well as the pleasure principle, seeking instant gratification of desire, there is also a reality principle, which in face of the risks connected to instant gratification, enjoined 'the temporary toleration of unpleasure as a step on the long indirect road to pleasure'.

Freud was also, like Marx (and, to a less pronounced extent, Darwin) anti-religious. Religion was part of the childhood of mankind, mere fantasy or wish-fulfilment, an opiate against the truth, an evasion of our true situation and our true responsibilities. Reason – scientific reason – showed us that we were alone in the universe. If we were not wholly masters of our own fate, we should at least aim to become so as far as possible. At any rate, social institutions were human constructions and should be modified to respond to human needs and desires. Nobility, so far as it is attainable, consists in coming to terms with the truth of our condition, and taking charge of the future as much as it lies within our power.

The Achilles' Heel

But how could this Enlightenment ideal be realized, if, as Freud teaches, we are largely under the domination of motives and forces of which we are unconscious? If, as Marx teaches, historical materialism is true, and reason – or what we pride ourselves on as such – is largely determined by historical and economic forces, and far from being true for all time changes when conditions change? If, as Darwinism has it, our faculties and abilities, including our intellect and our reason, are simply strategies for survival, useful in specific evolutionary circumstances, but again with no title to delivering timeless truth or validity?

The problem is that when scientific reason is turned on reason itself, then our intellectual powers emerge as the products of rather less elevated causes and circumstances, good for specific survival tasks, perhaps, but with no claim to any truth beyond that – any more than our bodies are of any use in the depths of the ocean or in outer space. If in its first incarnation the elevation of human reason and scientific method seemed to elevate humanity, as time goes on it shows us to be little more than apes, buffeted by pleasure and pain, and all our powers and traditions no more than often misleadingly valued devices for coping with our sovereign masters.

Of course, neither Darwin, nor Marx, nor Freud applied their own analyses to their own theories. If scientific theories are no more than survival strategies (Darwin), in a bourgeois age devices of false consciousness (Marx), largely the product of unconscious and irrational forces (Freud), why should we take any notice of Darwin, Marx and Freud? After all, they are offering what purport to be scientific theories. Perhaps, though, the Achilles' heel of the great rationalists will turn out to be the basis of a deeper hope.

Constructive Rationalism

The potentially subversive effects of Darwin, Marx and Freud on our conception of ourselves as free and rational beings have been largely ignored by progressive thinkers in the twentieth century. In so far as one may speak of tone, the tone has been remarkably consistent throughout the century, from Wells, Shaw, Russell and the Fabians in the earlier part right through to today's modernizers and reformers. Even the two major episodes of the century – the rise and fall of Nazism and of Communism – have been largely ignored. They are treated as if they were just unfortunate aberrations, which have little to teach us in the 'responsible', 'progressive' West. Despite some residual reservations about economic planning resulting from the collapse of centralized planning in the Eastern bloc, the optimism remains largely undiminished. With a little more knowledge, a little better planning (even if not in the economic sphere) and the elimination of ancestral prejudice, better arrangements and a better world are within our grasp. (Anyone who doubts that this tone still exists need only scour the letters pages and the opinion columns of the *Independent* and the *Guardian* for a few days.)

The tone is that which has been dubbed by Hayek 'constructive rationalism'. Here are some characteristic examples:

My plea [is] for the spread of the scientific temper . . . [which] is capable of regenerating mankind and providing an issue for all our troubles

[No society can be regarded as] fully scientific [unless] it has been created deliberately with a certain structure to fulfil certain purposes

The new world order of social justice and comradeship, the rational and classless state, is no wild idealistic dream, but a logical extrapolation from the whole course of evolution, having no less authority than that behind it, and therefore of all faiths the most rational

If we want the world to become a consistent whole, we must think of it as a whole. We must not deal with state, nations and empires . . . if we want world peace we must deal with these divisions as secondary things which have appeared and disappeared almost incidentally in the course of a larger and longer biological adventure. Education can wipe them out completely.

Suppose your intellectual organization, your body of thought, your scientific men say and prove that this, that, or the other course is the right one. Suppose they have the common sense of an alert and educated community to sustain them. Why should not a dictatorship . . . of informed and educated common-sense some day rule the earth? What need is there for a lot of politicians and lawyers to argue about the way things ought to be done? Why make a dispute of world welfare?

Scientific development has finally destroyed . . . the idea that ethics and values are not a matter of our free choice but are rather a matter of obligation for us.

The first two examples are from Bertrand Russell, the third from Joseph Needham, the fourth and fifth from H. G. Wells and the sixth from Jacques Monod, but they could, of course, be multiplied and replicated in the tone and ideology of most of the progressive sages of the century: Wells, Shaw, the Webbs, Keynes (in certain moods), through to C. P. Snow and the visionaries of today of Charter 88, Demos and the rest (who, these days, often see the market rather than the command state as the means by which we will arrive at Needham's rational and classless state).

The particular points worth dwelling on – what makes the tone constructive and rationalistic – are: (1) an advocacy of the spread of the scientific method into human affairs; (2) social reconstruction, internationalism, classlessness and planning in the light of rationally determined ends; (3) the autonomy of value and the rebuilding of our moral sensibility in the light of scientific change, as dictated by scientifically educated experts. Utopianism is, of course, the proper word to describe the attitude, but the term has somewhat gone out of fashion. We have had several Utopias this century, and they are widely regarded even by their supporters as having failed, though generally without hint of apology or compunction. Eric Hobsbawm's sublimely insouciant non-apology for seventy years of communism 'the cause to which I devoted a good deal of my life hasn't worked out', is typical. (The other evasion is the threadbare claim that some allegedly scientific or planned system was not scientific or planned enough.)

But before the non-working-out was so obvious that even the most purblind, rationalist intellectual was forced to admit it, it is worth recalling what it was that Western Utopians originally liked about Soviet Russia. The Webbs, for example, praised the building of the White Sea Canal and its murderous direction by the OGPU, the KGB's predecessor, as not merely a great engineering feat but 'a triumph in human regeneration'. Shaw found that in contrast to prisons in Britain, where men entered as human beings and emerged as criminals, in the USSR they entered as criminal types and would come out ordinary men but for the difficulty of inducing them to leave. J. D. Bernal praised Stalin for his 'deeply scientific approach to all problems', while Wells found him unusually 'candid, fair and honest', and for the Dean of Canterbury he was leading 'his people down new and unfamiliar avenues of democracy'.

Lenin had once defined Communism as electrification plus the soviets. The Utopia that the Western intellectuals of the first half of the twentieth century were looking for was one with a scientific and technological base, a rational social organization and a new type of human being to fit. It would be clean, uncluttered and safe. It would be democratic and classless. Individuals would be educated in modern subjects and formed to behave in socially positive ways. Anti-social behaviour would be eliminated because its causes – poverty, ignorance, greed, etc. – would be removed through education, political reform and psychological hygiene (hence the interest in penal reform). Slums would be cleared in favour of new towns and new architecture. There would be a lot of modern design. Health and medicine would, like education, be dispensed by the state, as would birth control. Laws relating to sexual conduct would be repealed, except laws that forced sexual instruction on the young. Religious and racial discrimination would be outlawed, though society itself would be secular. Censorship would be abolished. Patriotism would be superseded by internationalism. Local and national credit arrangements would be replaced by a world economic directorate. And the new man would be fed and bred to an ideal specification.

Bred. One little remembered facet of progressive thought in the first four decades of the century was what amounted almost to an obsession with eugenics as the means *par excellence* to elevate and purify the human race. The problem, which particularly offended high-minded and often liberal intellectuals, was that the middle classes – from whom the high-minded and the liberal largely sprang – were being out-bred by the indolent, unhygienic and feckless lower classes. Morever, modern medicine was keeping 'weak and degenerate' people alive, and even permitting them to breed, perpetuating their weaknesses and degeneracy in future generations. This apparent subversion of Darwinian principles – and supporters of eugenics derived their premises from Darwin – had to be countered. The middle classes would have to be persuaded by social pressure and financial incentives to breed more. Conversely, the lower classes would be encouraged to use birth control. The feeble-minded, who, in Russell's words, are 'apt to have enormous numbers of illegitimate children all, as a rule, wholly worthless to the community', would have to be sterilized.

It is, perhaps, worth recalling that in the USA in the 1930s, twenty-four states had compulsory sterilization laws, under which 36,000 people had been sterilized by 1941. Social hygiene was by no means a theoretical issue. It was only the Nazi regime that pushed eugenics off the political agenda, just as the collapse of Communism has removed the possibility of arguing for socialist Utopias, at least when they are presented as socialist Utopias.

And yet the impulses that favoured these things are by no means dead. In the 1990s, they have simply been channelled into different forms. We do not have the crude and blatant eugenics of the earlier decades of the century. But we do have abortion on demand and on the state-provided health service. We do have genetic screening and genetic 'counselling', which often amounts to pressure to abort handicapped babies, not unreasonably objected to by the living disabled; we do have genetic engineering; the prospect of designer babies is imminent, as is the use of biological means to modify behaviour. We have the prospect of human tissue and even organs being grown in laboratories from cloned embryos for transplantation – imagine the outcry had it emerged that such things happened in the laboratories of the Third Reich. In a very real and intimate way, scientific advances are challenging our sense of human life as a sacred, divine gift, just as deeply as the ostensibly more violent and public campaigns of mass extermination earlier this century, but in a way more insidiously. This is because the proponents of genetic medicine are not fanatics in a political sense; and what they advocate seems, given the advances in medicine that they themselves are pioneering, to be inevitable.

If, during the course of the century, eugenics has not so much disappeared from the agenda as re-emerged, transformed into genetic medicine, what of Utopian politics? Here the situation appears more complicated. In theory we claim to have learned and applied the lessons of the failures of socialism. The state should no longer own and man the commanding heights of the economy. Market institutions are allowed to flourish, and formerly state-run utilities and industries are privatized. (And by a sublime transformation of the old Communist excuse, we are told by rationalists of the market that market failure – as in Russia – is due to its not being market enough.) On the other hand, as we shall see in more detail in chapter 6 (page 157–226), outside the economy the state controls and directs an extraordinary amount of our lives, as is indicated by the fact that even in Britain, even after the Thatcher revolution, 40 per cent or more of GDP is spent by the state and its agencies. And while it does not directly control industry or the newly privatized utilities, it hedges their operations about with ever-increasing amounts of regulatory policies and controls.

In any case, as far as the twentieth-century rationalist– scientific programme sketched in this section goes, much of it has been achieved and much of our current thinking and politics is predicated on it. Centralized state planning of industry has turned out to be an irrational mode of production and distribution in comparison to the free market. But how is the market justified, and what are its fruits?

Of course, it is possible to defend the market in terms of its tendency to force people to compete and to take responsibility for their decisions, good or bad, and libertarians of the right frequently do defend it in these terms. But, equally, the market tends to undermine tradition and hierarchy: not only does it promote and produce social mobility, it produces undreamt- of-wealth for the vast majority of the population (as compared with rival systems). It virtually eliminates real poverty (despite the misrepresentations of the poverty lobby) and promotes classlessness – and is often defended on precisely these grounds. In the name of the market, national customs and ancient institutions are swept away. The market is a solvent of old barriers and old structures – and, as anyone who has been to Poland or Czechoslovakia since 1989 will recognize, old values and moralities.

In the Eastern bloc, for forty or even seventy years, Com- munism did not kill off religion and traditional morality, but ten years of capitalism is doing it very nicely. In the gulag and the totalitarian state, people turned to religion to give their lives meaning and hope. But now, amid the cornucopia of choice and instant gratification that the market promises and supplies, thoughts and aspirations remain obstinately earthbound.

As the most efficient means known to man of providing the means for the greatest number to fulfil their desires, the market is strangely consonant with many of the demystifying tendencies of the Enlightenment, and instrumental in producing their realization. This is particularly the case when the market floats free of local or national roots, which, by virtue of its inherent internationalism, it naturally tends to do.

And even if the market in isolation might encourage individuals to stand on their own feet, we do not operate a pure market system. Much else in our society is designed to mitigate the rigours of market responsibility, and encourages precisely the opposite. In our socialized approach to welfare, we reward incompetence and fecklessness by refusing to distinguish between those who deserve help and those who do not. The civil servants and social workers who distribute welfare are taught not to make judgements as to who deserves help, but to distribute welfare in terms of need, and in terms of who is most 'at risk'. The more 'need' you can demonstrate, the more help you will get, and quicker, however that need has been brought about. Similarly, simply being (passively) 'at risk' is enough to trigger state intervention, no matter how the risk has come about. People are thus discouraged from getting themselves and their children out of risk, because if they do their benefits will cease. They are also discouraged from saving, because those with savings are not allowed benefits. We also encourage more and more people to describe themselves as having 'special needs' or disabilities so as to have those needs met or disabilities compensated. Patient and industrious individuals who struggle to keep going without pressing their demands, 'needs' or victim status are pushed way down the queue for benefits, below addicts and violent people who have made themselves destitute and homeless, and feckless parents whose neglect and absence of provision and foresight put their offspring 'at risk'. Strikingly, even though health and longevity have increased dramatically over the last twenty years, the number of people on disability benefit has quadrupled. (Many in our parents' generation would have done anything rather than suffer what they – but not we – regard as the shame of going on benefit.)

It is not just in the poorer reaches of society that responsibility and dignity are undermined. Presidents who sin are described as having an 'addiction to sex', and they 'share their pain' with their population; duchesses who get into debt suffer from shopaholism, apparently now a medically recognized condition, with the twelve-point programme of 'Alcoholics Anonymous'; government ministers and international sportsmen who cheat on their wives and leave the mothers of their children 'find themselves in situations'. All receive counselling, no doubt; all present themselves as victims; all seek to be understood and sympathized with; all see themselves and want the rest of us to see them as subjected to forces as impersonal and irresistible as volcanoes, earthquakes and hurricanes.

The severe and severely rational thinkers of the scientific Enlightenment would not have approved of any of this. They were certainly judgemental and highly so. They advocated self-reliance. Indeed, that was part of what they hoped universal rationality would bring. They believed that all genuine seekers of truth would come to agree on the truth both about the universe in general and human life in particular. They were not, in the reductive sense, democrats. They did not believe that the majority was necessarily right, particularly if the majority was unenlightened.

But at a deeper level they did think of man as subject to

scientific analysis, and ruled by passion and desire. Logically, judgementalism can play no role in a system that operates on causal, scientific principles. You can't blame an apple for falling or a wind for blowing, or a neurone for firing or a man's hand for moving if the movement is part of some predetermined causal chain, even though that movement is to hit another or to fire the shot that will blow off his head.

I do what I am determined to do, just like a bit of the physical world (which I am), and that is that. I am no more personally responsible for my desires or my actions than I am for the beating of my heart or the release of my digestive juices. I can no more be blamed for my impetuosity than for my short-sightedness. Both are brought about by factors over which I have no control. They manifest themselves in given situations whether I like it or not, and whatever I do. The violent or drug-crazed yob who 'had the red mist come over me' or 'lost it, doctor' when he beat up his pregnant girlfriend is only partially accurate. On the scientific view of mankind, he never had 'it' in the first place. And neither does any of us. All that can be done in society is to modify upbringing and the environment so that our desires will turn out to have more peaceable ends and violent behaviour will be conditioned out of us.

Britain, *circa* 1999, would be unrecognizable in all kinds of ways to the eighteenth-century rationalist, and not attractive. At the same time it can be seen as an application of Enlightenment psychology and anthropology. We have a market dedicated to the satisfaction of desire, operating pretty scientifically to ascertain just what those demands are. And along with the market as a rational system for the satisfaction of desire, we have a rationalism of the market, at times every bit as ideological and impervious to the complexity and messiness of human reality (that is of individual human beings) as the rationalism of socialist planning.

At the same time, our social structure is engineered to

emphasize our status as unfree and determined by social and psychological causes. How could the Enlightenment thinkers quarrel with any of this, however much they might dislike the implicit populism, the dumbing down and the vulgarity and mediocrity of it all? For isn't the Enlightenment teaching an attempt to demystify motive, to see us as under the sovereign masters of pleasure and pain, and to satisfy these masters as smoothly and as extensively as possible? Doesn't the implicit determinism preclude any judgements on the relative worth of different types of desire, except in so far as my desire impedes yours? In a curious way, the collective non-judgementalism of Herderian irrationalism converges at this point with individual non-judgementalism of Enlightenment psychology.

And again, doesn't the determinism implicitly see us all as patients or victims, rather than as active, responsible agents? It sees us as pushed around by circumstances, and thus having a legitimate call on circumstances and on society at large to accommodate our desires, or at least to mitigate the worst consequences of our acting on our desires – which we cannot, in any case, avoid. We are all, in a sense, addicts. We are not masters of our fate or our motives. It is just that some addictions are more uncomfortable to those who have them than others. But the cure is the manipulation of desire, not praise or blame; the condition of the addict is therapeutic, not moral. President Clinton asks us to be sorry for him because of the inconvenience of his addiction, as, one supposes, does the Duchess of York. Neither is to be blamed, only sympathized with and offered 'help'.

If we are living in an Enlightenment world, in that the human beings who inhabit modern society are very much those beings described by Enlightenment psychology, there is a yet more precise sense in which the 1990s are recapitulating the 1790s.

Faith in Science

In the first place, there is still tremendous faith in science as a form of wisdom, and in scientific methods. There are, of course, some who object to the various applications of science, and some who would question the truth and validity of scientific theory as such. Nevertheless, neither type of objection has done much to dent the prestige of science, and certainly not in governmental, industrial and administrative circles. How could it, given that modern life depends on science at every turn? Furthermore, for every fashionable deconstruction of science – which tend to be both implausibly exaggerated and written in impenetrable sociologese and so eminently containable in academic ghettoes – there is an equally fashionable Stephen Hawking, Roger Penrose or Richard Dawkins, writing brilliantly and lucidly, and capturing the popular imagination. Among the generally literate and well educated, science retains its fascination, as is evidenced by the remarkable upsurge in popular science books and in the attention paid to science and scientists in serious newspapers. Indeed, given the extent to which scientists and science writers purport to be educating and leading the population at large, and the extent to which the population at large is content to be led, it is clear that the notions of scientific enlightenment and of enlightenment through science are very much alive.

Scientific-style enlightenment also characterizes many political initiatives in the 1990s. In all types of areas, reform is said to be necessary, not because of some glaring deficit in the existing state of affairs, but because what exists does not meet some abstract principle of system of rationality. In Britain, for example, over the years the House of Lords has been reasonably effective as a second legislative chamber, but along with many politically literate people, the present government is, in Kantian style, offended by the role within the Lords of the hereditary peers. And in one sense they are right. It is not easy to defend a hereditary principle in an egalitarian, democratic age on egalitarian, democratic principles.

But why does this mean it has to be changed? Hereditary peers have a degree of independence, which is presumably what is needed in a second chamber. They are not dependent on the government or the electorate. They are not the creatures of patronage that a nominated upper house is likely to be, nor are they superannuated politicians rejected by voters, nor simply a replica of the lower chamber. And if we are going to attack the hereditary principle in this case, why not in all other cases? Why not, for example, in the case of the Prime Minister's efforts to get a better education for his children than the majority of children have, and which his own political party would not allow them to have? Nevertheless, rationality and modernity demand constitutional change, and it will come, not just in the Lords, but also in the voting system (again, antiquated, rationally indefensible, especially if you are a Liberal, but – just probably – better than as yet untried alternatives), in the union of England, Scotland, Wales and Northern Ireland, in Europe, and no doubt in much else besides.

What is striking is not so much the detailed cases – though, taken together, they represent a radical reform of the British state, as the government quite correctly claims – as the argument in their collective favour: modernity, efficiency, rationality. And here we are very much on Enlightenment ground. The only possible counter-position is that of the Burkean conservative: what does not seem 'reasonable' and 'modern' to the ordinarily educated mind in 1999 may, nevertheless – and despite appearance – be the fruit of long experience and accumulated wisdom gathered from many different points of view. Further: we do not know the costs of either demolition or reconstruction. All human action, all policy, has unforeseeable and unintended consequences. These will emerge only when it is too late, and the threads holding our life together have been severed.

There is also the question of sentimental attachment, characteristically overlooked by proponents of new, more rational and reasonable orders. In the economic sphere George Orwell was as convinced a rationalist reconstructor as any. He constantly argued in favour of nationalization and against 'the big capitalists, the bankers, the landlords and idle rich'; in an England 'true to itself' it would be 'goodbye to the *Tatler* and the *Bystander*, and farewell to the lady in the Rolls-Royce car' and on with an English version of the notion of human equality. Nevertheless, when it came to broader political and moral considerations, Orwell was implacably opposed to the clever, bloodless rationalism and internationalism of such as Wells and Shaw. In 1941, he wrote

> what has kept England on its feet during the past year? In part, no doubt, some vague ideas about a better future, but chiefly the atavistic emotion of patriotism, the ingrained feeling of the English-speaking peoples that they are superior to foreigners. For the last twenty years the main object of English left-wing intellectuals has been to break this feeling down, and if they had succeeded, we might be watching SS men patrolling the London streets at this moment . . . The energy that actually shapes the world springs from emotions – racial pride, leader-worship, religious belief, love of war – which liberal intellectuals write off as anachronisms, and which they have usually destroyed so completely in themselves as to have lost all power of action.

Orwell comments that, whereas for Hitler's sake a great nation has virtually destroyed itself, 'for the common-sense, essentially hedonistic world-view which Mr Wells puts forward, hardly a human creature is willing to shed a pint of blood'. He also points out the apparently ineradicable tendency of British intellectuals to Anglophobia, and also of one-time pacifists to switch to bellicism, so long as they themselves do not have to fight. Both points are worth bearing in mind in 'modern' Britain, where we have Anglophobia masquerading as Euro-federalism and air-strikes against Serbs and Iraqis from a government and a party whose members were once individually and collectively committed to unilateral disarmament and, to say the least, unenthusiastic about the Falklands campaign, in which British interests and heritage were directly involved. But they are probably wrong politically. I see no popular enthusiasm for a Balkan entanglement or for further erosion of British traditions and institutions by a European bureaucracy, now shown beyond doubt and for all its protestations and charters, to be hopelessly and probably irredeemably inefficient, wasteful and corrupt.

Of course, I am not saying, any more than Orwell was, that racial pride and leader-worship, religious belief or love of war are necessarily good things (though they may not in all cases be wholly bad either). The point is rather that modernists, like Burke's 'sophisters, economists and calculators', do not like them, would rather they did not exist, and so pretend they do not exist. But, as we see in Serbia and, to a lesser degree perhaps, in Iraq, they do exist, as they do in more benign form in our own country. Are such feelings irrational, as opposed to non-rational? Or are they potentially the basis of that 'mixed system of opinion and sentiment', having its origin in ancient chivalry which alone can furnish the wardrobe of moral imagination, giving rulers and ruled something they can warm to, and against the background of which the aridities of legalism and terrors of sheer power are held in abeyance?

His feelings of this sort, linking us to the past and future by imperceptible, almost mystical bonds, hold society together. Without them questioning, sophistry, doubt and the equally powerful feelings of self-interest will tear society apart. May it be only if everyone in a society feels him or herself bound by a higher law and a higher authority that social bonds will not dissolve under the relentless scrutiny of reason and criticism?

Unfortunately, though, if you want a hearing these days, this is not the way to argue, any more than genetic research or pornography are to be criticized on biblical grounds. Romantic conservatives, attached to Burke's 'ancient chivalry', and dog-matic religious believers have to disguise their true thoughts behind a veil of broadly utilitarian argument – defending the Lords for their qualities of debate and sagacity of deliberation, attacking genetic engineering because of possibly lethal side-effects. Even in the forms of debate, then, the discourse of the Enlightenment appears triumphant. In 'serious' discussion, it has swept away all other voices, all other frames of reference, to our impoverishment.

4

The Uncertainty of Progress

There is only one certainty in life, which is death. If the past is anything to go by, there is only one certainty about a civilization, a culture or an empire, which is that it will come to an end. There is only one certainty about a species, which is that it will become extinct. And if the second law of thermodynamics is to be believed, there is only one certainty about any form of order, which is that eventually it will run down, collapsing into decay and disorder.

We know these things deep down. We know that much of our activity is simply an attempt to evade their recognition. We know that, compared to the security and warmth and optimism and good health of childhood, the promise of the future is the chill of old age and the slow onset of chronic illness, decrepitude and pain. For those who permit it, nostalgia for lost time can become unbearable and overwhelming. We can think of some of the great works of art of our era: Proust's *À la recherche du temps perdu*, with its terrible final scene of the effects of age and time on youth and beauty; Schubert's *Winterreise* with its so poignant dreams of the spring that is lost; Poussin's *Four Seasons*, the paradise of spring and delight of summer leading inexorably to the ashen tones and glutinous morass of winter's deluge. *Carpe diem* – pluck the day while we have it – is a possible reaction to our fate, perhaps the only possible reaction for the earthbound, but it is an optimism founded on pessimism, a cheerfulness that can exist only in the face of the horror we know will come to us tomorrow.

'While we are talking, envious time moves on. Pick today's fruits, put little trust in what is still to come.' Horace's eleventh ode from Book I contains the wisdom of Rome, balanced only by Virgilian images of impossible and unattainable Arcadias. The Romans did acknowledge progress in the specialized sciences, but as the Roman empire went on expectations of further progress evaporated.

For the Greeks, fate is yet more unkind and implacable; the gods are capricious and cruel. The archaic smile was bought at a terrible psychological cost, the famed Greek 'cheerfulness' the reaction of the sybarite who can no longer face the realities of the tragedies and the *Iliad*. Nor should we forget Odysseus' visit to Hades, and his conversation with the shade of Achilles: he would rather be the most miserable servant on earth than ruler of all the lifeless dead in this place. For much of the classical period in Greece, the cosmogony was that of the poet Hesiod. The world was going through Five Ages, of which our age was the fifth, that of iron, the last and worst. In the fifth century BC, Prometheus became a popular hero. He who stole fire from the gods became a symbol of technological awareness, and of a corresponding transition from savagery to civilization. But he remained an equivocal figure, at least until the eighteenth- and nineteenth-century romantics; he was destined by Zeus for eternal punishment for having defied the gods and taken the side of humanity. Moreover, throughout the classical era, belief in scientific or technological progress was balanced by fears of moral regress.

Progress was an idea largely absent in the ancient world. If things got better for a time, this was at most a temporary phase in an otherwise hopeless existence. Even less was there any conviction that progress could be universally shared. What improvements there might be would be only for one particular group or people. Each tribe's gods looked after their own, if that, and looking after one's own was usually through making a footstool of one's enemies. So where, then, did ideas of universal progress come from?

In contrast to the pessimism of paganism, stands the messianism of the Old Testament. Since leaving Egypt, the Israelites were motivated by hope, specifically that Abraham's posterity should increase and prosper and enter the Promised Land. They did, but then their lands were halved, and the majority were led into Babylonian captivity. After this débâcle, messianism was given a more spiritual interpretation by some. In the Book of Maccabees earthly hope was transformed into hope for the next life, for the first time in Jewish history.

What is notable about Old Testament hopes is their restricted compass. Even in the New Testament, Jesus speaks of the Gentiles (non-Jews) as dogs feeding off the crumbs that fall from the Jewish table. It is only with St Paul that a nationalistic sect takes on universal significance, and opens its doors and its hopes to all, Gentile as well as Jew, barbarian and Greek, woman and man, slave as well as free man.

But what was it hope for? Opinions differ, but what it clearly was not was hope for a secular scientific Utopia on earth. Nor, for all the primitive communism that might have been practised in the early Church, did it constitute a political programme. How could it be, when Jesus had so emphatically renounced political ambition, and when the early Christians were apparently expecting the Second Coming in the near future?

It did not come. In fact, Christianity and the Roman Empire, whose religion it became, expanded. The Church took on an institutional, quasi-imperial form. Its spiritual success and stature became intertwined with material progress, embellishment and establishment. As the Dark Ages gave way to the Middle Ages, the Church took on more and more of a political role. The Pope became an earthly sovereign, and the Church attended increasingly to the material needs of its members, who were potentially, and according to its doctrines, the whole of humanity. It is tempting, then, to see the progressive hopes of the scientific Enlightenment as a version of Judaic messianism combined with Christian universalism, together with a gradual displacement of concentration on salvation in the next world to the corporal works of mercy in this.

Whig History

Whatever its roots, what I am calling Enlightenment progressivism and what others have referred to as the Whig view of history is and remains obstinately part of our self-image, despite the vicissitudes of the twentieth century. The view consists of two components: first, that history is moving in the direction of greater scientific sophistication and knowledge, together with a more rational, more inclusive and more equal social organization and corresponding material advances, and second, that this ineluctable trend constitutes progress in a desirable sense. This view is flattering to us, because it implies that we, in the Western democracies at the end of the twentieth century, occupy the apex of history, the point to which all other periods and eras have been tending, but of whose full realization they have, each in their own way, fallen short. This is, doubtless, partly why we hold it with such an unquestioning faith.

What we now need to do is to question the first element of the Whig view, the belief that all history is tending in a certain direction. This doctrine is at once highly plausible and deeply inhuman. It is plausible because, from our perspective, everything that has happened has contributed to the way we are now. This, indeed, is a truism. We would not be where we are now had the past been different. Maybe even quite minor differences in the past would have been magnified and amplified to produce great differences in the years that followed.

From popular science, we are familiar with the claim that minuscule differences in the first nanoseconds of the universe would have produced a very different universe from the one we inhabit, in which beings like us could never have evolved.

Then again, maybe if Cleopatra's nose had been just slightly different Antony would not have fallen in love with her, and the Roman empire would never have emerged. Perhaps, as Tolstoy argued in *War and Peace*, the fate of wars depends on the little actions of insignificant soldiers; perhaps if Napoleon had not had a cold at the battle of Waterloo, the French would have won. Perhaps the cowardly action of just one unknown French soldier was the pivot on which the fate of the whole battle swung.

But what, if anything, follows from the truistic point that the present is a cumulation of myriad past causes, any tiny one of which might have been sufficient to have changed the present? It certainly does not follow that the past was designed or intended to produce the future. And, truth to tell, the possible effects of minor contingencies are not usually what Whig historians are basing their progressivist views on. Generally they want to play down the role of random details like Cleopatra's nose or Napoleon's cold. What they claim is that beneath the eddies, these surface phenomena and the odd, unpredictable accidents of history, a deeper, irresistible current is moving forward and will flow whatever the individual incidents; something like the 'long march of every man' or the gradual, but apparently steady growth of science, liberalism and democracy. Often these views will be underpinned by a quasi-Marxist assumption that scientific and technological de-velopments and their economic effects are tending inevitably in a given direction, and that these developments and effects bring in their train corresponding social, political and cultural changes.

The first point to notice here is that, once again, we will be looking at things from our point of view. Of course, the modern world is characterized by the rise of science and the rise of democracy. One of the themes of this book is to chart aspects of this development. But one has to ask whether the development was inevitable or intended, whether it had to happen as it did, and also whether other ages and other cultures would see things from the same point of view. Over and above this Herderian point, we might ask whether it is inevitable that things will continue in the same way, and what, from the world-historical perspective, we can say about a trend that peters out after a few centuries. After all, it is not impossible that the rise of science will, in various ways, slow down.

It is possible that there will be a technological or ecological disaster, which will destroy our current levels of prosperity, or even some catastrophical climatic change. Even without conceding the wilder claims of the ecological doom-sayers, one cannot rule out such possibilities completely; nor is it possible to rule out some maverick political agent armed with technologically sophisticated weapons upsetting the current world order to retard scientific and technological development. Talk of global winters brought about by atomic weaponry is not as fashionable as it was twenty or thirty years ago, but if it was a real possibility then, instability in Russia and elsewhere surely make it a real, if slight, possibility now.

In various ways, then, like the antlers of the Irish elk, which became too heavy for it to bear and led to its extinction, the success and extent of scientific development could prove its – and our – undoing. Moreover, even in its theoretical core it is not clear that science is progressing. Optimism over 'grand unified theories', linking quantum theory and relativity has proved premature. The various conundra and paradoxes of quantum theory seem no closer to resolution than they were in the 1920s when they first became apparent. We seem no nearer the end of science in 1999 than we were in 1988 when Stephen

Hawking so confidently predicted its imminent appearance. In any case, we have been here before: every great scientific advance, Aristotle, Newton, Einstein and quantum theory itself, has been ushering in the end of science – only itself to be questioned and eventually overturned by a successor theory. The lesson history teaches us about science is not a steady, cumulative advance in understanding, but what philosophers call the 'pessimistic meta-induction': that the best theory of every age proves eventually to be misconceived, very far from an accurate picture of the universe.

Here, though, is a more disturbing possibility: that in a sense we *have* reached the end of science, but not in a reassuring way. In 1928, the great physicist Max Born was confidently predicting that physics, 'as we know it', would be finished in six months. This was because there were, Born thought, just two elementary particles, the electron and the proton, and the equation governing the electron had just been discovered. (At that time no one had heard of the neutron, let alone of quarks and anti-particles.)

However, just while Born was foreseeing the end of physics, the equally great physicist Niels Bohr was having other, rather more disturbing thoughts. The quantum world was so strange, so difficult to understand in human terms (particles jumping from one state or position to another without going through the intermediate stages, particles with position but no momentum, entities that were particles one minute, waves at the next). Might it not be that in getting to that level of smallness, we had reached the limits of human understanding? Might understanding be restricted to the common-sense assumptions of classical physics, assumptions that quantum theory shows do not hold at the sub-atomic level? Might it not be that the quantum world will be for ever unintelligible to us, even though we had had incredible success in predicting the outcomes of its operations? Indeed, the very predictive success of theories that are, in a deep sense, unintelligible to us if anything bears out Bohr's point. While in 1999 we can measure and manipulate the outcomes of quantum events to twenty decimal places, we are no nearer really understanding what is actually going on inside elementary particles (if, indeed, they are particles) than were Bohr and Heisenberg in the 1920s. If in that sense we are at the end of science – at the end of the science we *can* do – we will need radically to rethink our notions of scientific progress.

Whatever one might say about the progress of science in the narrow sense, social and historical progress is far more intimately connected with our self-image, and its inevitability or even general direction far more suspect. Immediately after the fall of the Berlin Wall, all the talk was of Francis Fukuyama's 'end of history' thesis. The claim, which derived from Hegel's view of history, was that now that liberal democracy reigned throughout the world, the end point of history had been reached. Liberal democracy was inherently stable and non-aggressive; it was the state that satisfied the wishes of the vast majority of any population in such a way that there would be no impetus for anything else, no need for a revolution, or for any further radical change. Moreover, it was to this point that history had been moving, the individual liberation of the masses. The thesis was decked out by Fukuyama with impressive and optimistic charts showing the extent and spread of liberal democracy throughout the world *circa* 1990 (from its presence in at most three countries in 1790 to its dominance in sixty-one in 1990).

Several things were interesting about this. First, Fukuyama's version of the 'long march of every man' was rather different from that of the Marxist socialists of the twentieth century. Instead of history moving towards universal socialism, it was actually moving towards free-market liberal democracy, a world characterized by respect for individual freedoms and rights and by private property. But the underlying impulse of thought was similar. The difference was that where the socialists cited Marx, Fukuyama relied on Hegel. But, then, Marx himself had turned Hegel on his head: instead of world history being the movement of spirit to individual freedom, rational and constitutional monarchy, to guarantee freedom and reason – Hegel's version – for Marx, it was the movement of physical matter into class-ridden human society and through to universal socialism. So Fukuyama could be seen as the post-Reagan, post-Thatcher revenge of the Hegelians on the Marxists. But, critically, both shared the view that there was a discernible and inevitable pattern to history, against which exceptions to the pattern were to be seen as no more than temporary and ultimately unavailing interruptions.

Of course, Fukuyama and the Marxists could not both be right – which ought to make us somewhat sceptical of the type of claim each is making. Already in 1999 the Fukuyama of 1990 looks dated. Liberal democracy and capitalism have not triumphed in the USSR, or if they have, it is the 'wrong sort' of liberalism and the market. The world of 1999 is far less stable economically, politically and socially than the gurus of the market had us hope a decade ago. Even now the ex-Marxists are reappearing from out of the woodwork intoning once more their mantras about the crises of capitalism. Not that Marxism, scientific or otherwise, had triumphed this century. Yet protagonists of both doctrines would have us believe that anyone who stood in their way was out of touch with their time, and should step aside (or, more likely, be pushed aside). And that is where we find the human cost of doctrines of inevitable progress. 'You can't put a clock back,' we reactionaries are arrogantly told as we, our families and our views are pushed to the margins or, as happened on numerous occasions this century, actually liquidated.

Putting the Clock Back

You cannot put the clock back: again a truism, in so far as it means that what has happened cannot unhappen. But this does not imply that history is moving in a set or particular direction, which is how those who speak in this way intend it to be understood. That understanding is simply not true. We can allow for the irreversibility of the past and for a sense in which what has once been discovered cannot be undiscovered. We cannot just forget the secrets of atomic weaponry, for example, even though many scientists might prefer that we would, and even though, as a result of unforeseen catastrophes, this knowledge might one day become lost. Nor can we undo things once done, again however much we wish we could. But none of this predetermines what will happen in the future; even though we feel the odds were stacked against us, those in touch with the spirit of the time, as they would no doubt put it, will not necessarily have things all their way.

I well remember sitting outside a pub in Moravia in May 1987 drinking beer with the late Peter Fuller and two friends from the clandestine discussion group in Brno we had come to address. This was one month after what, in retrospect, must be seen as a critical visit by Gorbachev to Prague, in which it was made clear to the Czech leadership that the Red Army would not intervene again in Eastern Europe, though few outsiders realized the significance of the visit at the time. 'Will all this ever come to an end?' Peter asked our friends about Communism and the regime that looked then so contemptuous of its opponents, so dismissive of opposition and, above all, so permanent and immovable – as, remember, did all the Eastern European regimes appear to those armies of Western 'experts' and university departments and research institutes dedicated to the study and, as it often seemed, to the promotion of Communism.

'Yes', said Petr Oslzly, dramaturge, organizer of Theatre on a String in Brno, friend and colleague of Václav Havel and focus of intellectual opposition in Brno to the Husák regime. He sighed. 'Yes, because in the end everything comes to an end. But it won't happen in our lifetime.'

And indeed, wrong as Petr was, it was not events in Czechoslovakia itself that brought about the fall of Communism there. It was what was happening in Poland, and in Moscow and, more indirectly, what had happened in Washington and London. If President Reagan and Mrs Thatcher had not upped the arms race, so bringing the Russian economy to its knees, if Poland had not produced Lech Walesa and the Pope (who in 1980 was the *only* world leader to foresee the imminent end of Communism) . . .

My point is not so much the detail of this story, though it was and remains a heartening one for those who were told over and over again during the Cold War that they had to face reality, move with the times, regrettable as it no doubt was, etc., etc. 'Regrettable' it certainly was, but immovable, permanent, unchangeable it was not. Great leaders and lots of courageous smaller people supporting them can change things in a big way. What, for example, if Jimmy Carter and Neil Kinnock or Michael Foot had been the leaders in the West in the 1980s? There would have been at least partial nuclear disarmament; there would have been no talk of the 'evil empire' (still scoffed at by many, even as each day brings more revelations of just how evil it was). Husák, or some Husák clone, would still be in Prague and the KGB in Moscow.

The trouble is, our imaginations are narrow and our memories are short. We are too complacent, too passive in the face of the world as it is. We look at everything from the perspective of the present, as if the present were all that there could have been, and as if the future were going to be just like the present. And narrow imaginations and short memories play into the hands of those in power today. Whig history becomes official, and complacent progressivism is embedded in the minds of thinkers and educators who tend mostly to reinforce the illusions of the day.

Indeed, as Saul Bellow has pointed out, in our century just as political leaders have posed as intellectuals and teachers, so intellectuals and teachers have aped the doctrines and attitudes of the leaders (on whom these minor civil servants are largely dependent). One thinks of Lenin, the Great Headmaster himself, a 'powerhouse disguised as a pedant', as Bellow puts it; one thinks of Sartre, a shallow thinker but a Leninist of the mind, and his countless followers, not least in Cambodia.

But we forget how precarious was the journey that brought us to where we are today, and how uncertain the future. And even with the fall of Communism, this phenomenon is alive and well. The radicals of the sixties we remember so well inveighing against the 'corrupt' institutions of the capitalist hegemony (that is, the rich, free and comparatively unmanaged universities of the time) are now the besuited deans, heads of college and vice-chancellors of the University of X plc, more ruthless and less principled in pursuit of their managerial grail than any genuine captain of industry with a care for his products and profits.

All we can see is where we are now, and we generalize from this to both past and future, as if all history is some irresistible surge forward to a goal rather like where we are now only more so and with the wrinkles ironed out. At any time, it would have been possible to look at history in this way, but it has only become deeply ingrained over the past two hundred or so years, for part of the image of modernity is just that: a steadily rising tide of scientific and political progress on the crest of which we are riding. In so far as people have become used to this idea, they have acted to confirm it, and used it to cow and subdue those who would stand in their way – who are written off as out of touch, negative and fearful, suitable subjects for counselling and staff development.

Rhetorical History

But it is all rhetoric. To the extent that recent history has confirmed progressivist rhetoric, that is not because the rhetoric is true in isolation. It is because we and our leaders have chosen to act in line with it. It is true that the media and politics are dominated by the lazy certainties of 'enlightened' thought, whether this takes the guise of quasi-Utopian socialism or managerial consumerism. But the impact is the same: nothing must stand in the way of scientific development, and the political and social policies such development makes possible. The fact that people who appeal to the future and would claim to be enlightened often offer diametrically opposed proposals (socialism, capitalism) should make us pause, as we have already observed.

But it does not. The rhetoric of 'moving with the times' overshadows the differences, which are obscured anyway by the common roots of both styles of political thought: the eighteenth-century Enlightenment, its emphasis on science and progress, and its hostility to religion and other more ancient, more traditional forms of thought and allegiance, which in its terms were irrational.

The sub-Enlightenment rhetoric of the steady progress of all humanity converging on a common and foreseeable goal doubtless owes a lot to the idea of science itself progressing and changing our lives in steady, predictable ways. But this is not a conception of science that is true either to science or to its history.

Deep theory is one thing, and problematic and unpredictable enough, as we have just seen. But even more uncertain are predictions of technological developments. There is, indeed, a good theoretical reason why this should be so. If we could predict tomorrow's technology to any degree of accuracy, we would be able to predict how it would work. But if we knew today how it would work, we would be able to develop it now. It would be today's technology. And, of course, technological developments have the profoundest effects on the way we live. So if technological developments are, in their nature, unpredictable, then there is a very clear sense in which the future will be radically unlike what anyone can foresee now with any degree of certainty or justification.

H. G. Wells may have predicted modern warfare, tanks, air and space travel, the destruction of the countryside, the megalopolis and biological engineering, but he did not foresee the way in which human individualism and market forces would triumph over Utopian social engineering. He did not predict the microchip, surely as significant a discovery as any he did predict; neither could time travel take place as he thought, nor has science led to the socialistic world government he foresaw. In any case, the details of the effects of the motor-car and air travel on the lives of literally hundreds of millions of people, and just how these things would transform their lives and society, were hardly foreseen by Wells or any of the Edwardian prophets.

Similarly, even in the 1930s and 1940s when the mathematics and the early technology were being developed, no one foresaw just how the computer would transform everyday life, or just how information technology would reach into every corner of society and practice. Do we, even now, understand this? Do we really know what the effects of computers and IT are in the present, let alone what they will be in the future? And all this uncertainty about technological developments and their direction is quite apart from the obvious and much belaboured point that any technological development has consequences both intended and unintended. Each technological development solves some problem, or it would not be a development. But it also throws up unforeseen problems of its own, some of which may be far harder to eradicate than the problems it solved – the motor-car, nuclear power and pesticides are only three of the most obvious examples.

In other words, the history of science and technology does not support the progressivist view that scientific and technological development represent a calm and straightforward trajectory towards more knowledge and a better future. So we should not be intimidated by claims about the inevitability and foreseeability of scientific progress into accepting without question analogous claims about the inevitability of particular trends in the political, social or human domains. Even less should we concede that changes which come about as a result of historical trends necessarily amount to progress, rather than to regress. As I am arguing throughout this book, there has been much regress over the past two hundred years, as a result of what many would regard as progress.

History and Evolution

But – finally – no more would the theory of evolution itself support any optimistic view of historical change. While human history differs from evolutionary change in the natural world in having elements of deliberate planning (on our part), in crucial respects there are similarities. In particular there is the point that both in nature and in human affairs a solution to one difficulty or problem will always throw up new problems of its own. In nature, a variant of a species that is much more successful than the norm in feeding and breeding will, in a comparatively short time, outbreed the rest and become the norm. But its very success may create new difficulties. Its numbers may grow beyond the food available. Before long there will be too many individuals to feed. New biological solutions will have to be found to this new problem, which was directly caused by the successful solution of old problems.

Indeed one could go further on the theory of evolution. Strictly speaking, the process of random variation and selective retention, which founds evolutionary development, will not afford progress in any absolute sense. What it does is to produce variations of animal and plant, which can do the job better than their predecessors and competitors in the specific situations they find themselves in. But if the situation changes, an advantageous variation may be at a disadvantage. To take an example, the long necks of giraffes give them an edge in feeding where food is high off the ground, but if, for some reason, they find themselves where there are no tall trees, their necks will not help, and the cost of having them will be high.

Not only that, but in evolution 'better' means better only relative to competitors. It does not mean perfectly adapted. One could be better in a relative sense yet still imperfectly designed for whatever task there is. Further, better in a given situation and relative to your actual competitors may actually mean becoming less complex and losing faculties which are costly only in nutritional terms but which are no longer needed. So, sightless creatures in dark caves and flightless birds in New Zealand are evolutionary successes (or were, in the latter case, until European ships brought rodents to the islands).

Countless nature programmes on television notwithstanding, Darwin himself was under no illusions about the *imperfections* of the natural world under a system of natural selection. He wrote in *The Origin of Species* that we ought not

to marvel if all contrivances in nature be not as far as we can judge absolutely perfect; and if some be abhorrent to our ideas of fitness. We need not marvel at the sting of the bee causing the bee's own death; at drones being produced in such vast numbers for one single act, and then being slaughtered by their own sterile sisters; at the astonishing waste of pollen by our fir trees; at the instinctive hatred of the queen bee for her own fertile daughters; at ichneumonidae feeding within the live bodies of caterpillars; and at other such cases. The wonder indeed is, on the theory of natural selection, that more cases of the want of absolute perfection have not been obscured.

The point is that in natural selection, success and failure are relative, both to specific situations and to actual competitors. Within this double relativity, apparently unfit creatures can succeed and flourish. But change either situation or competition, and what looked excellent adaptations can become fatally unfit.

Is the theory of evolution a theory of progress in any sense? Here, opinions are divided. Some see it as simply a theory of 'descent with modification', to use the phraseology of Darwin himself; an austere doctrine in which there is no room for notions of ascent, and where what is lost may be as beautiful, as complex and as intelligent as what eventually wins out in the struggle for existence over the long term. On the other hand, Darwin concluded *The Origin of Species* rapturously:

> from the war of nature, from famine and death, the most exalted object which we are capable of conceiving, namely, the production of the higher animals, directly follows. There is grandeur in this view of life, with its several powers, having been originally breathed into a few forms or into one; and that, whilst this planet has gone cycling on according to the fixed law of gravity, from so simple a beginning endless forms most beautiful and wonderful have been, and are being, evolved.

From amoeba to man, then, and beyond; a sort of progress, one supposes. But, in a letter Darwin also wrote that while to us humans intelligence in a creature seems the chief criterion of progress, to a bee it would no doubt be something else. This rather Herderian reflection brings us back from our digression on evolution to thoughts of human history and human progress.

The obvious differences between history and biological evolution aside, our history seems much more like evolution than it is on the progressivist account. The course of history is far less uniform, far more unpredictable and chance-ridden than the progressivists would have it. History is not a steady march forward, but rather more a case of one step forward and one step sideways. History's direction is not predetermined, nor is what happens necessarily better than what has been. It is not necessarily a sign of intellectual or moral stupidity to be out of touch with one's time, despite what Tony Blair and other modernizers in this country and Europe may say. Modernity, as this is understood in the political and scientific rhetoric of our time, may be the source of our ills rather than a pointer to the direction in which we should be going. It is time now to consider some thinkers for whom inspiration was to be found neither in the present nor in the future, but either in the past or out of time altogether.

5

Thinkers of Loss

Not all those who have thought about the course of human history have believed in the inevitability of human progress. Some, indeed, have regarded as symptomatic of decline the very features of our lives that today we think of as progressive. Up to the time of the Enlightenment, a yearning for what had been lost or for what could never be found on earth was more common than any faith in progress. In this chapter we will examine the views of some of those who have been unconvinced about progress, beginning with the first and the greatest of the anti-progressivists.

Plato

Plato lived in Athens from around 428 BC until 347 BC. It was not a good time for Athens. During his lifetime Athens suffered from plague and from a disastrous war with Sparta. The greatness of the middle part of the fifth century was succeeded by rapid decline in the fourth, culminating in conquest and takeover by the Macedonians in 338 BC. During Plato's lifetime democracy descended into demagoguery, and alternated with dictatorship. In 399 Socrates, Plato's beloved teacher, was put to death, by democratic decision. Plato, a natural aristocrat, found it hard to forgive. He had great hopes of a better type of political and social organization in Syracuse, in Sicily, to which he paid three lengthy visits, twice as a guest of the rulers, but these hopes came to nothing, and ended in mutual recrimination.

Doubtless Plato's pessimistic and anti-democratic views were coloured by his experience, though it would be a moot point as to whether on any objective scale of mass slaughter and disregard for human life and value classical times were any darker than ours. Alexander might have been a butcher, but by the standards of our century one of middle rank. In any case Plato's arguments and insights do not depend on the details of his biography and the circumstances of his time. They are weighty and perceptive enough and have to be judged on their own merits.

Of all Plato's many telling images and metaphors, none is more revealing and multi-faceted than that of the cave in Book 7 of *The Republic*. Plato asks us to imagine a cave, deep below the earth, in which groups of people are shackled. They are facing the interior wall of the cave and cannot turn their heads or move away. Behind them there is a fire, and between them and the fire and above their heads other people are moving statues and carvings. These puppets cast shadows on the wall in front of the prisoners. The prisoners take the shadows for reality.

This, in Plato's view, is the condition in which the vast majority of mankind live. They take image for reality, and have no sense of the true causes of things, rather like people today whose mental landscape is conditioned by television and the mass media. Television, indeed, with its relentless and captivating successions of flickering images and factitious emotions is a more vivid realization of Plato's intentions in the cave than Plato himself could have imagined: he would no doubt have seen the role it plays in the lives of so many as a terrible vindication of his views.

We are then asked to suppose that one prisoner is freed. Seeing the fire and the puppets for what they are, he comes reluctantly to admit that what he had been taking for reality was a distortion. Though his eyes are hurt by the light, and he complains, he is then dragged up out of the cave into the daylight. He begins to make sense of the upper world outside the cave. Eventually he looks directly at the sun itself, and comes to the conclusion that it is the sun which produces 'the changing seasons and the years and controls everything in the visible world, and is . . . responsible for everything which he and his fellow-prisoners used to see'.

What we have here is a vivid image of an ascent from the normal human condition, sunk in illusion, sensuality and desire, through gradual enlightenment to true wisdom. In this ascent, the stage at which the prisoner grasps the mechanism of the puppets may be compared to the illumination afforded by natural science. Through science we begin to understand the causes of what we normally take for granted. Our ordinary world-view is shown to be limited and, in various ways, illusory.

But Plato was no unqualified admirer of natural science. Apart from its own uncertainties and problems, what science reveals are the mechanisms of the world. It shows *how* things are done and brought about, but not *why* or for what reason. Science cannot reveal the intentions or purposes behind the world. Indeed, it tends to deny that the world has a purpose, or that natural processes are guided by intentions, divine or otherwise, and this implicit atheism is anathema to Plato. Nor can science tell us what is good or valuable or worth doing – a point we have already encountered in connection with Enlightenment psychology, according to which men are simply governed by pleasure and pain, but which allows no space for any genuine choice or evaluation of our motives.

For Plato wisdom, which goes beyond what happens to be and the mechanics of things to their true purposes and the nature of the good life, is the province of philosophy. The man who struggles out of the cave to look at the sun is, in Plato's terms, a philosopher. He has acquired the wisdom to see things as they really are and how they should be. He will no longer have his eyes and his desires fixed on earth. He will want to look at eternal things, and – in terms of Plato's quasi-religious metaphysics – he will want to return to the true world from which our souls fell when we were born on earth.

We do, indeed, have suggestions or intimations of this perfect realm, in our moral sense, in some of our thinking about mathematics and in our perception of beauty, but normally these intimations are pushed away by the impetuosity of desire and the strength of the illusions among which we live. It is only the philosopher – he or she who has looked at the sun steadily and unflinchingly – who is able to become really free of desire and illusion.

Here, though, there is a problem and a paradox. The cave, as *The Republic* overall, is in part an account of a certain sort of education, whereby a few people become truly wise through a long and painful process of enlightenment. But having made the ascent to true freedom, will the philosopher have any wish to re-immerse himself in the everyday world, to return to the cave? Of course he will not. But does he not owe it to his fellow-prisoners to help them to improve their lot, to enlighten them too, and to lead them to a happier state?

The Republic is not just about philosophy and education. It is also about politics and psychology. According to Plato, both the state and the individual human being have a tripartite division. The human soul has an appetitive part, which is the source of instinct and desire; a spirited part, which is the source of action and courage; and a rational part, which is the source of wisdom. When the other two parts are ruled by the rational part, the person is happy and contented. The instincts are held in check, and our courage is directed to positive ends, so it does not become angry, bullying or overbearing and we are contented.

In like manner, in the state there are potentially three classes of men: the workers – craftsmen and farmers, who correspond to the appetitive part of the soul; then the soldiers, corresponding to the spirited soul; and finally, corresponding to reason, the wise philosophers. In the ideally just state, the rational people, the philosophers, will rule and the other classes will also perform the roles to which they are suited by their nature. In the just society of *The Republic*, members of each class will be given the upbringing suitable to their nature and calling.

In the analogy of the cave, the philosopher-rulers will be those who have climbed out of the cave and looked at the sun. They will, therefore, not be people who want to rule in the cave or down here on earth, having higher and better things on their mind. Plato's proposal is that in a perfectly well-adjusted society, with each class of people performing the tasks to which they were fitted, they would have to be forced to rule, for the good of the whole community, whether they liked it or not; even though in a sense they would be compelled to live what in other circumstances would be a poorer life than they might be able to live if they had no social duties, in ruling they – as with everyone else in the well-run society – would be fulfilling the role to which their talents and education fitted them.

A great deal of Plato's *Republic* concerns the special type of life and special education the philosopher-ruler would follow. Plato proposes that the rulers should have no class or property, that in the rulership there should be equality of the sexes, and in order to avoid the narrow concerns and desires of family life, children should be had and brought up in common. Apart from these radical social proposals, there is definitely a sense in Plato that the ideal state would be one governed by ideally enlightened rulers, whose wisdom would be deployed in running what was an enlightened society. It is important, therefore, to see the ways in which Platonic enlightenment is quite different from anything that would be considered enlightened or progressive at the end of the twentieth century.

In the first place, the enlightenment of the rulers is not scientific or earthbound, nor is it anything constructed by mankind or due to human reason acting and judging autonomously, off its own resources. What the philosophers look to, and what draws them on, is something quite beyond this world. Like the sun in the cave story, the world to which they look is perfect and unchangeable; it 'transcends' any of the interests and desires we have as mere human beings. It is that which gives everything else light and to which everything else is drawn, whether it knows it or not.

Natural science is no route to Platonic enlightenment. Not only does science deal with causal mechanisms, rather than reasons and values, not only are its theories uncertain and conjectural, compared to the perfection and certainty of mathematic reasoning, but the world of which it treats is the imperfect physical world, a world subject to chance, loss and decay. This earthly world is very far from the pure other world on which the philosopher gazes, of whose crystalline perfection mathematical and geometrical reasoning gives us a hint. For we can know and prove absolute truths about pure shapes, circles, triangles, quadrilaterals and the rest, even though we have never actually experienced any such things, but only rough and imperfect representations of them. How can we know and prove these truths, except by occasionally glimpsing the other world, the world of perfect mathematical forms, then training ourselves to study it? And in studying it and in analysing other aspects of our experience, we realize that this other world is not just a world of mathematical perfection.

It is also a world of absolute justice, of complete goodness, and of a beauty and purified desire that our own experience of loving and of sexual attraction gives us but the remotest hint. But it does give a hint. For most of us the experience of sexual desire is the first time we are really taken out of ourselves and held captive by something other than ourselves. In the Platonic scheme of things the same type of magnetism draws the philosophic mind to contemplation of the world of forms, the world that contains perfect examples or forms of the things we see imperfectly copied on earth.

So Platonic enlightenment is not scientific enlightenment. Nor is there anything democratic or liberal about his political proposals. As we have already seen, he regards rulership as properly the province of one class only. Those who follow the feelings of the multitude, and who are swayed by the speeches and performances that sway them, will undoubtedly be mis-educated and misled on matters of taste and morality. Mass education and mass entertainment will almost inevitably cor-rupt, as indeed in our day they do, in ways Plato even in his worst fears could never have foreseen. We can be saved only by what comes from God, which is what the rulers learn to submit to in their long process of seclusion, education and training.

Members of each class have something in their makeup that makes them suited to one role or another in the republic. Plato intends this absolutely literally. Once individuals are identified as belonging to a particular class, they are to breed only with members of the same class. Particularly with the rulers, it is crucial to keep the line pure, otherwise the exercise of rulership itself will be compromised and diluted with motives and opinions proper to the lower classes.

Plato was, then, a eugenicist, and a genetic determinist. But calling him names is not enough to refute his views. We have already encountered strains of eugenicism in quite unlikely and politically correct circles this century. Plato is surely correct in suggesting that gifts, including those of wisdom and leadership, are unequally and sparsely distributed in most societies; and given that universal education for most of this century in Western democracies has not produced universal wisdom, it is tempting to conclude that some differences in attainment reflect differences in natural endowments, a point to which we return in considering Aristotle's notorious views that some men (and all women) are by nature slaves. And, given the generally poor quality of political leadership at the end of the twentieth century (Major, Blair, Bush, Clinton), Plato may well be on to something in preferring as rulers those who never wanted to climb the greasy pole of politics in the first place. Perhaps better would be reluctant rulers, with their eyes and desires fixed on higher things, or even those born and brought up to rule as a duty, as a matter of *noblesse oblige*.

Certainly Plato presents some powerful reasons for thinking that democratic rulers are going to be prone to some very particular and insidious faults of both character and leadership. In what is perhaps the first piece of theoretical sociology, Plato describes the decline of society from its best state to its worst. And, because of the corruption inherent in all created things, decline is, in Plato's view, bound to happen. Perhaps the only reason we find the inevitability of decline hard to accept is because we are so used to progressivist rhetoric. While we are perfectly happy to accept entropy (universal heat loss and increase in disorder) as a theory in physics, we are less ready to envisage decline in the human world.

Plato, though, sees even his perfect society under philosopher kings as prone to dissolution. This will be because of errors in breeding. Despite the controlled breeding programmes, the philosophers will have some children who are not as good as themselves, who are neither lucky nor gifted. Strife will break out. Disinterested and propertyless rule by the wise will give way to a form of aristocracy in which the well-born still rule, but as much for their own honour and for amassing property as for the good of the whole society. Eventually wealth will become the main goal of the rulers: the ambitious, competitive aristocrat is replaced by or transformed into the money-loving businessman. But when wealth predominates in a conspicuous way, the children of the wealthy give themselves over to luxury. The ruling class becomes enfeebled and loses the will to preserve its position, just as the poor and dispossessed become more resentful. This is the moment when democracy originates: 'the poor win, kill or exile their opponents, and give the rest equal and civil rights and opportunities of office'.

And what, for Plato, is democracy? It is, above all, a state in which every individual is free to say and do as he likes, in which authority is neither exercised nor recognized, in which those sentenced in courts still come and go among their fellows, 'with no more notice taken of their comings and goings than if they were invisible spirits', in which politicians abjure gifts of birth and character and excellence of education and merit in order to profess themselves the friends of the people, in which there is every possible type of human being, with each reluctant nevertheless to stand out as better than the rest.

The democratic man lives from day to day, and for the pleasures of the moment. He refuses to be told that some pleasures are good, or some desires evil. He 'shakes his head and says all pleasures are equal and should have equal rights'. (Isn't that exactly what we are told today by advertising, the tabloid press and television?) Then, just as democratic society is full of all types – in a rainbow celebration of diversity, described by Plato himself as a patterned dress – so the democratic individual is a master of inconstancy and versatility, prey to every changing fashion. One day it is wine, women and song, the next water and a strict diet; hard physical training followed by indolence; one minute philosophy, the next politics or even military efforts.

He is, in short, a master of the Third Way, or of the *Neue Mitte*, yesterday's unilateral disarmers (providing they don't actually fight themselves), today's sabre-rattlers and bombers, yesterday's political radicals and libertines of the sexual revolution, today's advocates of fiscal rectitude and family values (provided taxation and public spending increase and provided 'family' does not mean family), yesterday's civil libertarians and welfare-rights activists, today's advocates of toughness on crime and harshness on scroungers (providing we are not talking about hanging, flogging or longer prison sentences, and providing no 'claimant' in 'need' goes unbenefited into the night, however much his or her state of need is of his or her own making).

This is not, by the way, a comment just on New Labour. It applies equally to the governments of John Major and George Bush, and to the 'conservative' party of William Hague, as it would apply to any politics of 'inclusiveness', any attempt to fudge and fumble one's way through the choices presented by 'left' and 'right', socialism and capitalism, as if contradictions could somehow be resolved in a welter of surface gloss and presentation. But inclusiveness that makes no judgement is not in fact coherent. Sooner or later it, and the society that fosters it, will fall apart, being little more than an arena for war of competing interest groups, all struggling to appropriate the resources of that society for themselves.

Then again, just as Plato foresaw television and its effects, he also foresaw the conditions that would lead to 'Cool Britannia' and pop stars, film celebrities and disc jockeys in Downing Street and the White House. After having mentioned that in a democratic dispensation teachers, having lost authority, fear their pupils and pander to them, and are in turn despised, Plato says this: 'the young as a whole imitate their elders, argue with them and set themselves up against them, while their elders try to avoid the reputation of being disagreeable or strict by aping the young and mixing with them on terms of easy good fellowship'.

Of course, the young are not deceived by being patronized in this way. I do not imagine that Oasis and Chris Evans or their followers are impressed by their being cultivated by grey politicians who are old enough to know better, and who surely have more mature interests than what entertains young voters. Part, indeed, of the point of pop music and youth television is that it is a private province of the young from which the established and middle-aged are excluded.

Plato believes that the democracy he describes is inherently unstable. He thinks that its lack of principle or centre and its lawlessness will bring it down. A tyrant will ingratiate himself with the people, much like the standard democratic politician, but with more sinister intent. With the aid of persuasive propagandists and a private army he may take over the whole state. And so the best – rule by philosopher-kings – is transformed into the worst, a real tyranny.

Maybe the decline of democracy into tyranny is not inevitable. It happened in Germany, in the 1930s, and in Eastern Europe, but it is not, for that reason, inevitable. It has not happened so far in Britain or the USA, and there is no reason to suppose it will in any foreseeable future. Maybe, indeed, none of the transitions Plato describes are inevitable.

In a sense, in his doctrines of historical inevitability, Plato is simply the mirror image of the progressivists. Indeed, the sequence he describes – aristocracy, oligarchy, democracy – are exactly the same. But what for our age is 'the long march of Everyman' is for Plato a descent into mediocrity and anarchy and one which, in his *Laws*, he is determined to arrest as far as possible by forbidding any change at all in the laws of a correctly ordered state.

As philosophers we are always told to pay more attention to those who disagree with us than those who agree, with counter-arguments rather than with supporting arguments. We democrats, we enthusiasts for universal education and scientific enlightenment should attend to Plato's criticism of democracy and democratic manners, and not, as commentators and translators of Plato normally do, distance ourselves as fast as we can from what he says. Of course, we do not agree with Plato, and no doubt the rule of philosopher-kings would be intolerable. Perhaps democracy is the least bad form of government, but that does not mean that it has no inconveniences (and not just the obvious ones). What if there is actually truth in what Plato says? To me, at least, his descriptions of democratic manners are disturbingly accurate.

As is what he says about music and, by extension, the other arts. For what, in essence, Plato is saying in discussing music is that music matters, that it has a deep effect on the souls of men. Therefore it is of the profoundest importance to a society what kind of music and art is favoured in it. What Plato says assumes that music is capable of evoking particular kinds of emotions and moods, in such a way as to take over the judgement and sensibility of individuals who are listening. Much as philosophers may deny this, every lover of music knows this to be the case, even though, on all rational grounds, maybe it should not be so. But Plato and Nietzsche aside, no philosopher of first rank has seriously investigated the spiritual effects of music and the other arts.

Plato would outlaw dirge-like music, also languid stuff, which conjures up moods of drunkenness, softness and idleness. What we should have is music that expresses military virtue, courage and discipline, and also music evocative of graceful and moderate behaviour in peacetime. Lyres are to be preferred to flutes, and overscored music and music with wide harmonic range generally to be avoided.

As with Plato's remarks on democracy, what he says about music has been generally mentioned only so as to be ritually dismissed, no doubt partly because he wanted to censor the wrong sort of music and the wrong sort of poetry. But while censorship *may* be a bad thing (always? in every case?), this does not mean that the considerations which led Plato to advocate it are wrong. Nor, as a poet and as one of the supreme artists of our civilization, could he be accused of being a Philistine or unaware of the power of art. To the contrary, it was precisely because he was aware of the power of art that he was concerned about its effects.

We, though, seem to think that just because the Stalinists insisted on cheerful and positive music and the Nazis castigated 'degenerate' art, any consideration of the psychological and spiritual effects of art is out of place. In a world where publicly lauded and subsidized artists and performers are fast running out of space to shock, Platonic considerations are definitely 'uncool'. And there is also the old chestnut about the Beethoven-loving camp commandant.

It is, however, not part of the Platonic position that everyone who loves Beethoven is *ipso facto* a good man and a friend of freedom, any more than it is necessarily true that a producer of violent or pornographic works could not be gentle or faithful as an individual. But we have to wonder about a society in which pornography and violence are practically *de rigueur* in popular entertainment, whose music is unremittingly crude, mechanical and incessantly hedonistic and subversive, and whose most admired paintings include images of screaming skulls and of loveless homosexual couplings. What room is there in this mentality for graciousness, nobility or just plain, average decency? Or, indeed, for the view that human beings can strive for such things and, without hypocrisy, attain them? Can the thought that we might be children of God or modes of the divine mind survive such a tide of barbaric sounds and images? Leaving aside questions of technical ability (which would certainly not be to our advantage), scientific enlightenment and democratic politics do not seem to have produced progress in the artistic realm, when we look back to the sixteenth and seventeenth centuries – times, we should remember, as turbulent and uncertain as our own.

It is not just that in our art we have lost a vision they had. It is more that we systematically refuse to consider that we might have regressed spiritually and artistically. Which, in turn, is why we find Plato on music and the arts embarrassing and prefer not to take seriously what he has to say.

Aristotle

'Some men are by nature slaves.' Aristotle was no democrat, nor did he believe in progress. He lived from 384 to 322 BC, a pupil of Plato and, for a time, the tutor of Alexander the Great. As well as being one of the three great philosophers of antiquity, he was also its greatest scientist.

But Aristotelian science is not modern science. While Aristotle did not follow Plato in seeking the perfection of things on earth in another world altogether, he did think that each type of thing on earth had its own essence, timelessly given to it, which made it what it is and, in the case of living things, determined its development. It was against Aristotelian essentialism that Darwinian evolution, with its idea of constantly modifying species, was primarily directed. Aristotle also believed that the world was directed by impersonal and eternal intelligence (or intelligences) and that the heavenly spheres, which circled the earth, had a perfection that the earth, with its tendency to corruption and decay, lacked.

Aristotle held that the essence of humanity was our rationality. The highest form of life for man was the exercise of rationality in the contemplation of divine, eternal truths. Beyond that, we have to find our happiness in living well. Happiness, though, is not something we can aim directly at. It consists in doing well those things our nature determines as being the good life for man; the exercise of the virtues, in other words.

Aristotelian virtue is subtly different from modern virtue. It includes qualities like the magnanimity of the great-souled man, the man who is rich and generous and takes delight in spreading his wealth around. Aristotle did not admire humility, nor was he a lover of trade and technology. Necessary as these might be, an existence centred on them is inferior to one devoted to the exercise of the intellectual virtues, particularly philosophy, or one dedicated to the pursuit of aristocratic friendship.

Aristotle had an instinctive disgust at anything petty, inferior or small-minded. No more did he believe in progress. What was good was eternally good and eternally present. Unlike the heavens, beings and institutions on this lower earth, including political set-ups, are subject to cycles of generation and corruption. There is, therefore, change, but no assumption that what comes later is better than what came earlier. In the case of a being in its decaying phase, what comes later will, of course, be worse. Nor did Aristotle indulge in the contemporary piety of the twentieth century, that the élite virtues of contemplation and magnanimity are, or might be, shared around the whole of society. Some men are, by nature, slaves; and in the Aristotelian scheme of things, nature cannot be bucked.

What Aristotle finds in nature is that some people are naturally rulers and others are naturally ruled. The natural masters are those who can use their intelligence to look ahead, and to deliberate about goals and ends. The natural slaves have 'the bodily strength to do the actual work', but lack the reflective intelligence of the masters – as, even more notoriously, do women. Slaves, in Aristotle's book, are 'living tools'. They do not lack reason altogether, but have it only in so far as to recognize it in the masters. All – masters and slaves, men and women – are better off if they are guided by their natural masters.

Aristotle himself has some doubts about what one finds in nature. The tidy divisions between those with mental and those with bodily powers does not always obtain. Nor does he think that the actual historical divisions between slaves and free men necessarily reflect nature; they may reflect no more than accidents of birth or the exigencies of conquest. There is, moreover, plenty of evidence – not, admittedly, available to Aristotle – that some women can be educated, can philosophize and can rule better than most men.

Nevertheless, we do need to take into account the inequalities that exist between human beings in intellect, in virtue and in motivation. In practice, of course, those doing most of the ruling and controlling in whatever system will tend to be or rely on the more able in various respects. But how far differences between individuals should be *institutionally* recognized in democracy remains not just unanswered but largely unasked. As we saw in considering Kant, with us the fiction of abstract equality remains supreme, but that does not make it any less of a fiction. We are happy to accuse the Victorians of hypocrisy in sexual matters. May the greatest hypocrisy of our time not be the pretence of an equality in which no one really believes, but which no one may contest, and which simply fuels resentment on the part of those who are manifestly not equal in a supposedly classless society?

In his discussion of different types of state, Aristotle partly modifies the implications of his appreciation of human inequality. The best form of rule, in Aristotle's view, would be an enlightened monarchy, in which a wise man rules for the good of everyone else. But such a happy situation is unlikely. Slightly more likely is an enlightened aristocracy, where those who are naturally best rule in a society guided by virtue. However, examples of enlightened aristocracy are also rare, which takes Aristotle to what he calls polity or politeia. This is the republic of free men, a type of democracy uncorrupted by democracy's characteristic failings.

Aristotle actually suggests that polity has certain advantages over monarchy and aristocracy. For one, many people are less easily corrupted than an individual or a few. Also, where many are involved in ruling, there will be less resentment than is likely to occur when rule is vested in a few. Finally, if many people, and hence many perspectives, are involved in decision-making, better decisions are likely to be made.

What, for Aristotle, characterizes good forms of government is that the rulers are ruling for the sake of the whole community. However, each form of government – polity, aristocracy and monarchy – has its shadow, where the rulers are ruling for their own sake, not for that of the whole. Corresponding to polity is democracy. The common people use their power to enrich themselves at the expense of the rich. This form of democracy is also likely to encourage 'the democratic idea of justice', that in which there is simple numerical equality, not an equality in which equal merit is rewarded equally, and unequal unequally, each getting what they deserve and no more. Strict numerical equality, in which everyone gets the same, is for Aristotle not justice but injustice, because it means that people will not be rewarded according to their merits, but whether they deserve it or not.

Not that there will be true justice in the depraved type of aristocracy, which Aristotle refers to as oligarchy. Instead of the demagogic equality of democracy, oligarchs will rule simply to enrich themselves and the small group they represent. Unjust monarchy – the worst fate of all – is tyranny, where the tyrant rules simply for his own ends.

Many of Aristotle's comments on particular forms of government are perceptive and telling, though they lack the sustained brilliance and invective of Plato's analyses. But what is striking is the way in which, in his *Politics*, Aristotle describes many different constitutions, of all different shapes and characters. Nowhere is there any suggestion that history is moving in a given direction. Indeed, in so far as events in Aristotle's day were moving in a particular direction – that of Alexandrian

Hellenism – Aristotle failed to recognize it at all. In Aristotle, we can, indeed, through a combination of reason and experience, describe the conditions that would be likely to produce a state most conducive to happiness and virtue. But there is no guarantee that such a state will come about or that, having come about, it will stay in existence.

That is because of the extremely unmodern view that there will be no ideal state without citizens of education and virtue, schooled in practical wisdom. And this, in turn, is unmodern because Aristotelian practical wisdom is a matter of experience and of having acquired virtuous habits. No one, in Aristotle's view, can be wise, morally or politically, just by being clever. Cleverness could simply aid vice or moral stupidity, as we see in the case of thinkers such as Bertrand Russell, who theorized disastrously about matters such as marriage and education, in apparently deliberate contravention of the experience of the many and the wise.

But as, in Aristotle's view, wisdom in practical matters can only be the fruit of informed and virtuous experience, it is precisely the many and the wise to whom we should attend. However interesting they might be as intellectual exercises, policy proposals drafted by twenty-year-olds from supposed first principles will not win many plaudits from a follower of Aristotle: they are likely to lack just that responsiveness to the subtlety and complexity of human affairs that only experience can bring. Modernity's cult of youth and the Baconian forgetfulness of the past to which the cult is allied look, from an Aristotelian point of view, to be a wilful abrogation of the best resource we have, morally and politically.

Augustine: Original Sin and the Two Cities

St Augustine (AD 354–430) was, of course, a Christian. He did not share the pessimism of Plato; nor was his god the remote intelligence postulated by Aristotle. Augustine was not bowed down by the fatalism of the ancient world, nor did he see history as an endless and hopeless cycle of recurring meaninglessness.

Augustine's version of history was linear. In a sense there was progress. There was the history of the chosen people in the Old Testament, and there was the Incarnation and Redemption in the New. Christ's birth, death and resurrection were the pivotal moments of human history. Those of us who lived after Christ lived in the last era of time, that between Christ's first and second coming; we were on our way, where pagans and non-believers could only wait and hope. Moreover, we look forward to the final event of history, the Last Judgement, in which everything will be resolved and renewed. At that point, there will be a clear and complete separation between two cities, the heavenly city of God, founded on love of God and contempt of self, and the earthly city founded on love of self and contempt of God.

In the Christian era, even human institutions could be better than they were under paganism, provided they were guided by the Church. Indeed, Augustine felt that the Christian emperors had improved the situation in the Roman empire. But the gains there were not permanent, nor were they guaranteed, nor were they total. How could they be, when we are dealing with fallen human beings, even the best of them motivated in part by love of self, rather than love of God, even the best of them tainted like all of us by original sin?

Augustine contrasts Babylon, the city and fellowship of the wicked, with Jerusalem, the city and fellowship of the saints. But this Jerusalem cannot be fully realized on earth. On earth it lives like a captive and a stranger in the midst of the earthly city. It hears the promise of redemption rather than redemption itself, even though it can, for a time and in limited ways, improve the earthly city.

In his *Confessions*, Augustine had prayed to God of our hearts being restless until they rest in Thee. He had also spoken of the vision he and his mother had experienced shortly before her death:

> As the flame of love burned stronger in us and raised us higher towards the selfsame, we passed through all corporeal things, and the heavens themselves, from which the sun and the moon and the stars shine down on the earth . . . At length we came to our own minds and passed beyond them to that place of everlasting plenty, where you feed Israel for ever with the food of truth. There, life is the Wisdom by which all things are made.

For Augustine, God is timeless and changeless. We are made for God, and have our ultimate destiny outside time. Compared to God, and the heavenly Jerusalem, anything on earth is fallible and imperfect. Even the Church on earth consists of fallen and sinful human beings and cannot be expected to be perfect. In this respect if no other, Augustine is Platonic, clearly distinguishing other-worldly perfection from this-worldly imperfection.

So the heavenly city on earth is in a state of pilgrimage. It is mingled with the earthly city. While it remains on earth it has to live under the peace and laws of the earthly city. In so far as this is necessary for the maintenance of life, those dedicated to God are happy enough to live under earthly dominion and to enjoy its peace. Their situation is like that of the Israelites in captivity in Babylon. Not, indeed, that any of us are free from the distortion, greed, corruption and sensuality that make secular laws and punishments essential if there is to be any form of peace at all on earth. To the extent that the earthly city upholds earthly peace, even those who are part of the heavenly city should obey its laws. This did not mean that they should acquiesce in abuses like slavery and torture: though they should be aware that the world's aims are not God's aims, but power, honour, wealth and sex.

Augustine, then, has a moderated pessimism about human life and human affairs. He would have been astonished, not to say horrified, by those medieval thinkers who, perhaps inspired by his own persecution of heretics, and by some of what he said, took the notion of the City of God to mean that states and empires should be run by popes and bishops. Secularizing the City of God in this way was a distortion of Augustine's considered view, ignoring our pervasive fallenness in this life and the truth that our real destiny was in the next.

Attempts, like those of Calvin in Geneva in the sixteenth century, to create theocracies – rule by divine decree – inevitably succeeded only in producing hells on earth. Keeping the city of saints saintly required draconian policing, a dictatorship in which citizens were encouraged to denounce each other, and in which magistrates imposed terrifying punishments on those condemned by the pastors. Augustine, though, would not have been surprised by this. Every human being and every human institution is a mixture of good and bad. He was well aware of the potential men have for turning even the best of institutions, even the Church itself, to providing for their corrupt ends. Life on earth is fraught with temptation, even for those on the pilgrimage to the heavenly city. Perfect peace and a perfect society will be found only in the next world. Augustine's views on the essential fallibility of all human institutions are themselves a consequence of his views on original sin. What we are in this world is due to the fall of our first parents due to which our nature is corrupted. Augustine was a thinker of loss, not because our present state was a decline from some better state earlier in history. Our loss was a cosmic one, due to the corruption of human nature in the Fall.

We have already noted how the earthly city is dominated by

the manifestations of our corruption: self-love, greed, anger and, above all, concupiscence, the destructive role played in our lives by sex. Men have no control over their sexual nature, and are prey to its irresistible impulses. In women, lack of genital and sexual control is paralleled by the pains and travails of childbirth. And it is through sex that both concupiscence and the taint of Original Sin are passed on to future generations. Moreover, those men – and women – who are prey to desire are, in the ancient Greek image, like urns with their base 'pierced', which, despite continuous pouring, are never filled.

Original sin and suspicion of our sexuality are deeply un-popular themes at the end of the second millennium. Indeed they have been since the time of the Enlightenment. Voltaire described the doctrine of original sin as 'the wild and fantastic invention of an African both debauched and repentant . . . tolerant and a persecutor, who spent his life contradicting himself'. He also waxed as eloquent as Rousseau on the subject of human nature: 'gather together all the children in the world, and you find nothing in them but innocence, sweetness and modesty. If they were born wicked, criminal and cruel, they would show some sign of it, just as baby serpents try to bite and baby tigers to tear.'

All this is in perfect contrast to Augustine who was con-vinced of the self-love and self-absorption of babies and that 'if infants do no injury, it is for lack of strength, not for lack of will'. Augustine also saw young children at play as the key to understanding the subterfuges and deceptions of adults nego-tiating deals. He would not have been surprised by the evils children can do, given the chance. But for Voltaire, human nature is not to blame. Bad upbringing and environment are the source of vice and crime, a refrain we have heard countless times since.

But repetition does not make it true, any more than un-fashionableness shows Augustine wrong on sexuality. Lust is, indeed, the most powerful feeling known to most of us, and brings with it not just destruction of social ties and commitments but a lack of self-mastery frightening in its intensity. It is also, in various ways, ridiculous, shameful and guilt-inducing, as are the jealousies and resentments it inspires. Rational adults should not be subject to such indignities. They should be able to handle even affairs of the heart without embarrassment – but that, of course, is the point. Sex has a nasty habit of making calm, rational behaviour impossible. In Augustine's words, the goal itself, sexual ecstasy, 'swamps the mind'.

Not to admit these things, and not to concede the extent to which every sexual act, however elevated, has its smidgin of lust, is to betray naïvety, or worse. Augustine's strictures cannot be laughed off as the ravings of a debauched African.

No less can his strictures on attempts to enlist an earthly city as the heavenly one. These days, quite apart from the overt tyrannies of the twentieth century, we are only too well aware of the potential of states to encroach on the lives of individual citizens, hells produced by paradisical intentions, and also of the way bureaucracies tend to serve their own interests rather than those of their clients and society generally. At a time when developments in European law and institutions are allegedly based on Catholic social teaching, a kind of soft, bureaucratic socialism, we should welcome the astringency of Augustine's realization of the ways in which ostensibly beneficent institutions can become vehicles for group egoism.

Renaissances

From the time of Vitruvius in Augustan Rome, recovery of lost beauty has been a recurring theme in the arts. The very name Renaissance (rebirth) conjures up images of a lost classicism to which we can only aspire.

Vitruvius himself wanted to contribute to the splendour of

imperial Rome by reviving traditional styles of architecture. This meant principally classical Greek architecture and building types: forums in the form of a square, Greek theatres, palaestras, peristyles, and saloons in private houses. He gave detailed directions for the construction of temples and villas, and for the planning of towns, all based on a careful study of Greek and Hellenistic models.

The face of Rome and other imperial cities was transformed by Vitruvian precepts, a phenomenon to be repeated, time and again, in Europe and in the USA, and in the centuries to come. Vitruvius's own ideas and writings were influential in their own right. His *De Architectura* was an important influence on the Romanesque and hence on the Gothic. He was much studied in the Renaissance itself. Later architects, such as Inigo Jones and Christopher Wren, wrote commentaries on his work.

But more than Vitruvius itself, the spirit that Vitruvius was the first to express and articulate appears over and over again in European history. The notion is of a classical golden age, which has been lost and which can, with study and devotion, be retrieved. It was this notion that received its most explosive expression in Italy in the fourteenth and fifteenth centuries. Against medieval theology, Gothic art and architecture and domination by churchmen and kings were posed neo-Platonic philosophy, the art and architecture of Greece and Rome and, in theory anyway, a form of civic humanism.

The sense was of a whole invigorating current in our culture, which had been pushed underground in the medieval Church. A new cult arose of sensuous and bodily beauty, a repudiation of the repudiation of the flesh, the bold claim that man was the measure of all things, and a deliberate mixing of pagan and Christian symbols (neatly encapsulated in Alberti's self-consciously Vitruvian treatise *De re aedificatoria*, in which he refers to churches as 'temples' and God and the saints as 'gods'). Pagan and Christian myths and earthly forms were all taken alike as symbols of a mystical neo-Platonic universe. This universe was ruled by the harmony and proportion which Renaissance artists, architects and musicians sought in their creations. Humanity was the microcosm by which the macrocosm was to be understood, and vice versa. From the perspective of fifteenth-century Europe, an old wisdom, secret but known to the ancients and subsequently lost, was being recovered.

Ironically, after the Medici in Florence, the popes in Rome became the most munificent of Renaissance patrons, particularly in the second half of the fifteenth century – a fact that contributed not a little to the fervour and austerity of the Protestant reformation in the sixteenth.

Eventually, religious revivals notwithstanding, classical motifs and mythology became the staple diet of European art and architecture from the sixteenth to well into the nineteenth century. Naturally, the interpretations of classical reality varied considerably. Palladio was very different from Alberti, and Schinkel different from either. At different times there were different emphases. Neo-Platonic philosophy aside, Rome provided the model for the Italian Renaissance, so much so that at the end of the eighteenth century Winckelman and Goethe took themselves to be rediscovering a specifically Greek form of classicism. And their Greek civilization, calm, noble, simple and Olympian, was quite different from that of Nietzsche, for whom Apollonian clarity and beauty rested precariously on an abyss of Dionysiac tragedy, turmoil and suffering.

Nevertheless, beneath all the differences of emphasis and content, there was a passionate sense of loss and of an old wisdom and beauty to which we moderns could only aspire, and never reach. And if, to our eyes, many of the works of the Italian Renaissance exceed their classical models in beauty and greatness many times over, might this not be precisely because their creators were in awe of what they felt they had lost, and whose perfection they were striving, in their view, fruitlessly to reach? If, in the Renaissance and subsequent classical revivals, progress was made, it was made in the belief that our history had been one of decline interrupted only occasionally and by dint of great effort and devotion to the past.

Reverence for the classical past was the distinguishing feature of the Italian Renaissance, and of the subsequent classical revivals that have done so much to enliven European art and thought. It is precisely this reverence for the past, together with the sense that mankind is part of a wider cosmic whole, which makes Renaissance humanism a profoundly unmodern movement. It was, indeed, against reverence for the past in general that Bacon was campaigning, and specifically against the worship of classical authorities. In their mysticism and also in their assumption that man was the measure of all things, scientific progress depended on the dropping of that aspiration, as Bacon correctly pointed out. Renaissance beliefs and ideology were unmodern and unscientific.

Renaissance ideas were also, in a certain sense, unChristian, but this did not make them unmystical or materialistic in a scientific sense. They were unChristian only in the sense that Christian and pagan myths were seen alike as pointers to another realm beyond our own, a realm whose lineaments we foreshadow in ourselves and in our perception and appreciation of the physical world. This was a very different form of humanism from the unmystical utilitarianism and scientific psychology of the modern world.

De Tocqueville and the Mediocrities of Democracy

Obviously Herder, Burke and de Maistre, key thinkers of the Counter-Enlightenment, are enemies of theories of progress. They are certainly thinkers of loss, and much of what they say is to the point here. However, arguably more damaging to progressivism than their all-out assaults are the extraordinary reflections on the direction of modern society by Alexis de Tocqueville towards the end of the second volume of his *Democracy in America* (1840). They are damaging because they are not written by one hostile to the democratic ideal, or to Enlightenment thought.

Quite the contrary, in fact. De Tocqueville had lived through the same revolutionary events as Burke and de Maistre. Like them, he disliked the violence of the French Revolution intensely. But he also disliked the extremist politics that he believed had brought it about, and in his condemnation he included the inflexibility and inequality of the *ancien régime*. He looked, therefore, with hope to the other great revolution of his time, the American Revolution. To a considerable degree he found his hopes for the future fulfilled by what he saw in America. In America he saw gradual and inexorable progress towards equality. Democracy had destroyed the feudal system and monarchies; it would no more be held up by inequalities of wealth and power.

In many ways the trend towards ever more egalitarian democracy was benign. In democracies men would no longer kill each other for honour or ideology. They would settle their differences peacefully, by legal and institutional means. With increasing prosperity increasingly spread around, they would become far more interested in their private lives and private concerns than in the public causes for which people routinely take up arms.

De Tocqueville pointed out that in America the principle of the sovereignty of the people had produced sixty years of peace and unprecedented increases in wealth and population, while all the nations of Europe had, as he says, been ravaged by war or torn by civil strife. While most of Europe had been convulsed time and again by revolution, America had not even suffered from riots. In America, the republic upheld and preserved rights and safeguarded property. There anarchy was as unknown as despotism. Moreover, in America there was a host of private organizations and institutions, which were energetic and enterprising. These institutions created the civic spirit that might otherwise have been missing in the absence of feudal hierarchy and ceremony, and they also provided a buffer between the individual and the state.

De Tocqueville was not blind to the difficulties posed for American democracy by slavery and its after-effects. Nevertheless, like Fukuyama in our time, de Tocqueville may have exaggerated the merits of American democracy and seen it as more seamless and unproblematic than, in fact, it was or is. He praised democracy for giving to the people the ownership of the laws of the state, and did not really appreciate the potential of all democracies, even the American form he extolled, for capture by special-interest groups and self-perpetuating bureaucratic and political élites. Nor did he take enough account of the professionalization of politics, and the development of party machines, with all that that entailed for access to political power.

But it is precisely his admiration of democratic society that makes his subtle, ingenious and prophetic criticisms the more telling, particularly as they have nothing to do with the difficulty of including slaves or ex-slaves in the process. His criticisms are of the likely effects of a benign democracy on those who would normally be regarded as its beneficiaries.

De Tocqueville's negative insights stem from the connection between democracy and equality. In aristocratic and feudal societies, individuals have their places and status assigned to them. Up to a point they accept these differences and their limitations (though de Tocqueville believes strongly that the divine will is for the fundamental equality of mankind to be recognized). Acceptance of social divisions implies that in aristocratic societies differences in attainment, ability and wealth are, by comparison with democratic societies, easy to accept. This is because when there are no generally accepted differences of breeding and rank, inequalities of other sorts also become offensive. Compared to the clearly demarcated groups and roles found in feudal society – groups and roles that produce within them feelings of solidarity and membership – in a democracy there is only a huge, formless mass of people, none of whom wishes to stand out from the rest to any great degree, and, more to the point, none of whom wishes others to be significantly different from the norm.

In democracy, instead of espousing grand public causes, which depend on people having ambition and visions beyond what are available to each individual, people concentrate on small individual pleasures and readily shareable material comforts. In democracy there is much ambition, but it is not lofty ambition; nor does it license or revolve around privilege. The citizens of a democracy are desperate for small material improvements and physical comforts. These they attain with effort, but indulge with anxiety, ever fearful of losing their little gains. The contrast is with the aristocrat who, being born to riches, takes them for granted and without too much difficulty, can do without them altogether (rather like the old Etonian who finds prison no great hardship). The aristocrat is also likely to be inspired by thoughts of honour, as much as by the benefits of trade and the market.

In a democracy, by contrast, social barriers are lowered. Inequalities become offensive in themselves. And while passions are gentler, and people more reasonable, desires are baser and the reasonableness utilitarian looking for nothing in excess. At the same time, while bonds of caste and class are replaced by feelings for the whole of society and the whole of mankind, the universal feelings, being diffused over a wider constituency, are inevitably weaker. In practice the democratic man tends to retire into his own individual private space and that of his close family. He is reluctant to obey, or to serve, unlikely to respond to calls to duty, such as those uttered by Jack Straw or Tony Blair. Each man chooses his own road, or so he thinks. In fact, he tends to choose the same road as everyone else.

In a democracy a great multitude of other, similar people stands against the individual. And in so far as the democratic individual sees himself as small and alone against that mass, his confidence in his own judgement and ability declines. This is the obverse of the stubborn democratic belief in intellectual and social equality. If none is better than me, I am better than none. So each individual craves the endorsement of public opinion and needs the support of the whole community. In democracy, therefore, newspapers and the state take on an importance unimaginable in closed, stratified societies, in which people had a robust sense of their stations and their duties, and a spontaneous and uncentralized social organization that made their fulfilment possible.

In a democracy the state provides the security to ensure the peaceful and prosperous enjoyment of private life, against the political incursion of the multitudes outside. In doing this it listens to the pleas of individuals and groups who insist that state interference is minimal, except in connection with their own favoured projects. The upshot is that the tentacles of the state fast reach into every nook and cranny of life, providing security and safety, helping the disadvantaged to achieve the ever-retreating goal of mass equality, and creating the illusory uniformity of the 'level playing field'.

Rather against his faith in the vitality of private institutions in the first volume of *Democracy in America* (1835), in the second de Tocqueville was less sure: 'In Europe in the old days almost all charitable establishments were managed by individuals or corporations. They are now more or less under government control . . . the state almost exclusively undertakes to supply bread to the hungry, assistance and shelter to the sick, work to the idle, and to act as the reliever of all kinds of misery.' True in Europe, if not in America. Education, too, becomes a national concern: 'The state receives, and often takes, the child from its mother's arms to hand it over to functionaries; it takes the responsibility for forming the feelings and shaping the ideas of each generation. Uniformity prevails in schoolwork as in everything else; diversity, as well as freedom, is daily vanishing.'

That this prophecy was alarming in its time as well as prescient is confirmed by John Stuart Mill's very similar sentiments in *On Liberty* in 1859:

A general state education is a mere contrivance for moulding people to be exactly like one another: and as the mould in which it casts them is that which pleases the predominant power in the government . . . in proportion as it is efficient and successful, it establishes a despotism over the mind, leading by natural tendency to one over the body.

What are we to make of all this, when state schooling, national curricula and governmental strategies for childcare and preschool socialization are taken absolutely for granted by politicians of all parties? When people who would balk at receiving from, or giving to, private charity (except when these are political campaigning organizations) expect, as of right, state support 'from cradle to grave'? Do we feel all this as despotism?

So inured are we to it that we do not feel it at all, either as despotism or anything else, except, of course, when we complain about the inadequancy of the 'resourcing'. But despotism it is, albeit mild and bureaucratic, and in a sense even worse and more insidious for being mild and bureaucratic, as de Tocqueville makes clear:

I see an immense multitude of men, all alike and equal, constantly circling around in pursuit of the petty and banal pleasures by which they glut their souls . . . Over this kind of men stands an immense protective power which alone is responsible for securing their enjoyment and watching over their fate. That power is absolute, thoughtful of detail, orderly, provident and gentle. It would resemble parental authority if, fatherlike, it tried to prepare its charges for a man's life, but . . . it only tries to keep them in perpetual childhood . . . It gladly works for their happiness but wants to be the sole agent and judge of it . . . It covers the whole of social life with a network of petty, complicated rules . . . It does not break men's will, but softens, bends and guides it; it seldom enjoins, but often inhibits action; it does not destroy anything, but prevents much being born; it is not at all tyrannical, but it hinders, restrains, enervates, stifles and stultifies so much that in the end each nation is no more than a flock of timid and hardworking animals with the government as its shepherd.

Well, not hardworking, perhaps, but otherwise not a bad description of our state in Western Europe, *circa* 1999. Perhaps, indeed, there is something to be said for institutionalized timidity, though not so much for the abrogation of freedom, independence and sheer adulthood that all this ever-so-well-intended regulation and legislation implies. Administrative despotism and popular sovereignty; or more, if de Tocqueville is correct at all, administrative despotism *because* of popular sovereignty. And, as he says, 'under this system the citizens quit their state of dependence just long enough to choose their masters and then fall back into it'.

A problem which de Tocqueville bequeathes us in his description of democracy is that the individualism and egalitarianism that go with democracy are inherently corrosive of communal feeling, public virtue and grand projects, except those relating to the pretty speedy improvement of man's estate. In ages of faith men accomplished lasting achievements culturally, architecturally and environmentally precisely because they had settled distant goals. The rigidities of their social structures meant their eyes were on the future and the past rather than on the political present, so they built cathedrals and estates over centuries, rather than spatchcocked millennial domes with no lasting purpose or value.

In democracy, where individualism and the rights of the individual reign supreme, men have no interest higher than self-interest, and self-interest as directed to material comfort and prosperity. Social instability goes hand in hand with instability of desire, with constant movement and constant activity, but all for instant gratification and easily quantifiable and immediately achievable goals. In the early days of the American republic there remained a residue of Protestant and Puritan virtue. Then self-interest was understood to have a cosmic dimension: it had transcendent perspective, beyond this life, the upshot being that in this life men would on occasion put moral concerns above expediency.

But what happens in a democracy when religion declines and we lose the extra-terrestrial underpinnings necessary to render self-interest long-term enough to be truly moral and truly virtuous? Will society not revert to a democratic war of all against all, in which the timidity and peacefulness of the early- and mid-twentieth century democracies are revealed as no more than a stage on a longer, more worrying journey?

No doubt some of the forms of democracy will remain, in particular the bureaucratizing of every aspect of life. But, as those of us who have worked in governmental bureaucracies can testify, bureaucracies themselves become increasingly subject to capture by groups and individuals wanting nothing more elevated than an increased slice of the national cake. This temptation is particularly potent when 40 per cent or more of the national wealth and power typically resides in state bodies, and when politicians are terrified of the bad publicity that well-organized special-interest groups heap on their heads – for example, the disabled, ethnic minorities, the aged.

In his bleaker moments, de Tocqueville foresaw the possible outcome:

> when social conditions are equal, every man tends to live apart, centred in himself and forgetful of the public. Should democratic legislation not seek to correct this fatal tendency, or actually favour it, thinking that it diverts the citizens' attention from political passions and avoids revolution, it might happen in the end that they may bring about the very evil which they seek to avoid and that the moment may come when the unruly passions of certain men, aided by the foolish selfishness and pusillanimity of the greater number, will in the end subject the fabric of society to strange vicissitudes.

No more than Plato or Aristotle, then, was de Tocqueville unaware of the susceptibility of democracy to demogoguery and anarchy. Like them, he sees that democracy can foster the very spirit which will lead to such things.

De Tocqueville does, it is true, encourage democratic leaders to inspire citizens with distant and grander aims than those of democratic trade and comfort. But where are they and their followers to find the necessary inspiration? Not, it seems, in democratic religion: in one of his most striking observations, de Tocqueville speaks of a kind of impossible pantheism as being the natural religion of democracy. As social conditions become more equal, each individual becomes less significant, more replaceable. Thought is only for 'the people'; the concept of unity (what we call inclusivity) becomes an obsession. In this unifying project, barriers of all kinds are broken down, including the ultimate barrier, that between creator and creation. We see ourselves as part of one great system, in which the individual and his or her acts and responsibilities are hardly significant. We are also part of one community, animals as well as human beings, the differences between animals and humans, and our distinctive freedom, rationality and agency ignored.

In a terrifyingly convenient synthesis, pantheism – whether New Age mysticism or environmental Gaia-worship – at once fosters our pride and soothes the laziness of our minds. It fosters our pride by implying that we are part of a greater process; but it soothes our mental and spiritual laziness because it is not our individuality that contributes to the success of the process, but rather a kind of passivity repudiating effort, ingenuity, intelligence and real individuality. We can all feel good about the Spirit Dome because it sounds uplifting, but it means nothing, makes no distinctions and is entirely without content. Unlike all previous religions, democratic pantheism abrogates difficult choices and hard decisions. In this new religion the only difficult choice is to do everything one can to avoid difficult choices.

Nietzsche

Nietzsche is modernity's most trenchant critic. To a degree, what he says echoes the strictures of others. At a descriptive level there are striking similarities between him and de Tocqueville, for example, though the tone is quite different. What makes Nietzsche critical for our story is that – again like de Tocqueville – he is not simply lamenting aspects of the modern world. He shows that the very strengths of modernity contain the seeds of its undoing. I want to elaborate this point by focusing on what he has to say about knowledge and about equality.

It is precisely knowledge as enlightenment that is problematic for Nietzsche. In his earliest book, *The Birth of Tragedy*, Nietzsche had denounced Socrates, the patron saint of philosophy and of all enlightenment. Along with the playwright Euripides, who put common people on the stage and had them spout their common feelings and indulge their vulgar emotions, Socrates had destroyed the archaic culture of ancient Greece, and hence its greatness. They had started questioning the myths, they had attacked the gods, they had thrown them off their pedestal, they had annulled the distance between gods and men, they had destroyed tragedy.

In a sense there was nothing new about this. It was, after all, the theme of Aristophanes' *Frogs*, and Aristophanes had mercilessly lampooned Socrates – though in 1872, twenty-eight-year-old professors of philology like Nietzsche were not supposed to take ancient literature that seriously. (Are they today?) What was new in what Nietzsche had to say was this:

> First, the sublimity and poise of Greek culture, the archaic smile, the beautiful bodies, the luminosity and order of the temples: all this, which even today casts so glowing, genial and golden a light on antiquity, was a tremendous pretence. It was an act of will of the most powerful imagination the world had or has ever known, in a deliberate attempt of a whole people to conceal momentarily from itself what would otherwise have crushed its spirit totally: namely, its all too profound sense of the horror and pain of existence.

Through tragedy particularly, and through the myths on which the tragedies were based, the ancient Greeks made the horror of existence beautiful, and hence livable. Just as their sense of horror was made beautiful through the tales of the gods, their plastic art and their temples, so did their sense of beauty quiver on a tightrope slung across the abyss.

For Beauty's nothing
but beginning of Terror we're just still able to bear,
and why we adore it so is because it serenely
disdains to destroy us.

Not Nietzsche, but Rilke, in the first Duino Elegy, but very
Nietzschean. For Nietzsche, though, beauty is not just the
beginning of terror. As opposed to mere prettiness, it grows
out of terror, and it gives us hope. But it has this power only
because of its symbiotic relationship with terror. It is not, in any
conventional sense, optimistic or conducive to optimism.

So, in Nietzsche's view, beauty in the classical sense is
intimately linked to terror and to myth or illusion. Socrates
is the destroyer of Greek tragedy, what it stands for and makes
possible, because he uses reason to blow away its mythical
underpinnings. He shows the gods to be, in essence, no more
and no better than mortals, and the myths to be unbelievable.
Socrates is the ordinary man, who questions to destructive
effect; by his example he encourages other ordinary men to do
the same. 'Socratism', as Nietzsche observes, depreciates all
known art and ethics; wherever its piercing gaze 'alighted' it
found only a lack of insight and the power of delusion, and
deduced from this that the prevailing situation was both
misguided and reprehensible. In that sense the Enlightenment
is right to take Socrates as its patron saint: Socrates is a believer
both in science (=the power of reason) and in liberalism
(=democracy – anyone has the right to question, and hence
to subvert).

Above all, Socrates made what Nietzsche thought a fatal
identification of virtue and knowledge. The identification was
fatal, because if virtue is what conduces to life and to a healthy
culture, then it cannot be identified with knowledge. Because,
once again, knowledge undermines myth, which psychic and
cultural health depend on.

The Birth of Tragedy is itself a work of poetry and feverish, almost uncontrolled imagination. Nevertheless its key features recur throughout Nietzsche's work. At the beginning of *Beyond Good and Evil* (1886), Nietzsche says this:

> The falseness of a judgement is for us not necessarily an objection . . . The question is to what extent it is life-promoting, life-preserving, species-preserving, perhaps even species-cultivating . . . To recognize untruth as a condition of life – that certainly means resisting accustomed value feelings in a dangerous way.

Including the accustomed value feelings, one might add, of those weaned on the customary pieties of the Enlightenment.

Nietzsche is outrageously unfair to Socrates the man, but not to a shallow optimism of knowledge. In many ways truth is destructive, ugly and even dangerous. (Think not only of the tendency of truth to destroy ennobling beliefs, but also of its tendency to make dangerous discoveries.) But even worse than the tendencies of truth itself are the tendencies of those who claim they are driven by the desire to discover the truth, however difficult, uncomfortable or unpopular this might be.

'Truth-seeking' can be no more than a mask for resentment, a cover for a desire to bring down the good and the old, a desire to subvert the wisdom of ages. 'Truth-seeking' is an easy option, particularly in an age such as ours when it has itself become received wisdom, and academics and journalists award each other prizes for their 'fearlessness' in its pursuit. And think of the sort of character it encourages: a disrespectful cleverness, and an intellectual fleetness, nimbleness and dexterity to catch out any more leaden-footed wisdom or decency. (Not that our 'truth-seekers' are themselves happy, healthy or decent: as Nietzsche would doubtless have predicted, there can be few more potent breeding-grounds for rancour, petty-mindedness, intellectual conformism and self-serving posturing than the common rooms of our current universities and the newsrooms of 'investigative' reporters, filled with people whose vocation is supposedly nothing less than the disinterested pursuit and transmission of truth.)

It is only too easy to engage in a form of questioning that is cost-free to the questioner, and destructive of what is being questioned. Here Nietzsche's attack on Socratic interrogation converges with Aristotle's views on sophistry and wisdom. According to Aristotle, only someone who understands virtue through its practice is competent to discuss moral and political methods. Cleverness in areas where experience and the difficulty of decision-making are of the essence is no substitute for the judgement only maturity can bring. Mere cleverness, such as the young characteristically manifest, is no guide at all to what we ought to do.

In Nietzsche's mature thinking, Socratism can be seen as an aspect of a wider modern phenomenon, the rise of what he calls slave morality. Slave morality is what emerges when the naturally inferior and downtrodden manage to get what will help them accepted as the morality of a society. Instead of aristocracy, democracy; instead of hardness and nobility, pity and love of the victim; instead of reverence for tradition and respect for ancestors, a belief in progress and exaltation of the uninformed young; instead of contempt for the inferior, humility; instead of real originality and individuality, the values of the herd; instead of bold action, querulous thought and endless critical discussion; patience and industry rather than the impetuosity of the powerful and energetic; instead of lofty disdain for what is worthless, a care for public opinion; not contempt for the cowardly but compassion for those brought down by suffering, real or imaginary; feminism, passivity and womanly feeling rather than manly action or anything grand, adventurous or powerful; above all, a stress on utility and calculation rather than magnanimity, superabundance and display of the spirit.

It is Nietzsche's view that anything great or worthwhile in human history has derived from superabundance and display of the spirit, and that nothing truly worthwhile is to be expected from the accountants of utility. Nietzsche, unRuskinian in every other way, would have echoed his anti-utilitarian and anti-industrial adage, that there is 'no wealth but life'. But, in a way, in our civilization it is already too late.

God is dead (not something welcomed by Nietzsche, for all its inevitability and his own anti-Christian diatribes). The world is empty and the stage set for mankind alone, thrown on our own resources. The creature of the immediate future is the last man.

The last man is the man who is more concerned with comfort, ease and immediate this-worldly satisfaction than with anything distant, challenging or hard. He is averse to risk and danger. Because he is reasonable, he believes in nothing he cannot verify in his own mediocrity. Because he believes in nothing his imagination will not allow him to comprehend, he seeks to avoid conflict and confrontation. He is, in the modern jargon, non-judgemental. Above all else, he desires happiness for himself and for everyone else. And because he regards pain and suffering of any sort as the greatest misfortune to befall himself or anyone else, his main attitude to the world and to others is pity.

Yet, as Nietzsche urges, 'The discipline of suffering, of *great* suffering – do you know that only *this* discipline has created all enhancements of man so far?' To avoid struggle and suffering is to avoid what alone can make life worthwhile. We all know in our hearts that our most precious achievements have been bought through struggle and suffering. To pity another, to make him comfortable and remove from him his pain and agony, is actually the cruellest thing we could do. It is to remove from him the one thing necessary. It is to belittle him.

As is the refusal to disagree with his beliefs, the easy-going insistence on 'non-judgementalism'. But as Fukuyama points out in his essay on the last man, relativism does not lead to the liberation of the great or the strong, but of the mediocre. From our point of view, ancestral battles and wars of religion are pointless, crimes against humanity. We congratulate ourselves on our enlightened attitudes to all that. As Nietzsche's Zarathustra puts it, 'For thus you speak: "Real we are entirely, and without belief or superstition." Thus you stick out your chests – but alas, they are hollow.' Not men, then, but husks of men, mere machines for pleasure and pain, without enterprise or vision, blown this way and that, all victims, all sharing our pain, even among hitherto unimaginable material comfort and prosperity.

Yet, in the progress of our enlightenment, isn't this what our psychology reveals us to be? And isn't enlightenment a deconstruction of the very myths that would ennoble us, that would set our minds and hearts on something higher, that would produce a creative distance between one individual and another, that would distance each individual from his mere animality, that would allow us to love and respect what we do and believe 'infinitely more than it deserves to be loved'?

It is precisely this 'infinitely more' that in previous eras has bootstrapped us out of mediocrity, out of the sense that nothing matters beyond pleasure and pain, and into the mentality that some things are worth doing beyond the present and the foreseeable future, and that certain lines of conduct are dishonourable, whatever the price. Has enlightenment progress rendered such bootstrapping ever beyond us? That is Nietzsche's message as we move into the third millennium.

The Pessimism of the Nineteenth Century

The nineteenth century is often seen as an age of confidence and of progress. It was certainly an age of progressivism. Comte, Mill, Marx and a host of other thinkers all saw the age as one of progress away from old superstitions and prejudices towards more rational ways of doing things. There was also the rise of technology in the industrial revolution. Science seemed to hold the key to the material future, and scientific thinking promised to unlock the secrets both of nature and of the human heart.

But beneath the expansion, the confidence and the brashness of the age, there were deep veins of melancholy. The industrial revolution and the growth of towns were not experienced as so benevolent by those most directly affected, or by thoughtful observers. Ruskin's diatribe against industrial practices and the division of labour – as manufacturing everything except men, breaking men into small fragments and crumbs of life – were expressed extremely, but were not atypical. They were echoed in Marx. Wagner's *Ring*, the greatest and in some ways most characteristic work of the mid- to late-nineteenth century, was, among other things, a deeply felt protest against both the ambitions and the methods of industrialization. It was also a work celebrating – if that is the right word – the submerging of all human and political hopes, and a return to an innocent and unsullied nature. Wagner and Ruskin looked back to the Middle Ages for a more organic and healthy form of life than that of their time. As did Pugin, whose call for a 'revival of Christian architecture' was as much social and political as aesthetic, for the Gothic approach to building was supposed to embody values of community and wholeness, which modern planning and modern life had lost. (This last point is particularly striking, as the style of building Pugin singles out for criticism is the utilitarian classicism favoured by Bentham for buildings such as his panoptic prisons and almshouses,

designed to facilitate easy supervision and regular, easily ac-
countable toil by the inmates.)

Novelists such as Dickens and Zola who described city life
were certainly not describing Utopias, however much they
may have had hopes of better things to come. More profound,
and more profoundly pessimistic, were the great Russian
visionaries, Dostoevsky and Tolstoy. The one looked for
salvation to a fideistic form of Christianity, and the other to
an idealized peasant life and religion. Both were Slavophils,
deeply suspicious of the direction Europe was taking. The
point is not that either was right, but simply that each of these
powerful observers, in his own way, rejected the modern world
and all it stood for, particularly anything smacking of scientific
enlightenment.

Even with many not committed to a form of medieval
revival, the atmosphere is of resigned regret, rather than of
enthusiasm. Matthew Arnold's 'Dover Beach' is typical:

> The Sea of Faith
> Was once too at the full and round earth's shore
> Lay like the folds of a bright girdle furl'd.
> But now I only hear
> Its melancholy long withdrawing roar
> Retreating to the breath
> Of the night-wind, down the vast edges drear
> And naked shingles of the world.

One of the problems with Enlightenment optimism is a startling
inability to recognize what has been lost in the demystification
of the world. It is as if the world had never been enchanted in
the first place, and mankind's highest vocation was to live in
scientifically designed industrial towns (in conditions of modern
hygiene and comfort), working for an industry that pays for and
produces our material plenty.

It will doubtless be said that the pessimists who have been mentioned represent only a reactionary obscurantism, and that they fail to appreciate the strides made through technology and industry, just as their present-day followers similarly fail to recognize either the gains achieved by what they object to, or its inevitability (globalization and all that). Maybe, too, development in Britain has been held up particularly in the twentieth century by a lack of scientific and industrial know-how among opinion-formers and political leaders.

However, at this point one is reminded of the observation of the nineteenth-century American philosopher C. S. Peirce, who held science in the very highest esteem. No reader of the journal *Science* is, says Peirce,

> likely to be content with the statement that the searching out of the ideas that govern the universe has no other value than that it helps human animals to swarm and feed . . . the only thing that makes the human race worth perpetuation is that thereby rational ideas may be developed, and that rationalization of things furthered.

Is life tolerable if all we are here to do is to swarm and feed?

Science, post-Bacon, post-Enlightenment, has been brilliantly successful in promoting human swarming and feeding, and for all the concern with 'pure' science, in this century at least, its efforts have largely been directed to the relief of man's estate and other utilitarian purposes, often militaristic. But science itself, in its Darwinian incarnation, can give no account of human life or purposes except in terms of swarming, breeding and feeding. The pessimists are those who look for more, and who know that once there was more. Small wonder they find the optimism of the modernizers Philistine, a promise of endless bread and circuses where, deep down, we know we are capable of something rather more inspiring.

Spengler: The Decline of the West

In *The Decline of the West*, Spengler quotes Goethe as saying 'what is important in life is life and not a result of life'. History is not a linear pattern to some pre-ordained, distant goal, nor is my life simply a stage on a journey other people are taking to somewhere else. Each life and each historical epoch has its own form and possibility. It must be judged for what it is. There is no aim for humanity over and above the lives and aims of individual men. Similarly each culture has its own possibilities of self-expression, which, like flowers, arise, ripen, decay and never return. In this context, 'progress' is an illusion, the narrow perspective of the contemporary man whose imagination is so limited that he can envisage no form of life but his own as the summit of human achievement or even desirable.

To these Herderian reflections, Spengler adds some sharp and pertinent reflections on the condition of modern Western society. Central to his analysis is the distinction he draws between culture and civilization. Fundamentally, civilization is what emerges at the end of a culture, when its forms become dead and its influence diffused. Civilizations are pragmatic, materialistic and cosmopolitan, where cultures are local, soulful and, in a certain sense, idealistic. A culture is a unifying spiritual orientation of a whole people, enlivening and informing all their activities. In civilization, the unifying vision is lost. What counts are technology and administration.

The influence of Nietzsche on all this is obvious, underlined by the fact that Spengler takes classical Greece to represent a culture, where Rome has all the marks of civilization.

In civilization

in place of a type-true people, born of and grown on the soil, there is a new sort of nomad, cohering unstably in fluid masses, the parasitical city-dweller, traditionless, utterly

matter-of-fact, religionless, clever, unfruitful, deeply contemptuous of the countryman and especially that highest
form of countryman, the country gentleman.

Civilizations are typically centred on what Spengler calls
world-cities, of which Imperial Rome and modern Berlin
and New York are examples:

> To the world-city belongs not a folk but a mass. Its
> uncomprehending hostility to all the traditions representa-
> tive of the Culture (nobility, church, privileges, dynasties,
> convention in art and limits of knowledge in science), the
> keen and cold intelligence that confounds the wisdom of the
> peasant, the new-fashioned naturalism that in relation to all
> matters of sex and society goes back far beyond Rousseau
> and Socrates to quite primitive instincts and conditions, the
> reappearance of the *panem et circenses* in the form of wage
> disputes and football grounds – all these things betoken . . . a
> quite new phase of human existence – anti-provincial, late,
> futureless, but quite inevitable.

Money and accountancy are the universal currency of civilization. They weaken religion and traditional institutions; they
dissolve taboos and prohibitions; they loosen local roots and
loyalties; and they colonize other parts of the world through
military conquest initially, but then through the softer but
ultimately more insidious weapon of trade.

Along with his breaking of taboos and local links, modern
man is Faustian – that is, he uses his knowledge and machines to
control nature, and then in turn his way of life is largely
controlled by them. Spengler talks of the 'modern sorcerer',
at his switchboard of levers and labels on which he can call
'mighty effects into play by the pressure of a finger without
possessing the slightest notion of their essence'.

Spengler is, not unreasonably, taken to be a prophet of doom. Certainly that is how he was read; and the title of his book is, after all, *The Decline of the West*. However, he stresses that he believes the development from culture towards civilization to be inevitable. He also writes that he 'would sooner have the mind-begotten forms of a fast steamer, a steel structure, a precision lathe, the subtlety and elegance of many chemical and optical processes, than all the pickings and stealings of present-day "arts and crafts", architecture and painting included'. He loves the Colosseum and the massive brick constructions of Rome far more than 'the empty and pretentious marblery of the Caesars'.

His point is that a time of civilization is a time of technical achievement. It is not a time for art or culture. It is better that a time should be what it is, up front, rather than pretend to be what it is not. 'Of great painting or great music there can no longer be, for Western people, any question,' he says; better, then, not to attempt art but to stick to functional design.

Spengler's invidious comparison between culture and civilization can also be given a far more civilization-friendly spin. Yes, it is true that 'civilization' uproots old loyalties, tears up old proscriptions, encourages movement and undermines instinctive moral attitudes. But are these not the conditions of the wealth it brings? Was there not something stifling and oppressive about many 'cultures' of the past, compared to the global freedom of ideas and communication we enjoy today? Isn't the anonymity and fluidity of the city at times preferable to the curtain-twitching of the village and the social stratification of the country? And is it not significant that Spengler's blood and soil notions enjoyed great success in Weimar Germany and played a not insignificant role in the rise of Nazism?

To each of these questions, the answer may be a qualified 'yes'. Spengler's comparisons are one-sided, and his distinctions are too rigid. His ideas did have unhappy associations. But none of this means that he was not pointing to genuine features of modern life, such that its conditions are indeed unpropitious for art and in other ways too. What, though, is most questionable is his analysis of progress. While he was right to question the idea that progress is a linear movement from primitive life to modernity, he is surely wrong to imply that modernity, as he describes it, is our inevitable fate, that our world is bound to be one of steamships rather than cathedrals. Of course it is actually neither, yet another illustration of the short-sightedness of those who affect to discern the direction of history (even while, in Spengler's case, denying there is any).

In this chapter we have explored the thinking of some of those who did not take the assumptions of the modern world for granted. In earlier chapters we examined the paths by which we have arrived at where we are now. It is time now to examine significant features of the modern world directly, with a view to relaxing their hold on our mental landscape.

6

The Twentieth Century

Profit and Loss

It is time to take stock. We are at the end of the twentieth century, two thousand years after the founding of Christianity and two and a half thousand years after the great efflorescence of culture, sensibility and thought, which we now think of as classical Greece. Christianity and ancient Greece: these are the influences that have formed us. But through the rise of science and the Enlightenment, and the reactions to it over the past two hundred years, Christianity and ancient Greece are, for most of us, dead.

For most of our contemporaries to walk into an art gallery devoted to the work of the Italian Renaissance, say, is like walking into a foreign country. The subjects depicted mean nothing. The style moves them not at all. They are in a museum. The resonance of the works has to be reconstructed, painfully, item by item; it can be retrieved only through some laboured comparison with a contemporary film or by reference to some psychoanalytical interpretation.

Church is no better. 'A few cathedrals chronically on show', in Philip Larkin's words, and the rest, as R. S. Thomas wrote, 'frowsty barns', hard ribs of bodies that 'our prayers have failed to animate'. For all anyone knows, there are now as many committed Muslims in our country as Christians. They certainly seem more direct and enthusiastic, less pathologically defensive. Apart from weddings and a decreasing number of religious funerals, most of us would as soon go into a mosque as into a Christian church, and understand as much.

Two years ago I went to the Christmas service at Winchester Cathedral. Instead of any sense of awe and reverence for the mystery we were about to celebrate, people talked loudly and gossiped openly. Among the cathedral staff there was an officious jollity. During the course of an unwanted conversation with one of the sidesmen, I learned that William Waynflete had been one of the medieval bishops of Winchester. Waynflete! I knew, already, that New College, Oxford, had been set up by William of Wykeham, the founder of the present cathedral, and I had reflected from time to time on the fact that New College had always seemed to me to contain more than its fair share of dons militantly or superciliously atheistic. But Waynflete, too, is the name of one of Oxford's principal chairs of philosophy, its recent incumbents showing little sympathy for the faith of its medieval patron.

My first reaction was of depression. But this, I later concluded, was misplaced. It was all but inevitable that Christian institutions of learning should end up subverting their original purpose and the intentions of their founders.

Just as Socrates was a product of the Athenian enlightenment and proved its nemesis, so Christianity contains within itself the seed of its own destruction. The Olympian gods could not survive the Socratic questioning that Athenian culture promoted. Similarly, Christianity teaches that Christ is the way, the light and the truth, that human reason is given to us by God to understand His truth and that the natural world is God's handiwork. Both philosophy and science, then, are part of the vocation of the true believer and encouraged by his faith; but if pursued far enough, they gnaw away at the beliefs of those who founded the medieval cathedrals and colleges, eventually undermining the whole magnificent fabric.

In this sense, then, the scientific revolution and the Enlightenment are not just the undoing of traditional Christianity. Christianity, along with Socratism, also produced them, just as it produced the characteristic morality of the Enlightenment. For where else did notions such as fraternity, the equality of man and universalism stem from? What, indeed, does brotherhood mean unless we have a common Father? In what sense are all men equal, except in the sight of God? Despite the optimism of Kant, rationality seems unequally distributed, and we are certainly not equal in any other way. How can we say that the warring tribes and conflicting values of the whole of human history point to a deeper human unity?

It was only through the ideal of universal salvation and unity, which it was the genius of Paul to introduce into Christianity, transforming it from local cult to a religion with universal appeal, that mankind gains the conception of itself as one kind, one species. Finally, along with equality and fraternity, the Enlightenment's stress on liberty and Kant's notion of autonomy are direct descendants of the Christian sense that within each of us there is a power of choice through which we forge either our ultimate salvation or our ultimate damnation.

But just as Christianity hardly survived the scientific quest for truth, it could not cope with the liberty and universal fraternity it had helped to generate. For, as we saw with Kant, Enlightenment autonomy meant that man took himself to be the sole judge of value, not God; while Enlightenment universalism sat ill with the imperialistic claims of Christianity to be the sole religious truth in a world with other major, and in some ways equally admirable, religious traditions.

However, for a time at least, it proved possible for ideals that had their roots in Christianity to survive in secular, Enlightenment form. The past two hundred years have seen astonishing progress not only in science and technology but also in the assertion of universal rights, in the growth and spread of democracy throughout the world, and in the shrinking of the world into one ideal global community. However fractured the world is in practice, the dominant ideology is against local boundaries and traditions, and for globalization.

Further, within those countries most characterized by enlightened thought, there is the sense that society as a whole, through the state, has to provide for the basic needs of each and every individual. There has also been a growing conviction that human reason provides the key to how we should organize our lives, with a simultaneous insistence on individual health and happiness, physical and psychological. And to these ends all else is sacrificed, all else becomes subservient. Nothing must stand in the way of human happiness; nothing must impede what reason can do to achieve what individuals see as happiness.

But there is an altogether more equivocal side to Enlightenment and post-Enlightenment progress. In elevating human reason and individual human happiness we have, at the same time, cast down the old religions and the old hierarchies. When the autonomy and the right to happiness of the individual becomes paramount – a right enshrined in the American constitution – it becomes problematic to tell an individual that there are things that he or she must not do, that there are barriers which may not be crossed. The old taboos are immediately under threat; a parlous situation once we realize that any sense of the sacred necessary to underpin the sanctity of human life itself depends on taboo, on the sense that these are things which absolutely must not be done. Yet one by one the taboos surrounding human life have been eroded by reason, always in the name of desire–satisfaction: abortion, euthanasia, homosexuality, divorce and soon the growing of body parts in organ farms. Some of us rage at capital punishment, world poverty and war (distant war) in the name of an abstract conception of human rights, while in our daily and intimate life every proscription sanctifying 'birth, death and copulation' is systematically taken apart.

Reason, of course, can take an individual or a collective form. We have seen both tendencies this century, collectivism alternating with consumerism. But either way the focus is resolutely earthbound. As such, far from the exaltation of human beings, we are witnessing our degradation. Science tells us that we are nothing more than the products of chance, survival machines destined to eke out a short, meaningless existence on a cosmically insignificant planet circling an un-remarkable star in an unremarkable galaxy. We are, moreover, subject to far cruder and more basic forces than we like to think. Human dignity, freedom and even reason are largely illusions unsustainable once we recognize our true origins and motivations and the true causes of our behaviour.

If each life is ultimately insignificant and pointless, then it makes little sense to think of some human beings or some activities as better than others. There is a democracy and equality of taste and judgement. The task of reason becomes simply that of allowing as many preferences and needs as possible to be satisfied simultaneously. In the end, that is what our contemporary discourse of rights amounts to.

The unanswered question is whether need and preference are enough to sustain any conception of right in which dignity plays a role. If the needs and preferences are those relating from the utilitarian psychology of pleasure and pain, it is hard to see how they can. Anything that contributes to pleasure and relieves pain is good, and anything that does the opposite is bad. There is no more to the dignity of the individual or the sacredness of human life than that – and that is tantamount to denying both.

As already remarked, during this century we have seen both collectivist and free-market attempts to bring about the satisfaction of as many needs and preferences as possible.

Collectivism has proved both inefficient and oppressive, so we are left with the market. But while the market is a better enabler of taste and preference than socialism, its calculated refusal to make any judgements of value makes it, to say the least, an uneasy partner in any quest to raise our sights above the satisfaction of immediate desire: while socialism and the market are in one sense antithetical manifestations of human reason, in another, deeper sense they share a common presupposition: that we are nothing beyond material existence, and that there is nothing sacred beyond the satisfaction of our desire. Reason, to the extent it exists, is just the means by which to achieve desire satisfaction.

In the twentieth century, in seeking to elevate man by stressing his reason and his autonomy – against the gods of our ancestors – we have in fact diminished man. Man has been reduced to no more than a naked, ignoble ape, at the mercy of all kinds of internal and external forces we can hardly understand or control. It is time now to examine the effect of twentieth-century rational demystification and rational reconstruction on key aspects of our lives.

Religion

Well, not perhaps *our* lives. For most of us the sea of faith has ebbed so far that not even our toes are touched. And that is hardly surprising as, with certain notable exceptions, Western religion in the twentieth century has lost its centre of gravity.

The notable exceptions are, of course, Catholicism in Africa and Eastern Europe (as represented by the Pope) and Protestant fundamentalism in Ulster and the USA. Most religious people I know regard both phenomena with the same horror our grandparents reserved for the 'enemies of religion': 'militant atheists', 'godless' Communists and scourges of the pious, such as Bertrand Russell and A. J. Ayer. In doing so they are implying that the sacrifices their grandparents and their fore-fathers made to keep the faith of their fathers alive were a complete waste of effort and time. Nowadays you can be a Christian, even a Catholic, without respecting any of Christianity's traditional practices, beliefs or prohibitions. Liberal Catholics in this country will single out the Pope for special condemnation: the Pope actually tries to censor priests and theologians who reject traditional Catholic teaching in faith and morals (but not very effectively, it seems, because 'Christian' bookshops are full of their works).

What we are seeing in the Churches at the tail end of the twentieth century is the final stage in their post-Enlightenment post-scientific transformation. Even as late as the first half of the nineteenth century it was perfectly possible for men of science to be swayed by William Paley's *Natural Theology*, which argued that the perfection and intricacy of the natural world was explicable only if it were the work of a divine intelligence. True, geology was showing the world to be considerably older than the biblical calculations of Archbishop Ussher (Creation at 4004 BC), but that was perfectly compatible with a reasonably generous reading of the Book of Genesis.

Darwin himself recorded his early admiration for Paley and Paley's persuasiveness, but the law of natural selection blew the optimism of natural theology apart. After Darwin it was no longer possible to see the living world as a divine masterpiece. It was chance-ridden, wasteful, cruel and, above all, purposeless; and man was part of that nature, hauling himself out of the mire, if at all, only temporarily, with struggle and by good fortune.

At the same time as Darwin was destroying the intellectual foundations of the traditional world-view, biblical scholarship, especially in Germany, was demonstrating the precariousness of the scriptures. They appeared to be neither unique, nor historical, nor divinely inspired, rather a somewhat motley and haphazard collection of myths and half-truths, rather characteristic of the backward time and place from which they rose. The miracle stories in particular were subject to relentless demythologization.

Demythologization is the keynote of twentieth-century theology. From the 'modernists' of the turn of the century, such as Baron von Hügel and Father Tyrrell, through Bultmann and Tillich down to the Bishop of Woolwich in the 1960s and the Christian Marxists and Don Cupitt today, theology becomes an increasingly desperate and unconvincing attempt to squeeze some essence of truth out of the Middle Eastern myths and medieval dogmas. Inevitably this means in practice that, despite all appearance, Christianity is saying the same thing as the latest secular thinking, be it scientific, philosophical or ethical.

The early modernists were Hegelians seeking philosophical truth beneath theological clothing. Bultmann and Tillich flirted with Heideggerian existentialism; their followers saw Christianity in terms of 'situation ethics' (that is, the relativism of deciding what to do in each new situation without any general principles). The Bishop of Woolwich was clearly influenced by the logical positivist doctrine of the strict meaninglessness of emotive and evaluative language, Cupitt by Nietzsche. Liberation theology, meanwhile, turns Christ into a precursor of Marx just when the rest of the world has tired of Communism.

In my view, the greatest Christian thinker of our century was Karl Barth if only because he had no truck with attempts to accommodate Christianity to the secular world in any sense. His moment of truth came in 1914 when he discovered that, almost to a man, the most admired theological authorities in Germany came out strongly in favour of the Kaiser's war, corrupted in Barth's view by secular currents of thought.

For Barth, salvation and truth were to be found only in the person of Jesus Christ, as revealed in the New Testament and not in religion in any conventional sense. Religion was the enemy of faith most to be feared he said, 'the most dangerous enemy a man has on this side of the grave', precisely because it attempts to harmonize revelation and secular truth, and to deny the distance between man and God. Jesus is where salvation lies (and only in Jesus); but, echoing Paul in the Epistle to the Romans, God's self-revelation in Jesus is initially the greatest of all stumbling blocks. Belief in Jesus is 'the most hazardous of all hazards', particularly because believers in Jesus are all too prone to water down the message, to make it acceptable to human reason and the secular world, to deny its paradoxical nature, and to commit the unforgivable sin of thinking we can reach God through our own efforts.

It didn't work. There was the problem of knowing just who or what Barth's Jesus was; was he the Jesus who walked in Galilee, the Jesus of the Epistle to the Romans, or the Jesus whom the believer met in prayer and faith, or all or none of these? But even more, the very insistence on God's utter distance and difference, which makes Barth's work so impressive, is in the end its undoing. For if God is so different, so totally other, can we in the end know anything of him at all, even through Jesus?

Barth's theology leads inevitably either to an indefensible biblical fundamentalism or to the same death of God that the followers of Bultmann and Nietzsche reached by other routes. A God of whom we can know nothing and who does not communicate might as well not exist. Church becomes a place of silence, where – in R. S. Thomas's words – 'God hides from my searching'.

Only it doesn't. As Pascal taught long ago, silence is just what humankind cannot tolerate, religious humankind least of all. Into the silence of religious truth powers a cacophony of secular busyness, the *mysterium tremendens et fascinans* and its language and rites evicted by officious niceness, the language of the bureaucrat and ill-focused social work.

Religion, if it is anything, is hard. It cannot compromise with the secular world, or it is dead. Paul, the Church fathers, Augustine, St Francis, St Thomas, Luther, Calvin, Wesley, Newman and a host of ordinary and not so ordinary Christians all understood that. It is not a criticism of a religion that it is out of touch with 'the modern world'. As we learn from the New Testament itself, from Paul, from Augustine, from Luther, from Kierkegaard and from Karl Barth, that is what it is meant to be. Thus, the very idea of a religious '*aggiornomento*' ('todaying') – the motif of the Second Vatican Council – looks like a contradiction in terms, even more so where that world has actually defined itself in terms of its repudiation of religious belief and value.

Over the past thirty years we have seen in both Catholic and Anglican churches a wholesale destruction of liturgy and language. Latin, plainchant, the Book of Common Prayer, the King James Bible, were all dignified, mysterious, resonant, powerful and historically sanctified symbols of a transcendent reality. All have been largely kicked away by Church hierarchies indistinguishable in attitude and lack of conviction from secular bureaucracies. Though, for all their protestations of niceness and reasonableness, the new clerical panjandrums have plenty of anger left for any members of their flocks unreasonable enough to cherish old-time religion or its rituals, as Catholics discovered when they wanted to keep the Latin mass, and as Anglicans who object to women clergy are today finding out.

And as the dogmas of judgement, incarnation, sin and redemption have been progressively eroded, the Churches have increasingly accepted the half-truths of vulgar Marxism: that in modern society, individual responsibility is a myth, that systematic political activity and campaigning is preferable to 'merely palliative' charity and good works, and that poverty and 'institutional' racism are the cause of crime and other social disorders.

Individual clergy, meanwhile, adopt ever more extreme political opinions (like the bishop of twenty years ago who blamed the Americans for the fact that hundreds of Vietnamese were taking to boats, with only a fifty–fifty chance of survival, to escape the barbarism of the Hanoi government). Religion has an inbuilt suspicion of the way the world is, as we saw in connection with Augustine. This suspicion is legitimated and elevated by reference to the Heavenly City. Unfortunately, with Christianity demythologized the suspicion of the existing order remains, but transposed from a theological to a political key: we should not be surprised that modern Christianity is an easy bedfellow to a whole variety of progressive political creeds.

It is hard to condemn those who, for philosophical or moral reasons, cannot accept the doctrines and morality of Christianity (or any other religion). It is also hard not to have sympathy for Christians struggling with doubt. But what is hard to sympathize with is the transformation of Christianity into the enfeebled thing it currently is. One could be Spenglerian about this: a great dogmatic, other-worldly, authoritarian religion, once the backbone of an equally great culture, is eventually destined to decline into an all-too-easy quasi-secular, non-judgemental encounter group, only loosely connected to the religion whose name it bears. Nevertheless, in abandoning the traditional Christian scheme of the fall, original sin to which we are all subject, the incarnation, crucifixion and redemption, the source of Christianity's strength is also abandoned. And so are the deep truths about us and our condition, which underlie each of those doctrines.

Christianity has declined, so in our culture science has prospered. Despite what self-publicizing scientists often claim, it is far from the case that science has been marginalized, even intellectually. Even though science is not as popular in schools and universities as, say, English or business studies, this has more to do with its difficulty than with its prestige. To judge by the number of works of popular science, at the end of the twentieth century, when our educated contemporaries want instruction and uplift they go to scientists. On television there are any number of well-made films extolling the wonders of the natural world, and almost universally presenting the orthodox neo-Darwinian account of it. In newspapers and the media more generally, far from scientists and advocates of the scientific world-view being unable to get a hearing, one is sometimes under the impression that it is impossible to hear any other perspective, at least where fundamental questions are concerned.

In other words, the 'two' cultures, of which C. P. Snow complained, simply do not exist. We are one culture, in which the prevailing orthodoxy is that science holds the key to the good life both pragmatically and intellectually. Publicly religion is hardly taken seriously at all. Our morality is conditioned by the way science can increase utility, collective and individual. Art and literature, for all their popularity, operate in the margins of serious life, as entertainment or provocation, but are certainly not seen as offering wisdom or truth.

But, while science and scientific rationality are officially predominant, and orthodox religion hardly even in retreat, it is not the case that science is loved or that people are spiritually satisfied. As G. K. Chesterton famously remarked, once men stop believing in God, they do not believe in nothing. They start to believe in anything. And so it proves to be. It is not mere impression that belief in ESP, the occult and New Ageism is on the increase. Sociological surveys have shown that belief in the paranormal has, if anything, increased over the past century.

One's first reaction would be to say that this is despite science and science education, which, as already remarked, currently enjoy unprecedented prestige and patronage. But, on reflection, is it despite or because of? Science offers a reductive view of the world, of nature and of human life, all of which are taken to be explicable in materialistic terms and according to scientific laws. Science, moreover, is widely perceived to be destructive in intention and careless of the environment. Many people feel threatened by the hegemony of science and its pretensions. They know that in their lives there are things for which science cannot account.

But religion has failed, at least in its intellectually respectable forms, and people look elsewhere. The co-flourishing of science and New-Age mysticism is no paradox. In the circumstances, it is exactly what would be expected, the one simply the inverse of the other. It is precisely because of the Enlightenment interpretation of rationality as scientific rationality that irrationality flourishes as the semi-articulate cry of the human spirit against the reductionisms of the modern age.

Philosophy

If that cry could not be answered by religion, how about philosophy? After all, it is less then two hundred years since Hegel pronounced that the journey of the spirit was a journey from inanimate matter to philosophy, passing on the way organic matter, animal life, consciousness, and human history, including the development of science, the institutions of the state, art and religion. But philosophy was spirit knowing itself directly, and not via the occluded media of art and religion.

As will be clear even from this briefest of summaries, Hegel did not see science or the study of the physical world as the highest human activity. This was because in science we are confronted with the brute facticity of the physical world. Beyond knowing how it is, we cannot see from looking at it as it is presented in the natural sciences why it has to be as it is. Human activity, on the other hand, is guided by reasons and intentions that make it intelligible, transparent to the observing consciousness in a way mere matter can never be. In philosophy the conscious mind understands itself in a state of complete understanding. It is the understander turning its understanding directly on itself; there is further for Hegel a sense (never fully explained) in which individual human understanding and self-understanding are themselves part of a cosmic process by which the world-creating spirit became aware of its own essence and nature.

Hegel elevated philosophy to a position it had never occupied before – or since. Such hubris had to be followed by nemesis, and indeed it was swiftly. This century, far from philosophy standing way above natural science and putting it in its somewhat lowly place in the universal scheme, philosophy, at least in the analytic tradition, has come to regard itself as little more than an adjunct of natural science. This was partly because Hegel's reasoning and that of his followers proved obscure and unconvincing to outsiders.

Critics objected particularly to the way in which Hegel purported to show that all kinds of developments in human history and culture were necessary stages in the development of the world spirit on the way to its final goal. Not only did this belittle the sufferings of these whose lives were crushed *en route* to the end of history – a theme to recur, of course, in Marx's version of the Hegelian system – but to those moved by a Herderian view of culture, Hegel's whole philosophy looks like the *reductio ad absurdum* of Enlightenment progressivism.

Even more, while during the nineteenth century speculative philosophy seemed to be getting nowhere, sinking ever further into oracular pseudo-profundity, science was becoming ever clearer, more accurate and more successful. Finally, at the turn of the century, as a result of the work of the logician Gottlob Frege and of Bertrand Russell, mathematical logic was installed at the heart of the philosophical enterprise. Formal logic would provide the method for philosophy. Philosophy's main tasks were now conceived to be the purification of language (to guard against the woolliness and vagueness of religion and Hegelian guff) and the elucidation of science and its theories. In true Enlightenment style, philosophy was to take on the task of ridding language and thought of unscientific dross.

At the end of the twentieth century there is no doubt that the philosophy which enjoys most prestige among professional philosophers in the English-speaking world is that done in the Frege–Russell manner. The central topics of interest are language, the mind and scientific knowledge, and the methods used are formal and logical. Language is seen as a system, analysable in terms of formal logic. The mind is seen as identical to the brain, the only problem being to show how our mental life is related to the physical events underlying it. (As one who does not share the materialistic faith, I will simply assert at this point that, in my opinion, *no* progress whatever has been made on this problem, despite thirty or more years of intensive effort, probably because the very notion of the mind *being* the brain is at root unintelligible.)

Human knowledge is characteristically seen in what are called 'naturalistic' terms – that is, as the result of our minds (or brains) being honed by evolution to cope with the environment. Even ethics is dominated by attempts (often deriving from the mathematics of game theory) to show which moral rules and institutions would be required to allow as many preferences or rights as possible to be satisfied simultaneously without trampling on other rights and principles. The methods used in analytical philosophy are predominantly technical and formal, so that if you look at a philosophical journal you might think that you had inadvertently picked up a collection of scientific or mathematical articles.

Of course, philosophy being philosophy, there are dissenting voices. In the English-speaking world the main focus of dissent is Ludwig Wittgenstein. If mainstream analytical philosophy is the descendant of Enlightenment thinking, Wittgensteinianism is the Herderian reaction.

Wittgenstein was originally identified with the Frege–Russell project to the extent that he saw philosophy's task as the laying bare in quasi-mathematical form of the logical structure underlying language. But he was never an uncritical believer in scientific progress, and later he rejected the idea that there was just one ideal form of language, or, indeed, of thought or culture more generally.

For the later Wittgenstein, there were many different human languages and practices, each serving its own function, each adequate in its own terms. It was not the job of philosophy to criticize these languages and practices from a supposedly ideal perspective, particularly not that of science, which was no more valuable than any other. There is no Archimedean point from which everything else can be perceived and judged.

What philosophy could and should do was simply to expose the elements of each language game, and to demonstrate how one differed from another. Above all, philosophy should be a defence against the pretensions of one language game or culture to be a universal touchstone of language or truth. This becomes a particularly pressing matter when we observe in our own culture the pretensions of science to explain and reduce everything else to its own terms.

Wittgenstein's generous humanism can certainly be applauded in the face of scientific reductionism and imperialism. Things, though, become more difficult when he *appears* – in Herderian mode – to defend the validity of the world-views of primitive peoples against those of modern science, even on the truth concerning purely physical facts. In other words, Wittgenstein's anti-scientific position seems ultimately, like Herder's anti-progressivism, to rest on a problematic relativism.

I say 'appears' and 'seems' because, in his later work, Wittgenstein was either unable or unwilling to say what he meant in such a way that readers could be confident they had grasped his meaning. Similar studied ambiguity suggestive of great but ever elusive profundity is the hallmark of philosophy in the European tradition for at least the latter half of the twentieth century. In reading Martin Heidegger, its most admired exponent, one is immediately faced with the difficulty that the writer plays around with language to a vertiginous degree. Part of the justification for Heidegger's obsession with rebarbative neologisms was his belief that from the time of Plato onwards language had falsified the truth and distorted thought. This would be fine, were Heidegger's purified philosophical language accessible, consistent even, but it is not. Indeed, he made obscurity a virtue, claiming on one occasion that 'to make oneself understood is suicidal to philosophy'.

In Heidegger I frequently have the feeling that there is at bottom some religious insight with an obscure notion of nothing replacing God or traditional religions. There is in Heidegger, as in Hegel, more than a whiff of 'spilt' religion. I have a sense that Heidegger is wanting to say that the world is being created by some nameless and ungraspable ground of being with whom or which human beings are in a special relationship. We humans are shepherds of (this) being, bringing being to light by our making, acting and knowing:

Are we perhaps here just for saying: House,
Bridge, Fountain, Gate, Jug, Fruit Tree, Window
– possibly Pillar, Tower? . . . but for saying remember,
oh, for such saying as never the things themselves
hoped so intensely to be . . .
Many a star
was waiting for you to perceive it. Many a wave
would rise in the past towards you; Or else, perhaps
as you went by an open window, a violin
would be utterly giving itself.

But that is Rilke (Ninth and First Duino Elegies); and I do not know whether it corresponds to what Heidegger really believed.

That indeed is Heidegger's greatest failing – not his Nazism, but the way in which his portentous talk about being and nothingness, about authenticity and decisiveness and our being 'towards' death, and the need for youth to commit itself lent itself so easily to interpretation as Nazism. It did not *follow* from any of this that the only hope for the individual was identification with a *Volk*, or that in 1933 the 'time for decision' was past, having 'already been made by the youngest part of the German nation' or that 'the Führer himself and alone *is* the present and future German reality and its law', though these were the conclusions Heidegger himself drew. Actually, Heidegger's philosophy could just as easily be interpreted in other ways: and that's the point.

Shifting and systematic ambiguity is not the vocation of a philosopher, even for one who, as Heidegger did, insists that the modern world has lost its soul. Perhaps especially not for such a philosopher, because if he really knew where to find it, it would be vital for him to show the rest of us where to go. As it is, what is mainly communicated is contempt for anyone vulgar enough to seek a straight answer to a straight question (a reaction one also sometimes gets from Wittgenstein and his followers).

Heidegger was, as just remarked, a Nazi. It is one of the marvels of the modern age that his work is the source of much contemporary 'Continental' (that is, non-analytic) philosophy, whose protagonists, almost to a man (or woman), are left-wing feminists. So are most of those who today read Nietzsche, who was, to put it mildly, neither left-wing nor feminist.

What today's so-called deconstructionists and post-modernists take from Heidegger and Nietzsche are principally two things. From Nietzsche they take the idea of unmasking and the will to power. Morality as practised, the conventions of civilized life and, at the extreme, reason itself are all taken to be merely devices by which one group reinforces its power over others. These things are held to have no timeless validity. A lot is made of the absence of any Archimedean point from which impartial judgements can be made. But if no judgement is impartial or objectively sound then the only question which remains is *cui bono?*. Whose interests are being served by the erection of such arbitrary prejudices into dogma? At this point, of course, Nietzsche converges with Marx, and we get the sort of left-wing Nietzscheanism associated with Foucault and his followers.

From Heidegger, over and above a lofty disdain for the everyday world, are derived the ever more arcane and self-referential outpourings on the nature of language and subjectivity, which are associated most famously but by no means exclusively with Jacques Derrida. As with Heidegger, for Derrida and his followers, behind language is nothing, behind us is nothing, we are nothing. In Derrida's scheme of things, all we are left with are endless fragments of speech circling round themselves, at the core of which is, once again, nothing.

The net effect is to disperse all confidence in language (and hence in reason itself) and any remaining hope in the idea of the substantial human subject as the source of its judgements, actions and beliefs and able to get some kind of rational control over them. Here so-called 'deconstructionism' converges with much contemporary analytical philosophy of mind, which also sees the human subject as an illusion foisted on us by primitive ways of thought. These trends are 'post-modern' because they involve a rejection of the modern Enlightenment view that we are free human subjects judging and valuing things by purely rational criteria and thus sometimes, at least, arriving at genuine truth.

We all know, of course, that none of this is true. We do not and cannot act as if truth and reason are simply masks for power (nor, indeed, do deconstructionists and post-modernists treat their own claims as just masks for power, any more than Nietzsche did his own writings). We act on the assumption that our beliefs are true and our values and commitments genuine. Nor can we act as if the human subject is nothing but a vehicle for ethereally existing ideas, which somehow, virus-like, capture it for a time (or indeed for genes to propagate themselves, in the Darwinian version of deconstruction). We cannot act in this way either, in respect of our own ideas, values and behaviour for which we know that we, as subjects, are responsible.

Nor can we treat those around us as no more than blank slates on which 'texts' somehow inscribe themselves or in which genes are mysteriously serving their own purposes: we love, we hate, we praise, we blame, we discuss, we enter into friendships and relationships – all on the assumption that we are dealing with people, subjects of experience, initiators of action and bearers of attitudes to us and, for the most part, sincere in what they say and do.

All this raises the question as to why so many highly intelligent people are attracted to the denial of these common-sense, but nevertheless profound, truths. For once Nietzscheian unmasking really is appropriate. People are attracted to the nihilistic ideas of contemporary intellectual life first because they answer to a profound unease with and hostility to the existing social order and its institutions, which many intelligent people feel; maybe (Nietzsche here!) this is because they feel themselves superior to the world as it exists, yet impotent to change it.

This sense of vain superiority is then fed by the impenetrable jargon, invented usages and opaque argumentation of much modern Continental philosophy. Heidegger is the source of this mystagoguery, rather than Nietzsche who prided himself (rightly, for the most part) on the clarity of his style. Only people as clever as us can follow this stuff or produce it. There is a Gnostic attraction in actually reading Derrida, or Lacan or Irigaray, and imagining one understands something from it. One is in touch with a quasi-religious revelation, to which only the (very clever) initiated can be party. But it is not religious. It is actually the opposite of religion, for it amounts to the denial of everything religion stands for: truth, beauty, goodness, legitimacy and the human subject itself.

Modern philosophy offers us little hope or consolation. The scientism of analytic philosophy, the cultural relativism of the Wittgensteinians, the 'hermeneutics of suspicion' of the Continentals – all in their own way, contribute to our malaise, to the sense that humanity and its works are but the froth on some ultimately meaningless cosmic process, encapsulating neither freedom nor dignity.

Art

After religion and philosophy, art. For perhaps a hundred and fifty years there was a sense that through art, including literature, we could encounter a deeper reality than orthodox religion or philosophy could offer. For much of the nineteenth and twentieth centuries, art became 'epiphanic', to use Charles Taylor's phrase, or revelatory. To put it very schematically, 'epiphanic' art had both romantic and rationalistic modes.

The romantic phase is most dramatically symbolized in music – above all, in the music of Beethoven and Wagner. Particularly in his later work Beethoven initiated an explosion of musical form to intimate a sublime reality. Could there be a classical piano sonata again after the Hammerklavier or Opus 111? The late quartets took their hearers into regions undreamed of in any previous art of music. And in the Ninth Symphony, with its cosmic scale and suggestiveness, Beethoven once and for all demolished the classical symphony, demonstrating its inadequacy to what had to be expressed.

Of course, none of this was literally true. The world did not end after Beethoven, neither did classical music, nor even the classical sonata or symphony, but he, more than anyone before or since, incarnated the vision of the artist as seer, as prophet, as redeemer, even.

The artist as redeemer, and the people as redeemed by the artist: this is to take us into the world, or rather worlds, of Wagner. '*Erlösung dem Erlöser*', redemption to the redeemer, the final words of *Parsifal*, Wagner's last opera, styled by its composer *ein Bühnenweihfestspiel*, a sacred stage festival. The words were also used at Wagner's own funeral.

Wagner was not the only musician who conveyed the impression that he was offering his listeners insights of a sublimity and depth beyond ordinary speech and far more real than the stale and threatened dogmas of orthodox religion. One thinks also of Schumann, of Liszt, of Bruckner and of Mahler to name but a few of music's most tantalizing visionaries. One thinks, too, of Turner, at least as interpreted by Ruskin, of Coleridge and Baudelaire, of Tolstoy and Dostoevsky, of all the nineteenth-century artists who, in their work and achievements, would claim to be the unacknowledged legislators of mankind. But how could it be that art and music could do what religion and philosophy between them could not? And how could we take the 'redeemers' seriously, given their own lives were so often and so signally unsatisfactory?

To go back to Wagner how could the same man write one opera in which there is redemption through sexual love and death, and another celebrating celibacy, compassion and the Catholic liturgy, one opera celebrating the triumph of civic order and another in which all order, all contract are submerged in a supreme denial of the will and which, to boot, attempts to revive a pre-Christian Germanic paganism? Does any of it add up? Doesn't the fact that when it is heard each in its own way is experienced as utterly convincing cast doubt on the nature of the magic that has us in thrall? Isn't it all just musical and dramatic sorcery, not in the clear light of day to be taken seriously? Such, at least, was the complaint of Nietzsche regarding Wagner, which has been echoed ever since. In defence of Wagner, Thomas Mann stressed that Wagner was a man of the theatre and that the theatrical approach to truth is unlikely to commend itself to philosophers, concerned as they are with virtues such as consistency and literalness. But what sort of defence is that? Can we really be led to our ultimate destiny through a temple made up of illusions produced by greasepaint, costume and mime, and created and staffed by morally ordinary and venal characters?

Answers could, and perhaps should, have been given to these questions. Through aesthetic experience we have intimations of significance, that human life has more to it than can be revealed in scientific or biological terms. However compromised the messenger, artistic expression can be powerfully evocative of aesthetic experience, particularly because in contrast to the unplanned beauties of nature, it is intended to do precisely that. Nineteenth-century artists and musicians were powerfully motivated by a mission to reveal deep and uplifting truths through their art. The problem that haunts the twentieth century and its art is not so much the human frailty of the messengers as fundamental questions as to whether in the universe or out of it there are uplifting truths to be revealed. Could there be redemption for the redeemer if there is no transcendent cosmic order?

There was, inevitably, a reaction to nineteenth-century artistic hopes. First, the means of expression came to seem increasingly overblown: élitist in form, theatrical, manipulative and insincere in intent, as Nietzsche's criticism of Wagner had it. Second, and more fundamentally, in the absence of any religious underpinning and with the rise of scientific accounts of humanity, the mission itself came to be seen as misguided. The history of art in the twentieth century can be seen as a series of attempts to wrestle with these problems. As a result, at the end of our century there is precious little being produced that would in previous eras have been regarded as art.

To take means of expression first: in the early part of the century, there was a deliberate attempt in literature, in music, in painting, in sculpture and in architecture to purify the means of expression. 'Ornament is crime,' proclaimed the Viennese architect Adolf Loos. Meanwhile, Schoenberg set about creating a new language of music on rational mathematical principles. Cubism and abstractionism looked like attempts to set painting on a course of purity, where it would be uncompromised by extraneous literary associations and unthreatened by the representational virtuosity of mechanical techniques such as photography. In literature, Pound, Rilke, Eliot and, in his own way, Joyce looked for a truer, more authentic means of expression than the overblown rhetoric and sub-medieval imagery of their Victorian and Edwardian predecessors,

In a certain sense early artistic modernism was rationalistic, a clearing away of old debris, a starting afresh on new and clearly excogitated principles. This rationalistic spirit comes across particularly in the writings of the architects and composers. In order to secure the intellectual purity of the new music in 1918, Schoenberg formed the Association for Private Musical Performances, at which applause was forbidden, while Le Corbusier, the most forceful of modernist architects, proclaimed that architects of the future needed to 'eliminate from their hearts and minds all dead concepts in regard to the house and look at the questions from a critical and objective point of view'. For some modernists, as for Le Corbusier in architecture or Schoenberg in music, that meant forging a new language on first principles. For others it meant a conscious aping of primitive forms, such as Picasso in his pre-Cubist period, the Stravinsky of *Firebird* and *The Rite of Spring*, Matisse and the Fauves in painting. Some figures had feet in both primitivist and rationalist camps. All, though, were agreed that by the beginning of the twentieth century their art was worn out, formally, conceptually and ideologically. A fresh start had to be made, sweeping away the tired beliefs and practices on which Western art had been based for centuries.

The early modernists, rationalist and/or primitivist as they may have been, were clearly not seeking popular approval. Anything but, as we see in the case of Schoenberg. For Le Corbusier, the architect, by his arrangement of forms, realizes an order that is a pure creation of his spirit. And if, when modern architecture reaches the general public, the public does not like it, too bad. They will simply be told, as Nicolaus Pevsner told them in 1943, that 'amenities to which we have been used are being replaced by something more exacting and more elementary', thus echoing, consciously or not so con- sciously, the Leninist/Stalinist dogma that if contemporary humanity does not like the policies of the political (or archi- tectural) vanguard, that just shows that contemporary humanity needs further 'organizing' until it does.

After eighty or more years of 'organizing' and of relentless propaganda and bureaucratic censorship in favour of artistic modernism, whether in music or in architecture or in the visual arts, modernism is no closer to being loved than it was in the early years of the century. As its proponents deliberately and self-consciously deprived themselves of any and every means of seeking to woo or win over the general public, this is hardly surprising. It shows the difficulty of attempting to create forms of art that do not depend on a fund of deeply felt and traditional feelings, and resonances.

It also shows the extent to which the pioneers of modernism were élitist. For the first time in the history of Western art, the organic progression from popular culture through to high art was deliberately and artificially broken.

In the first decade of our century, Mahler had famously brought brass-band marches, folk songs, hymn chorales and street songs into his serious music. But so had Bach, Haydn, Mozart, Beethoven, Brahms and pretty well every other great composer before Schoenberg, With Schoenberg, however, 'serious' music became hermetic, élitist, self-enclosed and self-referential, and in the early part of this century much the same happened in the other arts, which were also busily cutting themselves off from popular forms and models. It is as if artists and composers had to prove their seriousness by their inaccessibility, and by the way their art depended on theory and manifesto rather than by its appeal to the sensibility and taste of the ordinary educated and well-disposed public.

Of course, there were great artists in all fields who bucked the trend of élitist modernism. In music, there were Richard Strauss and Sibelius, Elgar and Vaughan Williams, Shostako-vich and Britten; in architecture, Scott and Lutyens; in the visual arts, David Bomberg and Winifred Nicholson, Henry Moore and John Piper; in literature, figures as disparate as Thomas Mann and Evelyn Waugh, John Betjeman, V. S. Naipaul and Iris Murdoch.

But, with the possible exception of literature, in histories of twentieth-century art the non-modernists have routinely been written out of the script (literally so in the case of Lutyens, on any account an architect of genius, but who is not even mentioned in Pevsner's *Outline of European Architecture*, which can still find space for a lyrical description and illustration of the Arnos Grove tube station). The ideology is that any art that is not founded on 'challenging' new theories, that does not continually question its own origins or standing, but that relies on the accumulated sensibility of centuries is lazy, inert and behind the times; it will find no room in histories of art that self-consciously take themselves to be describing the onward march of the human spirit.

The early phases of modernism in the arts were élitist and, in many cases, spiritual, even revelatory in intent. To the scandal of historians and commentators, some of the early modernists took their élitism and their concern for the spiritual into their politics and their religion. Think of Schoenberg's return to Judaism, think of Eliot's Anglo-Catholicism, think of Klee and Kandinsky's spiritualism, think of Lawrence's hatred of the democratic industrial present and his invocation of darker, older gods, think of Mussolini's patronage of modernist architecture and the Fascism of Pound and Céline. Many of the early modernists, even while rejecting the forms of the past, often had, at the same time, a despondent respect for the work of the past. They manifested something approaching a despair that they were unable to create in the unselfconscious way of artists at home in their tradition, who are able to build on it easily, naturally and organically.

'These fragments I have shored against my ruins,' cried Eliot in *The Waste Land*. Meanwhile, Manet's attempts to re-create the spirit of Titian and Giorgione in nineteenth-century Paris proved prophetic of the efforts so many twentieth-century modernists, of whom Picasso was only the most notable, to rework the masterpieces of the past. It was as if, even as they struck out on their own, they could not but reflect on what they knew had been lost. But in the end, the élitism, seriousness and revelatory ambitions of the early modernists proved unsustainable. For one thing, as the century went on the faith in the human spirit and its progress, which inspired early modernism, declined dramatically. This was due not just to the decline of formal religion. The great social and political projects of the first half of the twentieth century themselves turned to dust and disillusion. For those with eyes to see – and this included many artists – it became harder to envisage the human spirit as on a progressive journey at all. Modernism gradually ran out of steam. There was no longer a single way forward, no longer really any sense of progress, no longer a tradition, old or new, no longer the confidence a tradition could engender.

All there was was individual choice, weightless, insubstantial. As Jean Baudrillard put it in 1984: 'one is no longer in a history of art or a history of forms. They have all been deconstructed, destroyed . . . it has all been done . . . all that are left are pieces, playing with pieces . . . one is in a kind of post-history that is without meaning.'

The Stalinism of modernism has thus given way to the consumerism of post-modernism – a chaos of artistic form in which, because nothing has any significance, anything can be done, without reference to any rules, principles or standards. Post-modernism is, indeed, a reflection of a situation in which – and not just in art – there are no rules, principles or standards.

In years to come, I predict that the characteristic artistic innovations of the twentieth century will prove not to be the bold modernist experiments of its early years but rather Dada and Pop. In a sense, Dada was the precursor of what is today referred to as post-modernism. Dada was the ultimate response to the loss of faith, both in art and humanity; while Pop is the art form *par excellence* for the democratic age. If the human being is, as scientific materialism would have it, nothing but an unsavoury mixture of warring impulses and discordant messages over which we have no control, surely art should not attempt to portray the human being as noble, intelligent, virtuous or graceful. And, to be sure, there has been plenty of art this century that has emphasized human grossness, depravity, cruelty and lust. Many of the works in question – from Otto Dix to Salvador Dali to Francis Bacon to Lucian Freud – have been created with no little skill and artistry, and also in a recognizably traditional manner.

But, one wonders why, if the message is so bleak and

humanity so worthless, why go to all the trouble? In particular, why use artistic techniques – such as those of the oil painting and epic novel – devised and developed for the elevation and idealization of humanity, to present exactly the opposite message? These questions condense and coalesce around the strange figure of Marcel Duchamp, the archetypical Dadaist. Duchamp was the great liberator and democratizer of art in the twentieth century. In his universe, to be an artist you did not need to be skilled or trained in a traditional technique, such as oil painting or the carving of stone or the casting of bronze. All you needed to do was to designate something, anything, a work of art, and get it accepted as such. It was in 1913 that Duchamp exhibited a bicycle wheel, calling it *Bicycle Wheel*, and in so doing he revolutionized art. *Bottle Rack* followed in 1914, and in 1917, the notorious urinal exhibited as *Fountain*, by R. Mutt.

It may be that the Dadaist Duchamp did not intend to be taken entirely seriously. It is also true that Duchampian practice did not become dominant in the art world until the second half of the century. But since Andy Warhol's 1960s invocation of Brillo boxes and Campbell's soup cans, anything, absolutely anything, can be a work of art, and somewhere probably is: old washing-machines, teddy-bears, basketballs in boxes, graffiti, pornographic photographs, used nappies, sheep in formalde-hyde, casts of the underside of chairs, going for a walk, bricks, human faeces, artists getting drunk, aborted foetuses.

What has been lost in the Duchamp–Warhol transformation is the conception of art involving the transformation of ma-terials for an uplifting aesthetic purpose. Does any critically acclaimed artist today actually believe, as Klee and Mondrian believed less than a century ago, that through painting and through abstraction one could somehow evoke the spiritual mystery and power that underly the visible flux of the material world? Many artists claim to find this end of art as it has been traditionally conceived as highly liberating. The problem with the liberation in question is that all now depends on the artist's ability to get him or herself noticed, not on his or her vision and skill in working in some material or other. The upshot is that art comes closer and closer to advertising, a matter of superficial style rather than of any real form or substance.

When the only criterion of success is getting noticed, qualitative judgements lose all basis in reason. It is no coincidence that Andy Warhol's first career was in advertising, nor that the advertising mogul Charles Saatchi is the Maecenas of contemporary art. Except that in art, as opposed to conventional advertising, what is primarily advertised is the artist, rather than any honest, free-standing product. Warhol's notorious 'fifteen minutes of fame' is not just the condition of the contemporary artist: it is the criterion by which some otherwise talentless individual comes to be recognized as a significant contemporary artist. Self-expression becomes paramount, rather than the disciplined sublimation of self through wrestling with the intricacies and subtleties of a formally sophisticated tradition of artistic expression. The romantic view of the artist as primarily displaying his or her personality – which was never wholly true in the case of the nineteenth-century-romantics who worked in media with long and venerable traditions – becomes actual truth with the post-Warhol avant-garde.

Inevitably, in this situation, what rises to the top is the loudest, the newest, the most garish, the most perverse, the most shocking. The general public, which still has a feel for traditional art, is affronted, but as a legacy of early modernism the art establishment has long since stopped taking any notice of the general public. Meanwhile, artistic panjandrums like Sir Nicholas Serota, the director of the Tate Gallery, justify what is going on in meretricious spectacles like the Turner Prize in terms of the publicity generated and in the potential of works to 'challenge' old assumptions and preconceptions. This, though, leaves two problems, a law of diminishing returns in the challenges, which have to become ever more extreme, and the poverty of the thinking of the artists. If you really want deep thought on life, society or morality, Damien Hirst or Rachel Whiteread or Tracey Emin would not be the most obvious sources of inspiration.

And while the general public is cut off from 'serious' art, whether modernist, post-modernist or Dadaist, pop culture puts down ever deeper roots in popular consciousness: by means of radio, television, video and IT, Pop has become the universal art form of the end of the twentieth century, the first truly universal style in the history of the globe. To some extent, Pop tries to address universal human concerns with a directness and, at times, even a positiveness lacking in most serious art. But in the simplicity of its forms, the crudity of its lyrics and plots, its mind-deadening rhythms and volume, it is incapable of transmitting anything but the most banal of messages, by turns sentimental, violent, hedonistic and, above all, cynically pandering to the lowest tastes of its main constituency, the young.

Pop artists, musicians and writers have never been in danger of overestimating the intelligence or sensitivity of their audiences. They know that to do so would be to risk professional suicide. The divorce between serious and popular art has been disastrous – not just for the increasingly hermetic and self-enclosed world of high art. The traffic used to be two-way, with the language and taste of higher forms finding their reflection in the songs and imagery of mass appeal. With nothing but unformed and debased popular taste to influence its productions, popular culture remains immured in stupidity and worse. It is incapable of engaging the intellect or refining the sensibility, or expanding sympathy, understanding or awareness, just as Plato feared and predicted would be the fate of the art forms of democracy were they left uncensored and undirected from above.

Even worse in our non-élitist day, when academic and political careers are made on the basis of denying any differences in quality or ambition between high and low art, between Shakespeare and soap opera, between Schubert and the Beatles, one risks condemnation as an outright snob if one points out that the easy 'compassion' of Band-aid and 'I Ran the World' is no way to solve any serious problems of hunger and food distribution; that 'Candle in the Wind' is a triumph of saccharine sentimentality; that the studied glorification in so much pop music of self-engineered ignorance and drug dependence would have no place in any true civilization (let alone be fêted by its political leaders); and that the most authentic feature of Irvine Welsh's *Filth* is its title; but, as I say, at a time when our leading newspaper can seriously tout the drug-crazed, cacophonous and destructive Jimi Hendrix as brilliant and innovative, and as a hero to all the great guitarists of his time (Segovia? John Williams? Julian Bream?), in its 'People of the Century' series, such home truths are likely to receive scant attention and less respect.

In comparing the artistic scene of the late 1990s with that, say, of the 1820s one cannot but be struck by the erosion of hope. We have moved from a world of great artistic expectations such as those of Beethoven and Schubert, of Wordsworth and Coleridge, of Turner and Ruskin, of Pugin and Schinkel, to one of largely unrelieved and cultivated banality (to use a phrase of F. R. Leavis) – even though there are more artists and artistic subsidies than in the whole history of the world, ever more inflated claims are made by artists and bureaucrats for the civilizing power of art, and there is more talk than ever of culture and communication.

In our time art, as a living thing, has been destroyed largely by a combination of two Enlightenment tendencies. The first is the scientific erosion of the shared symbolic order, which was necessary to sustain an elevated role for art. The second is increasing democratization, which makes judgements of quality as between works more and more problematic. In the world of public subsidy and funding, administrators and politicians succumb to this refusal to judge, insisting that high art has to make itself 'accessible', even though there are empty seats at most opera and ballet performances in London, at prices below what punters would pay for football matches, pop concerts or commercial musicals, and even though at the same time they lavish funds on those very exercises in Dadaism designed expressly to insult the taste of the opera- and ballet-going public.

To return to the relationship between art and religious faith, the writers, artists and musicians of the nineteenth century were not, in the main, orthodox believers – but in their works, they still lived off the capital and hope of the shared symbolic order of Christianity. It is partly the waning of that capital in the world as a whole that makes the predicament of artists today more difficult: for how can mere artists exalt the human spirit if there is no spirit to exalt and no cosmic power to do the exalting?

They cannot, so in all artistic media at the end of the millennium, they revel in our baser nature. It is also true that, for a large number of our contemporaries, encounters with the great art of the past provide the nearest they get to religious experience (and not only in explicitly religious works). Much of it retains the spiritual charge it once had, even in an age of unbelief, which partly explains why, to many people, that art seems more vital, immediate and compelling than anything being produced today. As I will argue later, this fact provides the basis for a limited optimism, even in 1999. But that optimism is unlikely to be sustained by the art of 1999 itself, certainly not by that which is publicly subsidized and critically acclaimed.

Education and Psychology

In both education and psychology, the aim becomes to realize human potential in each and every individual. Pre-existing rules, structures and forms of knowledge are seen as repressive, inhibiting and often serving the interests of the dominant forces in society. The only problem is that the notion of human potential is almost wholly underdetermined – except in contrast to the supposedly repressive forces holding it back, such as sexual taboos, didactic teaching and judgementalism, the tendency of those of whom one disapproves to lay down the law about what is right and wrong, good and bad, worth making an effort to learn or not.

The upshot in education is universal primary and secondary education – but which still leaves 40 per cent of children leaving primary school illiterate and innumerate to a greater or lesser extent, and 20 per cent or more pupils being categorized as having 'special needs', in which their 'self-esteem' is seen as more important than their objective achievements. As surveys show, time and again, the vast majority of school leavers are almost entirely ignorant of their literature, their history, and their cultural inheritance. More than a third of young people in institutions called 'universities', but which cannot fill places in maths, science and engineering, have, by government diktat, to offer remedial help in the 'key skills' that should have been mastered in primary school. Within institutions of education a constant and debilitating campaign of attrition is urged against standards and tradition.

As for psychology, as has already been mentioned, more people than ever feel dissatisfied, and say they need some form of counselling or therapy, even though there is no evidence that most forms of psychotherapy are more effective in dealing with mental illness than placebo treatments. (The main exception is so called cognitive therapy, which in essence amounts to the age-old remedy of getting depressed patients to focus on the brighter sides of their lives.) Nevertheless, we live in an age when 'counselling' is routinely offered, and accepted, for any kind of stress or difficulty, including many of those attendant on simply doing what in earlier times would have been regarded as one's job or duty. And so are damages for public service workers who find just doing their work particularly stressful.

How did education and psychology become so centred on the feelings and perceptions of the individual? Or, to put it more precisely, how did education come to adopt a child-centred psychology at the expense of the realities and perspectives beyond the understanding of the uneducated individual?

In a broad sense, the stress on individual happiness derives from the Enlightenment view that what matters in human affairs is the happiness of the subject, rather than any divinely or socially given role or calling. But within this general framework the decisive shift was made by the romanticism of Rousseau. Like the encyclopedists, Rousseau was a naturalist, but unlike them, his naturalism involved a love of nature and hostility to civilized life and scientific reason. Hence Rousseau's most famous aphorism 'man is born free, and everywhere he is in chains'. God and nature make things well, but we, through our meddling, our vanity, and our striving to outdo each other, produce the luxury and excess of civilized life and mess things up.

In education, and in our own lives, Rousseau believes, we should strive to get in touch with our true selves, our true natures. In education, this ought to mean an organic, natural development, in touch with nature and with the genuine problems of existence, as free as possible from the false values of book-learning and academic and fashionable competition. According to Rousseau, the traditional education of his time taught everything 'except self-knowledge and self-control, the arts of life and happiness'. A proper education ought to be based on our natural impulses (which were 'always right') and not the superficialities of high (and false) culture. If this meant mediocrity from an intellectual point of view, so be it: 'desire mediocrity in all things, even in beauty'.

Rousseau's main educational work, *Émile*, is a heady brew. It combines nature-worship, child-centredness, an emphasis on doing and discovery at the expense of reading and being taught, together with a pervasive suspicion of the existing order of things, from which the growing child must be protected. Its actual prescription (for a tutor to teach *Émile* in the country on his own away from all social intercourse) is obviously impractical. Nevertheless *Émile* and Rousseau's influence can be seen in every primary school in the Anglo-Saxon world. So, more pervasively, can Rousseau's advocacy of concern for one's inner self and a natural psychological equilibrium as being more important than the world beyond. I am not, of course, saying that Rousseau would have approved of the typical British primary classroom of 1999 or of the advice-column mantra that one has to find space for one's own development, but in reading Rousseau and his followers, one can see the roots of such attitudes.

If Rousseau was one determining influence on twentieth-century educational thought, the American philosopher Dewey was the other. In some ways, Dewey and Rousseau are opposed. Dewey rejected Rousseau's concern for the inner self and saw education in essentially social terms. He was also far more favourably disposed to science than Rousseau, and far more optimistic about the power of science to solve our problems. Nevertheless, key elements from both, as filtered through those influenced by them, coalesce to produce what amounts to the received educational wisdom of our day.

Dewey, who had been closely involved in experimental schools in Chicago in the 1890s, links meaningful education with the child's own attempts to solve problems arising from its own social experience. What he calls the full meaning of studies is secured only when it becomes relevant to the child's own present needs and aims, which in turn are social. Education thus becomes an initiation into techniques of quasi-scientific problem-solving in groups. Traditional education, by contrast, produces only barren residues of real knowledge. In addition, through its authoritarianism and certifications, it reinforces and perpetuates élitism and social divisions.

For Dewey, the classroom should be a social enterprise, in which all are engaged in communal projects. It is a sort of democracy in miniature, in which the teacher is not an 'external boss or dictator', imposing standards alien to the pupils' lives and experiences. Rather he or she is the 'leader of group activities', who gives the group not cast-iron answers but, rather, starting-points to be developed through the contributions of all involved, all of whom have a valid point of view.

While Dewey stresses practical problem-solving where Rousseau looks for the organic development of the pupil's inner personality, in fact the similarities and overlaps between the two are more significant than the differences. Despite his political and sociological commitments, Dewey sees education in terms of personal growth in a manner redolent of Rousseau. Education is all one with growing, he says; and since new problems, and hence new growth, will always arise, 'there is nothing to which education is subordinate save more education'.

Further, both Rousseau and Dewey share hostility to studying history and the classics. Both reject knowledge not stemming from the experience and/or problems of the child (or adult). And one imagines that Rousseau would not have dissented from Dewey's view that the most worthwhile knowledge was that which could be shared by the whole community.

It will hardly be necessary to underline the extent to which educational theory combining Rousseau and Dewey is alive today: stressing creativity and self-esteem, child-centred, focusing on practical problems, rather than on traditional learning and culture, dismissive of distinctions between education and training, anti-authoritarian, seeing education as democratic and egalitarian in scope and aim, and a lifelong process not to be circumscribed by syllabuses or exams. Taking Rousseau and Dewey together, what we have is an educational vision that sees education as, on one side, directed to the lifelong psychological development of the individual and, on the other, as a project of social engineering, aiming at producing a democratic-cum-egalitarian mentality through initiation in the classroom into techniques of communal problem-solving.

People who knew nothing about the educational views current in the Anglo-Saxon world at the end of our century might have expected schools to be concentrating on the straightforward teaching of the best that has been thought and known in the central academic disciplines of the sciences (physics, chemistry and biology), mathematics, literature, history, the arts, and religion (mainly, for obvious reasons, Christianity). They would have imagined teachers to be confident in what counted as the best, and confident in teaching it. They might have expected that the basic skills of reading, writing, spelling, punctuation and arithmetic would all be taught rigorously and systematically in the early stages. They would have wanted technical subjects taught, where appropriate, as if the pupil were apprenticed to a craft whose principles were well established and well understood. They would have expected differences of academic ability and motivation between pupils to be recognized in streaming and selection, particularly by the time of secondary education. They would also have been suspicious of any straightforward identification of education with personal growth. Growth is determined by what is within us (much of which may be undesirable) and compromised by aggressive selfishness and original sin; education, by contrast, ought to be determined by things outside us, by the subject matter and morality that have shaped civilized life, survived the test of time and the limitations of local cultures.

While in Britain, at least, they might, if they are lucky, find some of these traditional attitudes in independent schools, they will not find them, or not find them much, in the state sector or in the institutions that train teachers. Over the past century, partly in response to the thinking of Rousseau and Dewey and their followers, and partly because of growing egalitarianism within society as a whole, there has been a massive erosion of confidence in the sense that some things just are the best (and so should be taught) and a corresponding undermining of any sense that a teacher is, by virtue of his or her profession, an authority.

Teachers approximate more and more to counsellors or social workers, and schools (increasingly, universities too) become institutions devoted more to psychology and social engineering than to education in the traditional sense which is why Anglo-American pupils know so little after eleven or more years of compulsory schooling, even though, in the American case, expenditure on education is higher than anywhere in the world.

A recent and somewhat random inspection of documents from teacher-training courses (made when I was on the government committee in England regulating teacher training) revealed the following as characteristic of modern pedagogy: mathematics teaching that emphasizes practical applications and discovery methods, rather than abstract mathematical truth and formal proof (even though proof is the essence of mathematical method, that which distinguishes it from empirical investigation, and abstraction is the source of its universality); history teaching that stresses imaginative reconstruction, the investigation of sources and impressionistic social history, rather than the factual and political narratives necessary to make sense of any of these activities; music courses that emphasize pupil performance and composition, though without providing the essential technical basis, and which encourage the study of pop music, as if young people's minds and sensibilities were not already sufficiently assaulted and corrupted by pop outside school; a hostility to formal (phonic) methods in the teaching of reading, despite the now overwhelming evidence in its favour, and the fact that children who cannot read by the age of eight suffer thereafter from almost insuperable educational disadvantage (significantly, in 1898, Dewey had referred to a stress on reading and arithmetic in the first three years of education as a 'false educational god'); a hostility to any suggestion that there might be a 'canon' of great literature (and this in England!) and instead 'investigation' of such marginal forms as acrostics, haiku, tanka, 'dub' poetry, and rapping, together with 'teen' literature and the drearily inevitable Alice Walkers and Toni Morrisons; continual references in course documents to personal growth and crosscurricular themes, and to gender and race 'issues' (even though the school curriculum has now been skewed away from formal examinations and technical treatments so that girls do better in public exams than boys, and even though many ethnic minority groups do far better at school than indigenous whites); already watered-down science curricula further weakened by the introduction of low-level 'investigations' and the introduction into science courses of contentious social science and political elements; almost universal acceptance of the performance-depressing myth that educational under-achievement is due to social 'deprivation'; an implacable hostility to selection (grammar schools) and independent education; finally, and most corrosive of all, British history, the British empire, Christianity and Western achievement generally routinely undermined in the name of multi-culturalism.

In the 1990s none of this was new in the world of education. Dubious and contentious psychological claims have long been dominant in 'official' pedagogical thinking, displacing knowledge of the subjects to be taught from its rightful place at the centre of the educational stage. In a highly influential textbook from 1966, we find the following claims:

1. Concrete experience must underpin learning. It is said, as an example, that fractions should be taught by dividing chocolate boxes. Mathematics teaching that does not rely on practical apparatus and concrete applications is rubbished, no doubt a first step on the road which, in 1996, led to the prestigious London Mathematical Society complaining that university undergraduates in mathematics do not understand the notion of proof.

2. There are two main dangers in teaching: (i) that teachers do not ground concepts in the child's experience of the material world, and (ii) that they may attempt to teach what is beyond the child's ability to conceptualize. One of the main complaints of school inspectors in the late 1990s is that teachers — intimidated by this sort of thing, and by stereotypical views of their pupils' backgrounds – continually set their sights far too low. More fundamentally, why should teaching be limited by the child's material surroundings? Isn't part of the point of education to expand the imagination? Might it not be a good thing were teachers to hint at the limits of the material world?

3. Streaming depressed the general level of achievement. In response to the catastrophic failure of the experiments with mixed-ability teaching and comprehensive education, the Labour government of Tony Blair is beginning to question these dogmas but, like its Conservative predecessors, it is meeting implacable opposition from teachers and educational advisers.

4. Authoritarian teaching and discipline is less effective than 'democratic' regimes in classrooms. Pure Dewey – yet all teachers and most pupils know that without discipline nothing

can be done; moreover, what possible justification can there be for anyone purporting to teach (or organize teaching) who is not, to the relevant level, an authority?

5. Learning general techniques of problem-solving is more efficient than learning specific bits of information. Rote learning, as in the learning of multiplication tables, is 'essentially the unenlightened verbalizing of the child'. Similarly 'the amount of historical understanding derived from formal exercises in manipulating dates and dynasties or taking down notes is virtually nil'.

6. Primary-school classrooms should abandon the traditional 'confrontational' set-up, with the teacher at the front facing pupils seated in rows of desks. Desks should be arranged as work-tables, with pupils in groups and the teacher part of the class. The emphasis will be on 'active learning' and 'learning to learn'. (With the discovery that 40 per cent or more of pupils' time is wasted in the new type of classroom, and that each pupil has around two minutes of the teacher's time per hour, there has, recently, been a modest return to whole-class teaching.)

7. Punishment, criticism and competition inhibit learning, and should be replaced by praise and co-operation. (Interestingly, in the interests of 'encouraging growth', Dewey himself displayed, in the words of one of them, 'a deliberate refusal to be discriminating' about his students; no matter what was said, he would encourage them.) Finally, the 'traditional' stereotype of the teacher as standing in front of a class and telling is 'at odds with the view of educationalists'. In future teachers should keep abreast of 'developments' in educational theory and practice. They should see themselves not as didacts, but as 'controllers of systems of instruction' (yet it is the traditionalists who are routinely dubbed as technicist!).

To the pervasive psychology of education should be added the sociologizing, usually of a vulgar sub-Marxist variety. The structures of education (curricula, exams, institutions) are seen as part of the apparatus by which the dominant classes, genders, or races maintain and reinforce their dominance. The task of the radical sociologist of education is to unmask the mechanisms of this apparatus. These include the validity of subject boundaries, of curricular content, of the distinction between high and low culture, of canons of culture and correctness – all of whose real function is to regiment, classify and marginalize in the interest of the dominant groups and powers. This type of analysis not only links with the deconstructive tendencies of modern philosophy, it also provides an easy justification of the egalitarianism underlying the comprehensive movement, and of the hostility to testing and to subject- and content-based curricula still so prevalent among so many teachers both in schools and in institutions of higher education in the West.

To what extent, though, are the educational trends we have been considering by-products of modernity? They have their roots in part in the particular visions of Rousseau and of Dewey and of those who followed them. But these visions can be put in a wider context.

We can take first the utilitarianism of the Enlightenment, the belief that what matters and what motivates us are pleasure and pain, happiness and unhappiness. Against this background, any educational ideal that cannot be seen as contributing to utilitarian goals becomes immediately problematic, however much individual Enlightenment thinkers might have valued the pursuit of truth or of beauty for their own sakes. In this context, we can also understand the exponential growth in recent years in subjects (like business, tourism and psychology, therapy and counselling) that appear to be directly related to satisfying people's needs and wants rather than to more austere and disinterested goals. Looking at things from a slightly different angle, we can recall the Baconian ideal of the purpose of knowledge and of learning as being the relief of man's estate. The hostility to the ancient classics and to pure history, which we find in Dewey and his followers, looks very Baconian; but so, more fundamentally, does Dewey's stress on problem-solving and applied knowledge – a stress which, like Bacon's own philosophy, would make the study of pure science problematic and difficult to defend. Once again, hospital beds or symphony orchestras – or any other activity or enterprise engaged in for its own sake, for its own glory, and not for some crudely utilitarian, crudely egalitarian project?

Egalitarianism is the subterranean current running under most of our educational policies. In a democratic society committed to nothing beyond the greatest happiness of the greatest number, it is all but impossible to defend educational élitism and selection, particularly when everyone, through their taxes, is paying for education. What all cannot have, none shall have. So we have mixed-ability teaching in primary schools, neighbourhood comprehensives at secondary level, and mass 'higher' education, comprising 40 per cent or more of the age group. That all this involves dumbing down of curricula, rampant grade inflation and subjects of no intellectual worth or credibility is regarded as a price worth paying to bolster the self-esteem of those 'excluded' by a more discriminating approach to learning and achievement. It also becomes more and more difficult to defend or articulate the notion of the teacher as an authority: 'our young people face too clearly an unknown future. We dare not pretend that old solutions will suffice for them . . . Our young no longer accept authoritarian morals. We must then develop a point of view and devise a correlative educational system which shall take account of ever increasing change. Otherwise civilization itself seems threatened.' Thus wrote Dewey's disciple, W. H. Kilpatrick, in 1929, though even seventy-five years ago relativism and abrogation of teacherly authority might have seemed a bizarre remedy for civilization's impending collapse. Since 1929, civilization has become no more secure and teachers have almost universally

200

lost faith in their right to lay down the law on pretty well anything, which makes one wonder what their point might be.

Education is an extremely boring subject. What is interesting are history, maths, physics, English, literature, ancient Greek, the arts and so on. The depressing thing about 'education' is that it diverts attention from areas of great fascination on to an area of virtually no interest all: the personalities, characters and social background of the learners who, by definition, are uneducated, and who, knowing nothing, have little of interest to say or contribute. In this sense 'education' is the ultimate leveller. It conspires to convince uninteresting people that they might be interesting and that they might become happy were they to focus on their uninteresting personalities. In fact precisely the opposite is true. They will become interesting and happy only if they forget their own special needs and circumstances, turning their attention away from themselves and on to things of intrinsic value outside themselves. But as some, at least, of this intrinsic value is beyond the reach of the many, even to suggest such a thing becomes an offence in a society devoted to maintaining the fiction of democratic equality.

Education is, of course, only one aspect of a wider malaise. When people were religious and when they defined themselves in terms of their stations, and the corresponding duties, they sought and often found fulfilment in self-forgetfulness. They looked to God, or their family, or their vocation or their craft, rather than to themselves. Psychology becomes central in a society only when people forget God or lose any sense of their allotted roles and identity. This explains why, in our century, psychology and associated therapies have replaced religion and tradition as guides to how to live, and why more and more of us seek counselling of various sorts as the answer to our problems and why the domain of the mentally disturbed grows ever larger. The structures and ideals within which people in previous centuries operated have dissolved, so we are thrown back inward, on our own far from reliable resources.

These structures, indeed, following Rousseau and following Freud, have come popularly and well-nigh universally to be seen as repressive, precisely because they impose restraints and direction on our naturally given feelings and impulses. Anything that inhibits the free development of the personality has come to be seen as negative and oppressive. No matter that Freud in his later years came to admit that civilization actually depended on the repression of our natural instincts, and their sublimation into other, more positive and more regulated channels: by the late 1990s anything that constricts or restricts instinct is labelled harmful and negative. Psychologically the paramount duty is to get in touch with one's true self. Therapy looks more and more like a way to evade duty and responsibility in the name of self-fulfilment or realization of one's potential. Counselling is essentially non-directive, 'client'-centred and 'client'-directed, finding spurious excuses for what the 'client' always wanted to do but was held back from doing by rules of morality and society. The only duty of the counsellor is to be 'non-judgemental', to allow the patient untrammelled self-discovery.

It is true that all this is a parody of Freud and of the other fathers of psychotherapy, but it is how their message has filtered into general consciousness. Further, Freud and the founders of psychoanalysis were reacting against a moral atmosphere that might actually have been repressive. The psychologists most associated with today's non-directive counselling – thinkers such as Abraham Maslow and Carl Rogers – were themselves rooted in highly moral, if not moralistic environments. So when they initially spoke of self-actualization and authenticity, they blithely imagined that those seeking self and authenticity would find moral selves, truly brimming over with positive and unselfish feelings. They never expected that their 'clients' would take them at their word and seek 'self-actualization' in whatever direction their strongest feelings dictated. There was, in other words, no sense of original sin or of the often destructive effects of one's strongest feelings, or any inkling of the likely outcome of sudden lifting of repressive structures (an outcome perhaps best illustrated in the story of the Californian convent in the late 1960s that was literally decimated when the sisters introduced a Rogerian therapist into their spiritual deliberations).

In fact, an invisible thread connects the progressive educational views we have been looking at and the 'humanistic' psychology of the likes of Rogers and Maslow, as can be seen when Rogers states: 'The teacher or professor will largely have disappeared. His place will be taken by a facilitator of learning, *chosen for his facilitative attitudes, as much as for his knowledge* [my italics]'. But it has already come to pass: in today's universities people from so-called 'teaching and learning' units regularly help to design modules in subjects, such as mathematics and foreign languages, in which they have no qualifications.

Rogers goes on:

> The student's learning will not be confined to the ancient intellectual concepts and specializations. It will not be a *preparation* for living. It will be, in itself an *experience* in living. Feelings of inadequacy, hatred, a desire for power, feelings of love and awe and respect, feelings of fear and dread, unhappiness with parents or with other children – all these will be an open part of his curriculum, as worthy of exploration as history or mathematics . . . The student will *never be graduated*. He will always be part of a 'commencement'.

So education becomes psychology – a course of personal transformation and dominated by the rigmaroles of psychology. Group sessions, role-play, self-disclosure, examination of one's feelings regarding one's teachers become part of education.

And not just education in the academic sense. Almost any form of training, these days, will inevitably involve the manipulative techniques of psychology. Those whose moral sense or intellectual integrity causes them to resist or refuse will be labelled 'negative', scared or 'repressed' in the time-honoured psychological way, as if any criticism reflects on the character of the critic rather than on the legitimacy of the procedures criticized or on their intellectual vacuity.

And, as we have seen, school is only 'commencement'. 'Lifelong learning' means not just the compulsory acquisition of unnecessary certificates throughout one's life (a process worth rather more to state employed certificators than to the certificated), but also a continuing engagement with teacher-facilitators, now in the guise of counsellors, psychologists and therapists. All operate under the dubious assumptions that the aim of life is personal growth and autonomy and the removal of obstacles to that growth and autonomy. As the obstacles to growth and autonomy tend to include established moral codes (especially in the realm of sexuality), inherited and even acquired duties and responsibilities, it is easy to see where it is all likely to lead: not just to nuns leaving convents, but to the erosion of all standards in the matter of personal gratification and relationships.

An unhappy marriage of Enlightenment advocacy of personal autonomy to the Rousseauesque elevation of natural instinct produces the contemporary ideology of personal growth. It is inculcated through current orthodoxy in education and psychology, but when, as in so many cases, it leads to personal breakdown and to unhappiness, the remedy is for more of the very psychology and education that caused the problems in the first place. But this will only deepen the malaise.

For as Aristotle taught long ago, happiness and fulfilment do not come from looking within or seeking person gratification or autonomy for its sake. Within we are likely to find nothing very edifying or even coherent. The search for personal gratification produces progressively diminishing returns, as every Don Juan and drug addict knows all too well. And autonomy is valuable only to the extent that we choose well. Happiness comes, if at all, as the satisfaction from doing worthwhile things well. It is far more likely to come from responding to the needs of others and from immersing ourselves in rewarding activity, or even in prayer and contemplation than it is by cultivating personal growth. But more than that, and as Aristotle did not stress enough, there is the question of original sin, evil and ill-will. If, as we all know is the case, our characters are flawed, what guarantee is there that personal growth and the means to it will not emphasize the dark side of our self, particularly given that our vices are often stronger and more impetuous than our virtues? Rather late in the day, in his journal for 14 April 1969, Maslow wrote that encounter groups and the therapies associated with them had

> . . . no theory of evil, of how to handle . . . mean and nasty people. The implicit theory in . . . Rogers, *et al.*, is that if you trust people, give them freedom, affection, dignity, etc., then their higher nature will unfold and appear . . . But when there is not good will, but viciousness and hatred instead then you must be ready to counter attack . . . or else you let evil, wrong, nastiness win.

Warming to his theme, Maslow extends his analysis to the philosophy of education prevalent in America at the time. College faculties, he said,

. . . lack theory of right and wrong of evil and so don't know
what to do in the face of viciousness. This non-theory of evil
. . . is one peculiar verson of the 'value-free' disease (which is
the same as ethical relativeness, of Rousseauistic optimism, of
amorality, i.e. nothing is wrong or bad enough to fight
against) . . . What kind of educational philosophy is it that is
unprepared for ill will? . . . It's a philosophy in which
nothing is bad or sick or wrong or evil?

Strange, is it not, that in the century in which there has been
as much pure unadulterated maliciousness and evil as any, the
dominant psychology and philosophy should be one that
stresses autonomy – come what may – and denies evil?
Hitler, we are told, was not autonomous enough, but
dominated by unautonomous ideas. Serial killers are the
product of their upbringing and not responsible for what
they do. Bad actions are due to bad childhoods, repressive
education, and defective chemistry. Moral problems are
basically problems of hygiene.

At a deeper level, though, I have no doubt that Enlightenment and romantic ideas contribute to the evil whose
existence they deny. We do not believe in the devil, these
days, but as I remember from my Catholic childhood, that is his
ultimate triumph.

Politics, Media and Sport

The title of the sub-heading is not just a reference to the British
Labour government's absurd ministry of 'Culture, Media and
Sport'. As politics has become more democratic, less authoritarian and deferential, more mass, as it were, it has come to
exist in and through the mass media, and to define itself in
terms of the mass media. The mass media, meanwhile, centres
increasingly on sport, which in its turn takes on the values and

attitudes of the mass media. It is time to look at the *panem et circenses* of the twentieth century.

Politics

The twentieth century has been the century of politics. Politics has not just taken over government from hereditary establishments and immovable, secretive oligarchies pretty well throughout the world. Politics, in the sense of government by career politicians claiming some sort of popular mandate, has also taken over the running of people's lives to a hitherto unprecedented degree and, in the case of the mass mobilization of whole populations in times of war, their destinies and deaths too. Our century has also become the century of political spectacle, theatre and display.

Much of what has happened and what we see is almost too obvious to require further comment. Plato's worries about democracy being a prey to demogoguery have been amply confirmed, as have Aristotle's fears about democratic factions operating to enrich themselves at the expense of the rest of the city, particularly those whose property and services the democratic state routinely expropriates.

It is not just the rich who are expropriated: in Britain and America, taxation has reached epic dimensions compared with the few pence or cents of turn-of-the-century income tax. Standard-rate taxpayers in Britain have to surrender more than two-fifths of their earnings to the state in taxes, while in Euroland the figure is half. It is as if every year we are forced to work until May, or even later, for the government, whether we like it or not. Only then are we allowed to keep anything of what we earn for ourselves (a predicament not unjustifiably dubbed slavery by Robert Nozick, slavery being when one is forced to work for another whether one likes it or not).

It will be said that taxes pay for things of universal benefit, such as health, education, pensions and social services, but we should not overlook the remorseless logic of bureaucracy. The first duty of any bureaucrat is to preserve yourself and your job, increase your power, influence and work, and when things go wrong, claim that the underlying cause is 'lack of resources'.

If a bureaucracy is charged with waste or fraud or with just being too big, then another bureaucracy will be set up to investigate . . . hence in Britain under John Major we had a civil service unit to investigate government red tape, while in Europe the European Commission set up its own commission of highly paid officials to investigate fraud in the Commission. Meanwhile, when our army is the smallest in our history, there are more civilians working for the Ministry of Defence than the total number of British troops and administrators in the Raj in the whole of the Indian subcontinent, many of them doubtless producing managerial policies, internal audits, and sex and race codes.

So used are we to the torrents of legislation flowing from democratic parliaments, is it even worth commenting that in America – the home of enterprise, the free market and limited government – central government issues seventy thousand pages of new legislation every year? In Britain under a government officially committed to pushing back the boundaries of the state, education law, to take just one example, increased from 1979 to 1997 from one slim volume to five fat folders.

The red-tape commission, by the way, found no evidence of waste, over-manning, or unnecessary bureaucracy in the Department for Education. This rather surprised those who had been entangled in its spider's web of statute, regulations, interpretation and 'advice' on every conceivable matter to do with education, from examinations and curricula through to school meals, discipline and policies on sex education and school assemblies (much of it actually replicated by government quangoes and by local government). It is as if once a bureaucracy is set up, for what seem the best of motives, no one, even with the best of intentions, can do anything to prevent its cancerous growth. I will explain shortly why this might be so.

It is not just capture of a nation's resources that democratic politics encourages. In so far as the state is providing services for all paid for by everyone's taxes, it becomes increasingly difficult to maintain standards of high quality in areas like education and the arts. Judgements of quality are inherently discriminatory: they exclude and they rank. They sit ill with pretensions to democratic inclusiveness, and prompt accusations of 'élitism' and calls for 'access'; so in Britain funding for the Royal Opera House has to be off-set by funding for ethnic and 'community' arts, dance and visual arts, and the opera house has to lower its prices and engage in patronizing 'outreach' programmes (never mind that many of its prices are already far lower than those for football or pop concerts); so grammar schools are abolished in favour of neighbourhood comprehensives so awful that our Prime Minister cannot bring himself to send his own children to them, and getting on for 40 per cent of the population are in effect frogmarched into institutions called 'universities' (though in reality many are nothing of the sort).

Meanwhile, democratic inclusivity and non-judgementalism means that social services and health are administered on the basis solely of need, however that need comes about and whatever are the prospects of the recipient. Social workers do not judge whether a 'client' is deserving of help: sex-change operations ('gender reorientation'), all kinds of infertility treatments, cosmetic surgery, contraception and abortion for very young girls, and much else besides, are provided on the National Health Service despite the moral objections that would certainly have prevented the state providing them twenty or thirty years ago. In 1999 even to utter thoughts about rationing treatment to the more deserving is to be 'divisive' (a term of abuse), as health secretary Frank Dobson discovered to his cost when he tried to limit the prescribing of Viagra on the NHS to certain categories of patient.

In these and many other ways, the indictable drift of democratic politics is to non-judgementalism. We are drifting towards what de Tocqueville saw as a state of universal mediocrity in which the state supplies many of the needs of everyone without, as it were, ever judging or saying no – providing only that the citizen accepts the poisoned chalice of state provision, and the right of the state to take over ever-increasing tracts of his life.

Meanwhile, political discourse and argument is increasingly infantilized, a process in which the mass media are readily complicit. Elections are run like advertising campaigns, with market research carefully designed to elicit just what will appeal to those groups of the population whose voters are crucial to swinging the result one way or the other. Hence the use of focus groups. In Britain in the 1997 election the reactions of middle-class housewives, in places like Welwyn Garden City, to particular policies and slogans apparently determined what went into the Labour Party election campaign. These reactions were not, one supposes, based on any deep study or explanation of the policies, for if they had been the ladies in question would no longer have been representative of the votes the pollsters were anxious to secure, and so would not have been the right 'focus' for the purpose.

If the state did nothing beyond the night-watchmanly tasks of defence without and police within, selling political parties like toothpaste or detergent would not matter very much. After all, worse things happened in eighteenth-century elections, as we see from Hogarth, yet Britain was then entering on a period of unprecedented growth, prosperity and imperial power.

But the atmosphere and ethos of eighteenth-century British political life was quite different from that of today. It was honestly and openly corrupt, about the honest pursuit and use of power. The great rationalist lie had not captured the soul of political classes, let alone that of the populace at large, who expected little from the institutions of the state, and certainly not that they should run their lives for them.

Rationalism in politics – to use Michael Oakeshott's telling phrase – is the quintessence of Enlightenment thinking. It is in this form of politics that the Enlightenment has had, and continues to have, a profound influence, even among those who have never thought about either politics or enlightenment.

Political rationalism underlies almost all political thought and activity today. It is far more significant than distinctions between, say, socialists and free marketeers, both of whom are, in the intended sense, rationalists. Enlightenment rationalism, it will be remembered, combined mocking scepticism about past belief and practice with unbounded optimism about the power of the unprejudiced rational mind (modernizers, in today's terminology). It elevated consciously thought-out technique, calculation and analysis over settled, unconscious ways of doing things. It was universalistic, in its espousal of the thought that there was one best way of doing things for everyone. It believed that once we had scientifically uncovered the true springs of human action, rather than those things to which people cravenly and hypocritically paid lip service under the dogmas of religion and the constraints of irrational authority, we could then set about devising political and administrative systems for the optimal satisfaction of everyone's real desires. It is, in other words, the ideology underlying both bureaucracy and the unthinking assumption of most citizens that the state should be in the business of running things and so solving all our problems.

Rationalism in politics is simply the practical application of these Enlightenment dogmas. Marxism was one form of rationalistic politics, advocating as it did the direction of the economy by the central state committee, but it was not and is not the only form of rationalism even in the economic sphere.

Experience has now shown conclusively that, quite apart from its propensity towards dictatorship, the command economy just does not work even in economic terms, as illustrated by the Polish joke from the mid-1980s about the shortage of sand occurring in the Sahara shortly after they nationalized the desert. Practically nowhere in the world now does the state presume to run industry directly. Some of the worst and crudest effects of political rationalism have disappeared, thankfully, with the ending of the Soviet empire.

But, in most countries, this does not mean that the state allows any free capitalist act between consenting adults. In the economic sphere state regulation has replaced state management. So in the European Union, which many initially believed was to be just a free-trade area, endless regulation governs employment, production and sale, all supposedly to create 'harmonization' and 'level playing fields' – as if the market could not be trusted to do any of these things itself. In fact, what it leads to is ever-burgeoning bureaucracies and systems of subsidy to redress imbalances – that is, it rewards inefficiency and creates endless opportunities for fraud and corruption.

The market, regulated or not, is itself a product of the Enlightenment, and in its key aspects can certainly be seen in Enlightenment terms. It is global, universal and unprejudiced. Through consumer demand it reveals desire; in entrepreneurial response to desire it maximizes both production and choice in a way centralized economies simply cannot. In other words, it serves the material needs of the man revealed in Enlightenment thought. In cutting through local prejudice and custom it also speaks to his psychological condition as well – rather successfully, in fact. As I remarked earlier, what Communism failed to do in half a century or more in Eastern Europe, tragically the global free market has made a pretty good start at doing in ten.

While the oppression of atheistic totalitarianism drove people back to their religious and national roots, the material plenty and amorality of the market teaches quite different lessons. For in true Enlightenment style, the market is no respecter of national roots, ancient customs or religious traditions. But unlike the militant assault of the explicitly atheistical dictatorship, the market does the Enlightenment's work gently and imperceptibly. Its material plenty simply means that people cease to dream of anything else.

Enlightenment politics is not just about the satisfaction of desire through the economy, whether market-led or command-driven. It is also what Oakeshott calls perfectionist: it promises the elimination of need, poverty, ignorance and sickness once the prejudices of the *ancien régime* are liquidated and its own scientific solutions and procedures are adopted. It is this scientific-cum-administrative perfectionism that most modern states have bought into, and it is this that provides the rationale for their takeover of the lives of their citizens who, as de Tocqueville predicted, become ever more infantilized, at the same time as, materially, they become better off and more secure.

Thus, in Britain's welfare state, we see the state promising to eliminate need, poverty, and ignorance. It takes over the health of the nation. No sick person will be denied state health care. No old person will be allowed to go uncared for or unprovided for. No child will be uneducated. Moreover these things are so vital to a civilized society that they cannot possibly be left to 'chance' – that is to private charity, individual initiative and responsibility. Health, welfare and education must all be planned, administered and provided by the state. In being planned and administered in this way, they become host to a mass of petty, benign and absolutely enervating regulation, as again de Tocqueville foresaw.

And not only state-provided health, welfare and education.

Activities not directly run by the state are subject to its regulatory zeal. In employment, as fast as the state denationalizes industries, it takes back through regulation. No one can run a business, these days, without a raft of policies, codes of conduct and provisions only loosely related to buying, producing or selling. But growth of state interference is not just in employment: every other aspect of our lives falls sooner or later under the state's supervision, often in response to some supposed abuse or scandal. The food we are allowed to eat, the animals we are allowed to own, the arrangements we make for the care of our children, the sports we are allowed to engage in, the clubs we are allowed to set up, the changes and improvements we are allowed to make to our own houses and property . . . All these, and many more aspects of what would not so long ago have been thought *private* activity are now subject to legislation and statute. Even sexual activity, though not subjected to legal prohibitions, is surrounded by government-funded programmes of advice, encouragement and for the mitigation of ill-effects.

Two aspects of this state-led encodification of our lives are worth remarking on. The first is the typically rationalistic assumption that 'good practice' in any area can be codified. We no longer see wisdom as arising from experience, inherited traditions and assumptions too deep for articulation. We know that, in many respects, people have lost their bearings – largely because of the Enlightenment's assault on the value of tradition, right feeling, ancestral morality and shared prejudice for the transmission of a living sense of the way things 'should be done'.

We think that this gap can be filled with reams of instruction. The fallacy of this is first that explicit instructions will leave out the crucial and necessarily unexpressed sense of how the explicit instructions are to be applied, sensibly, humanely and reasonably. They will, in other words, leave out that element of judgement or practical wisdom which, as Aristotle knew well, is central to a practice that is running well. This element of judgement and the wisdom underlying it is what inspires the spirit of the game, or the ethos of an institution or the unspoken assumptions and bonds needed to tie together those engaged on a common task or vocation.

To those who do not have this unspoken sense, explicit instructions will be meaningless, and are likely to result only in a form of bureaucratic literalism, by turns vexatious and laughable. To those who do have it, explicit instruction in the form of a code of practice is likely to be either redundant or crass or both.

To make this slightly more concrete, does any experienced teacher need to be told to treat his or her pupils with fairness and consideration or to pace their lessons appropriately? Yet this is the sort of thing we find in managerial codes of practice, of which the archetype is undoubtedly the bureaucrat Polonius's advice to Laertes, intended, of course, by Shakespeare as satire, but one that would pass our bureaucrats and management gurus completely by. The whole point is to know what it is to treat a particular pupil with fairness or just what the appropriate pace of a given lesson ought to be. And that sort of knowledge, which Aristotle calls practical wisdom, is gained only through experience, through having virtuous dispositions oneself, and through working with those who already know and understand these things.

We have our Nolan Committees, our Scott Reports, our 'last-chance saloons' for the press, and editorial codes of conduct, even government training for marriage, but does anyone, apart from those with a vested interest in these things, really suppose that public life is cleaner or the press less venal or marriage more solid as a result? Or that – without a change of heart on the part of those affected – their recommendations will have any real effect?

Managerial codes of practice exhibit the rationalist fallacy of thinking that what really matters in a practice is what can be written down, and that writing them down and having bodies to supervise their implementation will, by themselves, improve bad situations. But they have a second, equally insidious, equally destructive feature, particularly but not exclusively when they are drafted by governments.

They encourage ideologically motivated lobby groups and their representatives in government to use them as devices of social engineering. Thus, no advisory document on education or employment is put out by government today without the obligatory references to gender, race and special needs. Educational and employment practices are thus distorted to ensure that politics itself is transformed into a project of rationalistic social engineering: instead of political institutions being neutral rule-keepers, which permit groups within a society to work out their interrelationships themselves, political institutions became players in the game. They line up on one side or the other, responding to those who want more black judges or women engineers or C2s in universities. No evidence is ever adduced to show that simply having more black judges or women engineers or C2s in universities will itself improve the institutions in question.

Nor could there be: if someone is a good judge or engineer or academic it is not because of their race or sex or class, it is because they have the right training, ability, experience and motivation. There might be something to be said for attempting to improve these things in the supposedly under-represented groups, but this is not the aim of the social engineers. Their point is pursuit of some notional equality, combined with the thought that the existing 'establishment' (white, male, middle-class) is holding things up and preventing progress. Displacing one establishment, though, does not get rid of establishment; the first lesson to be drawn from revolutionary history, whether in France or Russia or black Africa, is the rise of new and often far worse establishments, after a revolution against a former establishment. And in so far as there is an establishment in Britain in 1999, it is not those with ancestral prejudices. Such dinosaurs as there still are find no place in contemporary politics or administration and are occasionally wheeled on to the media only for the purpose of being pilloried by right-thinking presenters and commentators. The establishment is manned precisely by those who hold a rationalistic view of politics, who are committed to egalitarian social engineering and who make no secret of their contempt for traditional morality and religion.

It is all a sorry illusion. The state has not eliminated need, poverty or ignorance, nor, judging by the ever escalating numbers claiming disability benefits, are we much fitter than we were before the state nationalized health. We were once told that the poor will always be with us. By whatever standards obtain in a society, there will always be needy and ignorant people. Ill-health and disability are part of the human condition. These things cannot be eliminated, least of all by political means, however much such means will undoubtedly enrich those charged with implementing them. Very likely they will also increase the levels of resentment, fraud and fecklessness in the politicized society.

What we need to do is to learn to come to terms with the frailties of the human condition. We need to learn how to live together without the intervention of political agencies. We need to treat those who are needy, sick, poor and ignorant without patronizing or demeaning them or turning them into 'claimants' in thrall to faceless and unresponsive bureaucracies.

We also need some sense of how to behave if we are needy, sick, poor or ignorant, remembering that to a greater or lesser extent, at one time or another, all of us will suffer from these conditions. In so far as twentieth-century politics pretends it can solve problems of poverty, ignorance and sickness once and for all, it not only promises what can never be delivered, it also prevents us from seeing what the problem is and how, Enlightenment hopes notwithstanding, science, reason and politics provide no ultimate solutions to it. Above all, in its pretence that it can abolish need, ignorance and sickness, it blocks us from ever understanding the spirituality of the Gospels and of St Francis – for whom poverty was not a curse to be abolished, but a state and a vocation to be sought and cherished, precisely to achieve a liberation and an autonomy undreamed-of by the radicals of Enlightenment, or their successors, political or economic. Political rationalism, in short, makes it impossible to grasp how, for a millennium, the dominant inspiration for Western mankind should have been that of 'the crucified saviour'.

Media

The legendary Lord Reith, the architect of the BBC and its director general from 1927 to 1938, once said that 'If the day should come, and I don't think it will, when broadcasting should play to the lowest rather than the highest in man, then the country will have fallen very low.' Few could doubt that, in Reith's terms, this country has indeed fallen 'very low', and so have most other countries.

It is pointless to waste time proving that this has happened. You need only turn on a television, go into a record shop, read a newspaper (maybe comparing the *Daily Mail* of 1910 with *The Times* of 1999) or surf the Internet to see that the worst of Reith's (and Plato's) fears have been amply fulfilled. Of course, amid the torrent of garbage sluicing through the airways, the pages of newspapers and in cyberspace (90 per cent of Internet traffic is consumed by pornographic images apparently), there are a few better offerings. But they are notable precisely because they are exceptions. And the places where they are to be found have overall been relentlessly dumbed down, as can be seen by considering the relentless popularizing of even our 'serious' papers' and the evolution of the BBC's Third Programme of 1946 into today's Radio Three. The one was severely intellectual, resolutely élitist and uncompromising – and *thereby* opened the gates of the temple of culture to the uninitiated, as many of us brought up in the 1950s can testify – with as much serious speech and drama as music; the other is largely music, including all kinds of jazz and pop, and increasingly dominated by gossip, chat and chummy 'presenters', and for a number of years was run by a man who professed to be unable to discriminate between the worth of Schubert and Bob Dylan.

'Presenters'. The incestuous and self-referential nature of the mass media is nowhere more clearly exemplified than in the way in broadcasting 'presenters', including newsreaders, have become more important than what they present. This is no exaggeration. The latest product from what appears to be the BBC's apparently unstoppable assembly line of finger-jabbing female Scottish presenters will be earning over four times more than the government ministers who are occasionally allowed on to her programme to undergo her not very penetrating questioning. In much of television it is difficult to know who is the star or who the 'celebrity guest'.

Situation comedies and soap operas plumb ever new depths in inanity and filth, linguistic and behavioural, the underlying tone being a relentless denigration of anything and everything but the lowest tastes and attitudes. And then there are the talk-shows of the 'nuts and sluts' variety, celebrating every kind of neurosis, addiction and depraved taste. The people on these shows, when not hired actors, are victims, as indeed we all are, but in their case especially praiseworthy for the courage of self-exhibition. The paramount value in the media is that, for both commercial and cultural reasons, no one must ever be excluded; and this leads to increasing reliance on the exhibition and expression of feeling, and the excision of anything hinting at superiority.

Nietzsche, it will be remembered, criticized Euripides for allowing the common man on to the classical stage. Today in the media it is nothing but the common man, or woman – and the commoner, the less idealistic or elevated the better. Anyone with pretensions to be better will be cut down and, if possible, exposed in his or her private life; and what television does not do here, the newspapers – quality or tabloid – will more than make up for. And the rest of us, while disapproving, slaver over the details – not, I suspect, so much for their salaciousness as for the casting down of the hero.

On television, superiority must not be shown or implied, for that would be judgemental and divisive, the worst of all crimes in an age of democratic mass media. This is why the television personality has to be an ordinary, regular guy with the accent and manners of the ordinary guy (even though he is actually a barrister educated at public school and Oxford). It also explains why on television politicians have to appear no different from the rest of us, and are never happier than when they can demonstrate their utter ordinariness, even down to appearing on the chat-shows, sharing their ordinariness and their pain with the rest of us.

It will, of course, be said by the producers of television and the editors of newspapers that the viewing and sales figures depend on dumbing down. And they are right, which says something both about the 'information explosion' and the market – and about the society we live in as reductively material in its ambitions as its science and philosophy would teach us. We have our answer to Bentham's poetry versus pushpin question. If you want to know what it is, simply look around a bookshop or newsagent, turn on the television or surf the Internet.

Public-service broadcasting, such as that of the BBC, at one time upheld standards. But in an age of political demagoguery, this is hardly sustainable. Why, we will hear from our tribunes of the people, should we pay for programmes that appeal only to snobs and fogeys? Shouldn't the BBC cater for all tastes, however mindless, and compete with the worst of the market? In its implicit answer to this question, the BBC throws its very reason for existence into question, becoming ever more desperate when viewing figures show that, for some reason, it cannot compete with commercial stations however low it stoops.

In 1969, in a television series called *Civilization* Kenneth Clark quoted Ruskin as saying that 'great nations write their autobiographies in three manuscripts: the book of their deeds, the book of their words and the book of their art. Not one of these books can be understood unless we read the two others, but of the three the only trustworthy one is the last.' Lord Clark then went on to compare the comparative rise and fall in the artistic reputations of the Apollo Belvedere and of the African mask once owned by Roger Fry (the one down, the other up). He continued:

> I don't think there is any doubt that the Apollo embodies a higher state of civilization than the mask. They both represent spirits, messengers from another world – that is to say, from a world of our own imagining. To the Negro imagination it is a world of fear and darkness ready to inflict horrible punishment for the smallest infringement of a taboo. To the Hellenistic imagination it is a world of light and confidence, in which the gods are like ourselves only more beautiful, and descend to earth in order to teach men reason and the law of harmony.

You wouldn't get away with that today even though it raises interesting questions. Nor can one imagine on television in

1999 any celebration of 'civilization' because that would imply that there was also barbarism (divisive, judgemental, you see). For all our talk of multiculturalism we do not want to compare or assess cultures. Multiculturalism means denigration of one's own culture in the light of a nodding acquaintance with the superficial aspects of others. And what if – as our cultural authorities assure us – television and film are the art forms of the twentieth century? How will future generations judge the book of our art?

Whatever future generations might think of us, there is no doubt that Plato would have been appalled. Our mass media generally, and television particularly, have all the unfortunate characteristics of Plato's cave. The only difference is that while the prisoners in the cave are forced to look at the wall, no one is forced to watch television or read the *Sun*. But the effects are surely the same. Image substitutes for reality. The critical faculty is so deadened that, like Plato's prisoners, we complain when we are torn away from our mental life-support systems. The world reduces to the images on the screen, intelligence is talked out by chat; everything is seen as it is construed in the television studio.

More: with its relentless flickering and movement, with its noise and colour like nothing outside itself, television is like a drug. It satisfies nothing in us, but it spoils our taste for anything else. Thus television prides itself on its nature programmes; but people who know nature only from television are often hugely disappointed by the real thing. The jungle looks nothing like the jungles of *Life on Earth*, nor has the real savannah the drama of the filmed chases.

You can understand why people come, Warhol-like, to believe that any reality other than that of the television screen is not really real. Ordinary reality lacks the pace, the colour, the excitement, the drama, and the sheer in-your-face assault of television. Of course, anyone who has been on television knows that it is not really like that at all. In itself the world of television is as mundane as any other world. It is also far less fulfilling than many others precisely because it is in the business of creating nothing more than image and ephemeral excitement. How many times do we need to be told that mere 'words' and mere 'ideas' are not sufficiently visual for television? How television appears is all that matters, but television's appearances corrupt all others.

If, as Pascal said, the sole cause of man's unhappiness is that he does not know how to stay quietly in his room, in our time and to our unease television and the mass media are major contributing factors. For while they require only our passive co-operation and make no demands on us, physical or intellectual, they might almost have been designed to stop us finding quiet in our selves. They are the perfect media for a society in which it is politically and morally imperative that everything tracks down to the lowest level of mental and intellectual challenge, and where people crave the opiate of continual distraction, stumbling from one factitious media-created sensation to the next.

The mass media create a passive, anaesthetized population, as cultural critics from old left and old right used correctly to complain. The mass media are hugely influential in reinforcing belief in equality of taste and therefore hugely influential in keeping aspirations down. They have to be, otherwise their products would not sell. But this leads to an impasse. More and more aspects of our lives take on the values of the mass media. But for most people the mass media are the only source of information about the world beyond their private circles. How, then, can the torpor the media induces be shaken?

Sport

Not, it seems, by sport, a major factor in our distraction by the media. Long before us the Romans understood the potential of sport to divert the masses, not surprisingly the more violent the better. The huge crowds, the febrile atmosphere, the gambling, the enclosed stadia, the spectacle fraught with danger and passion, the astonishing levels of skill; the only thing missing from the Roman Colosseum was television and the deification of sport and its heroes through television.

Half a century ago George Orwell wrote a short essay entitled 'The Sporting Spirit'. In it he elaborated most of the negative points regarding professional sport, particularly of the international variety: the violence of the players and their cheating; the viciousness of spectators, their mindless hate-filled partisanship and their xenophobia. Sport for Orwell, far from fostering goodwill between nations, feeds the lunatic modern habit of identifying oneself with large power units and seeing everything in terms of competitive prestige.

Almost everything Orwell says is true. The only point he does not sufficiently develop is the way even in 1945 (when he wrote his essay) sport was big business. He cannot, though, be blamed for not seeing the extent of the interdependence of sport and the mass media in our day, so he could not prophesy the unbelievable sums of money now available to top players, the successful promoters, agents and team owners, largely realized through television advertising and sponsorship, which in their turn rely on sport for audiences and sales. And yet, some countervailing points should be put, even in the century of the 1936 Olympics, the sovietization of sport, drugs scandals, bribery, football hooliganism and sporting terrorism.

Sport can be heroic, beautiful even, as we see in the funeral games of Patroclus in the *Iliad*, in Pindar's Odes and on countless classical vases. Further, the ancient Greek attitude to sport had nothing to do with any supposed 'Olympic spirit' or sense of taking part being the main thing. The ancient Olympics were highly professional, winning was everything, was often achieved by ruthless methods (that is, cheating), and secured the victor a city pension for life.

Moreover, cheating and Orwell's strictures aside, sport is an arena in which admirable qualities can be displayed and are sometimes rewarded: dedication, skill, finesse, strength, courage, fair play, fortitude in adversity, magnanimity towards the vanquished. Furthermore, uniquely in the modern world, sport is an area in which egalitarianism can get no foothold, in which excellence is prized and fostered, not denigrated and hidden, and where rewards to the successful – often of a colossal sort – are apparently not resented by the masses. Uniquely in sport the pieties of political correctness and the egalitarian efforts of social engineers are seen by everyone for the nonsense they are.

Finally, and again unusually in the modern world, sport is an area in which activity of a regulated sort is valued for its own sake, and not for the sake of something else. Whatever ulterior motives politicians, promoters and media moguls may have in using sport, and whatever financial and sexual rewards good players might get as a result of their playing, none of these side-effects would be possible, were playing and watching sport not regarded by most people as worthwhile in themselves, rather than as a means to some other end.

It is both the universal accessibility of sport and the intrinsic satisfaction it affords that explain its particular twentieth-century deformations. We should not, as Orwell did, denigrate or ignore its virtues. But we can still reflect on the fact that whereas the ancient Olympics took place as part of a religious celebration, which all Greeks observed (suspending wars for the duration), the modern Olympics are a media-fest whose vulgarity would have been embarrassing even in the Roman empire.

Sport in our day may not be an unfailing cause of ill-will, as Orwell asserted, though it frequently is. It is thoroughly permeated with the values of unbridled commercialism and this compromises its values. It is also one of the major distractions of the modern age. The defects of modern sport arise precisely from its mass appeal and its easy propensity for commercialization and for projection by the mass media.

But, at a more profound level, unlike ancient Greeks, we do not see the undoubted values of sport as intimations of something higher. Lacking an overall context for our lives as a whole, we have no context for sport either, a context in which sport can be valued for what it is, while at the same time being seen in its true place in the overall scheme of things. For the reflective person, even for one who, unlike Orwell, actually appreciates sport, our obsession with it is inevitably deeply unsettling.

Conclusion

At the end of the second millennium of the Christian era, humanity is in a morass. This is not just in those countries of the world where people are suffering from oppression and material deprivation. It is not even especially in those areas. For the most part, people in the underdeveloped world can think of nothing more desirable than life in or on the model of the affluent West. That form of life – our form of life – for much of the world provides the height of ambition and the summit of human achievement, to which we are, mostly unthinkingly, convinced mankind has been progressing over the centuries.

And that is our problem. Our situation has indeed brought amazing benefits at the material and political levels. As one who owes his life to modern medicine, who enjoys many of the fruits of industry (including, I freely and unfashionably admit, my private car), and also the stability and security afforded by liberal political arrangements, I would be far from denigrating any of these benefits.

But there has been a terrible cost, as I hope to have indicated in this book. It is not that of environmental catastrophe, which may be much exaggerated in any case. We should always bear in mind when there is a scientific scare story that the doom-sayers have their pride, their reputations and their self-interest too. They are not more likely to be wholly impartial recorders of objective fact than are the scientists working for drug companies or tobacco manufacturers. In addition, they provide amazingly good copy for newspapers and television. The cost is that scientific reason, whose technological and political applications have brought us in the main both prosperity and peace, has destroyed the visions which once inspired men. It is doubtless a confused recognition of this truth that underlies the popularity in the media of scientific scare stories and of superstition more generally.

Scientific reason has intimated to us that – in Nietzsche's terms – at one time men loved the Olympian gods, at another the God of Abraham, Isaac and Jacob, and at yet another the God of the New Testament, in all cases infinitely more than they deserved to be loved. Yet in this superabundance of loving, our predecessors gave themselves goals and aspirations that elevated them – and which still, even now, continue to elevate us, though diminishingly so – and that form the basis of our culture and civilization.

But, as a culture, we love the old gods no more. We have no comparable vision or hope. Science has destroyed these edifying and elevating beliefs. Physics and modern cosmology tell us that we live in a universe which is self-contained and self-sufficient, governed only by the impersonal operations of chance and causal law. In this vast universe we are no more than biological survival machines on an insignificant planet. We are dominated by the genetic imperatives to survive and reproduce, and the playthings of forces, biological and social, which we cannot fully understand, let alone control.

We see ourselves as living under the dominion of nothing more exalted than Bentham's twin masters of pleasure and pain. Under this conception of human nature there is no bar on anything science might do to further pleasure and reduce pain, whatever the cost in terms of human dignity or of the sacredness of human life. Indeed, there is now a groundswell of opinion according to which human beings are really no different from animals. After all, as Bentham emphasized, animals suffer, and are subject to pleasure and pain, just like us. Moreover, it is said, the higher mammals communicate, reason and manipulate tools (and each other), to a greater degree indeed than human babies and the mentally defective. We give babies and the brain-dead rights, so why not the great apes (who share 99 per cent of our genes), dolphins and other intelligent creatures? Why not accord them the respect we accord ourselves?

This argument entirely overlooks the differences between humanity as a whole and the rest of the animal kingdom, and also that very small genetic differences can produce vast differences in behaviour and constitution. It overlooks the way in which we humans can understand ourselves as rights-bearers, as owing duties to each other. We discuss among ourselves just what these rights might be and negotiate about them. The animal-rights argument also overlooks our sense that we ought to refrain from abusing others, both human and animal, even though we have nothing to gain from so refraining, a feature entirely absent from the non-human world, where we do not find members of other species manifesting compassion to other animals – or to humans, come to that.

More generally, the attempt to play down differences between animals and humans overlooks the way in which we use our powers of communication not just to send each other signals but also to reason and to seek the truth for its own sake. It overlooks the way in which, uniquely in the animal kingdom, we respect other human beings because they, like us, are free, rational agents, capable of formulating long-term goals and projects and liable to suffer when these projects are frustrated. It overlooks our sense of justice and injustice, both in the way others treat us and in the way we treat others. It overlooks our sense of ourselves as selves, with an integrity and a need to be respected as selves, over and above the considerations of immediate pleasure and pain, which wholly dominate the lives of non-human animals. The argument further over-looks our propensity to find beauty and meaning in the physical world, beyond its ability to satisfy our material and physical needs. And, crucially, it fails to see that we accord babies and the brain-dead rights because they belong to a species (us), whose mature and normal members have and do all these things, which even the cleverest of apes will never be able to do.

It is, though, hardly surprising that, after two centuries of scientific analyses of human nature, we are – for the first time in human history – inclined to play down differences between humanity and other kinds. For the inexorable drift of these scientific analyses has been to erode human dignity and free-dom, and the basis on which these notions rest, in particular any sense of ourselves as transcending the natural order of things.

If science has reduced our horizons to the merely human (or nearly animal), liberal morality and politics have chipped away at the contours of the human landscape. In the moral case nowhere has the change been more profound than in the area of sexuality. Ever since the time of Diderot, sexuality has appeared to enlightened thinkers to be surrounded by irrational taboos and customs that inhibit individual autonomy and deprive people of harmless pleasure. And it is perfectly true that marriage and traditional sexual morality did put all sorts of restrictions on sexual activity, which on the face of it are hard to justify, particularly if all that is at issue is a harmless pleasure, and it locked many people into situations from which they would prefer to escape. In the name of freedom and reason, divorce is made easier, sexual activity outside marriage becomes widely accepted, and 'relationships' are liable to be initiated and terminated at will.

We now know that in the main the effects of this revolution have not been good for the children of divorced parents, and even less for those whose parents never lived together. But even leaving this aside, has it improved the lot of those subject to transient and uncommitted relationships?

As Burke would undoubtedly have pointed out, the 'irrational' institution of marriage protects those liable to be hurt by the selfishness of those unprepared to make or honour commitments. It prevents sexual relationships from being, in their own way, a war of all against all, in which the stronger simply exploit the weaker, by using them then walking out on them when they feel like it, or by subjecting them to unwanted and humiliating advances, or worse. In linking sexuality to a sacred ceremony, traditional morality implied what is surely true, that sexuality is not just a matter of harmless pleasure but frequently involves deep emotions, which are hard to contain or direct. In this most fraught and uncertain of areas, marriage and traditional sexual mores provided a degree of order and dignity tragically hard to restore once it is gone – as we see in the futile and ham-fisted attempts of institutions such as universities to produce 'codes' against sexual harassment and the rest, whose purpose can only be to protect those (mainly women) who, far from having been liberated, have been made vulnerable by the removal of the old 'irrational' taboos. Their effect, however, once the intuitive sense of what is proper is lost, is by turns ludicrous and oppressive. They produce nothing more useful than an arena for the display of resentment on the part of those who feel affronted, whether justly or not, and for the playing of power games by bureaucrats, whose careers are made by meddling in matters that in a society with moral stability would be kept private and personal.

At a time when we are constantly being urged to be more rational and modern in all kinds of areas, the modernization of sexual morality that has occurred over the past thirty or so years can stand as a salutary reminder of the sort of thing that is liable to happen when we simply ignore the teachings and customs of our 'irrational' predecessors. Liberal politics, meanwhile, drives more and more towards the grail of equality, thereby making discriminations and judgements of quality increasingly problematic in pretty well any area except that of sport. Indeed, so committed are we to notions of equality that the mere fact of differential performance of different groups in matters such as educational achievement or appearances before the courts is taken to indicate 'institutional' racism or sexism on the part of the educational system, or the police or courts. Individuals, meanwhile, who for one reason or another cannot compete in society but who are fed on a half-understood diet of equality and human rights, become increasingly resentful and violent when they realize that they are never going to make the grade socially or economically. If we are to do something for the inarticulate and violent underclass of which we are seeing more and more, what we need is not, as President Clinton thinks, classes in conflict resolution. These people hardly attend school. What we need is some rethinking of the meaning of equality and the doctrine of rights.

In the absence of any serious thought in this area, the drive towards formal political and social equality continues unchecked, despite the implicit conflict with biology – the scientific wing of the Enlightenment – telling us that there are ineradicable differences of inherited intellectual capacity, even as between different racial groups. At the moment we seem unprepared for this scientific truth, if truth it is. Ideals of inclusivity reign which, with the exception of sport, depress and compromise performance and ambition in a million and one ways, obvious and not so obvious, while at the same time filling with vain ambitions those least able to come to terms with their inability to achieve them.

Whether or not there eventually turns out to be an irreconcilable conflict between the politics of Enlightenment egalitarianism and the science of Enlightenment biology, we are already confronted with a tension between Enlightenment globalism and the Counter-Enlightenment respect for tradition and local roots. Nationalism remains a key feature of political thought at the end of the twentieth century, on the face of it thoroughly unenlightened, particularly when we think of the Balkans.

On the other hand, in this area accommodations can be made, as enthusiasts for the European super-state also support Scottish and Welsh devolution without any apparent shame or embarrassment. In the United Nations itself we have both the Universal Declaration of Human Rights together with an insistence on the nation state and its right to infringe that declaration within its borders. The calm surface of this compromise is ruffled only occasionally by complaints that some nations are failing spectacularly to uphold human rights within their jurisdiction. Perhaps this contradiction is solved at the level of states: in the United Nations we have democracy and equality between states, rather than between individuals who live in different states with different (that is, better or worse) attitudes to individual rights.

However this may be, the other major Counter-Enlightenment theme, that of feeling, nature and spontaneity, has found its place easily and seamlessly in the context of Enlightenment thought. Human progress is not just a matter of material and scientific progress but of progress towards psychological freedom and self-fulfilment. As in the case of sexual behaviour, this turns out to be the liberation of our natural, spontaneous selves at the expense of repressive structures and traditions.

As in the intended sense, individual psychological fulfilment for all turns out to require a basic material plenty, whatever Rousseau may have believed about contented peasants, and democratic-cum-egalitarian social structures, and as the Enlightenment itself saw human fulfilment ultimately in psychological terms, there is no real conflict here. As far as individual lives are concerned, the rationalism of the Enlightenment and the romanticism of Rousseau and his followers (at least as understood in 1999) actually point in the same direction.

Overall, our era is one of technological progress, combined with the elaboration of individual rights (rather less of duties), and the attempt to satisfy psychological needs (increasingly unavailing as the needs multiply, the resources to fulfil them diminish and the facts of human inequality become ever more unavoidable). Despite a greater sensitivity to the environmental costs of material plenty for all, our mental landscape remains very much that mapped out during the period of the Enlightenment.

It is true that in 1999 with the demise of the Soviet Union we seem to have got beyond the stage at which enlightened politics is seen in terms of centralized state planning. Caution, though, is advisable. Even in 1999 British television can put on a prestigious series whose aim is to present the Cold War 'not wrapped in Old Glory, but from the viewpoint of both protagonists', and still rolling out the old chestnut of moral equivalence: 'in the Soviet Union and in America the Cold War was fought by fear'. In America, fought by fear? Fear to set aside anything in the USSR? A few screenwriters having to write under pseudonyms in the McCarthy era? A few trade unionists exposed as the witting or unwitting pawns of Moscow at a time when the Cold War was really a matter of life and death? A handful of atom spies – real spies, as we now conclusively know – given not show trials but real trials, according to due legal process?

And where are the TV programmes showing the Second World War 'from the viewpoint of both protagonists'? Thankfully nowhere, but why, even after the opening of the KGB files, do we have to accord such respect to the Evil Empire and its operations of subversion in the West? And where are the Gulag memorials to set alongside the quite proper Holocaust memorials and preserved concentration camps? Why isn't this a project for the millennium, a project celebrating the human spirit in the darkest of adversity? Is it because we still think of Communism as a basically good, rational and progressive idea, which, in the deathless words attributed to Eric Hobsbawm, 'just didn't work out'?

Indicative as all this is of the way progressivist rhetoric still holds us captive, to concentrate here on these questions would be to miss the main point. The main point is that the free market and its ambitions are as much products of the Enlightenment as socialism. Both accept the premise of material improvement through science, and that happiness in this world is all any society can aspire to. In one way the situation in the free market is more poignant, more pregnant with despair, and not just because in the affluent West our demands are higher. For whereas those who lived in the prisons of Eastern Europe could always aspire to something better on the other side of the Wall – and it was better in just about every respect – we have that better thing, with nothing better than it in prospect.

As we find more and more, what we have is not enough. Real happiness eludes us. There is little in our common culture to sustain ideas of genuine excellence in serious pursuits. It may be that there is not enough even to sustain the basic civilization and values needed to make our lives together more than a wearying and self-defeating war of all against all. Certainly there is not, if the images of man given to us in biology and neo-Darwinism are all we have, which is what scientific reason seems to be telling us. Nietzsche believed that once men no longer believed in God there would be a crisis of value; and although few Anglo-American philosophers have taken seriously this aspect of his thought, a walk around the average Anglo-American city in the evening does little to show that Nietzsche was wrong.

Saul Bellow observed towards the end of the Cold War that

more die of heartbreak than from nuclear war – or, one could add, from environmental problems. If, in the title of the film, this is as good as it gets, then one can safely predict ever more amounts and types of heartbreak, even as we surround ourselves with ever more choices between ever more sophisticated technologies and entertainments, with ever more means of averting risk, and immerse ourselves ever more in therapy and the discourse of rights. Maybe drugs, medical and recreational, legal and illegal, will still the pain. Perhaps, as in *Brave New World*, the state will be our supplier, and addiction to happiness drugs compulsory.

We may not even have, as the Marxists used fervently to hope, some 'crisis of capitalism' to upset the order of things. Problems there will doubtless be of an economic sort, but it is hard to foresee a system-shattering catastrophe. However demoralized we become, 'the system' is likely to continue to produce enough and more than enough on the material level to keep the liberal-democratic masses satisfied. Their existence may approximate more and more to that of the prisoners in Plato's cave or of the infantilized citizens in de Tocqueville's novel form of despotism. But the whole point of Plato's cave or of de Tocqueville's immense tutelary power is that those involved do not become restive or rebellious. They actually resent being told that their lives are less than fully human, less than ideally adult.

But they are: they are ill-prepared to face life's real difficulties or to aspire to its real rewards. Even as their minds are swamped with the diversions of the electronic age, and thought and true feeling made all but impossible, this ill-preparedness is the source of a nagging, unassuageable unease. Deep down we all know that even the ultimate rewards our society offers us – fifteen minutes of televisual fame, or even worse fifteen years, a Caribbean island or a country mansion – are in themselves empty husks, no true indicators of the meaning of life. And the meaning of life is just the little matter on which our official ideology of scientific enlightenment and liberal politics studiously refuses to pronounce; in place of anything like that, what we are offered are material prosperity, formal equality and political participation, and when these are not enough, drugs or therapy or yet more unrealizable political promises.

What, then, is to be done?

Nothing. Nothing is to be done. That is the short answer, but also the deep answer.

It is one of the great illusions of progressivist thought that there is always something to be done; that there is a solution to every problem that faces us, that we can discover that solution by reason, and that the solution consists in doing something, either politically or individually.

There are plenty of problems that can be solved, but what concerns us here is not yet another problem, nor is it anything on which science or social science or politics can help. What we are talking about here is not a problem, or even a dilemma. It is the human condition itself, as we saw earlier in considering the meaning of progress.

We all know well enough that there are some negative aspects of our existence to which there is no solution on earth, other than endurance. Neither politics nor therapy nor riches can remove from us the basic realities of death, of sickness, of disappointment, of inequality, of grief, of misfortune in love, of, at a deep level and in various respects, personal inadequacy. Only if we live in such a way to face these realities without illusion can we call ourselves happy. We have first to understand that the negative aspects of human life are as much a part of life as the positive ones, and actually necessary to our fulfilment. As Rilke put it in his tenth Duino Elegy, we are most of us 'wasters of sorrow'; we forget that our sorrows are

nothing else
than our winter foliage, our sombre evergreen, *one*
of the seasons of our interior year – not only
season – they're also place, settlement, camp, soil, dwelling.

Jubilation requires lamentation. Jubilation is only jubilation in balance with lamentation, though this is a message most of us are reluctant to hear, believing as we do that it is possible to lead a fulfilled or developed life without confronting trial and tragedy.

We seek diversion to hide the reality of sorrow from ourselves, but the diversions, which the market is far more adept at supplying than socialism, compound our inability to see life in perspective. This is partly why many wise and holy people see poverty and chastity as ideals to embrace, rather than as crosses to bear. They are seen as ideals because they help the adept to face what it is our condition to have to face.

But it might be an even greater blessing to be able to face our fates with equanimity, without cultivating virtues of non-attachment, in the midst of a normal human life; to be able, in other words, to take and leave what life has to offer, not just to leave it. After all, the goods of life are goods. They do not cease to be goods just because of the bads. They cease to be goods when they make us unable to accept the bads, when they put us in a state of denial regarding what we really are, when, as Nietzsche argued, they make us unable to see that achievement and struggle, fulfilment and suffering are complexly inter-related.

The criticism of scientific materialism and progressivist politics is not that they do not produce goods, but that they contribute to a state of mind that systematically denies the full context of human life, its realities and possibilities. Nowhere is this more agonizingly illustrated than in the pre-natal screening programmes for conditions such as Huntington's chorea,

Down's syndrome and spina bifida. As things stand, the only point of such screening is to prevent those with the conditions in question from being born. This not only suggests to those living with the conditions that they would have been better off not being born, a point rightly made by lobbyists for the disabled and the disabled themselves, who often feel that their lives are highly valuable, the difficulties notwithstanding, it also puts pressure on those who know they have conceived such a child to abort. And in its disregard for the sacredness of human life, it erodes the notion of the value of each and every human being.

Henceforth will only those human beings who come up to some ideal specification be valued, or even born? This dilemma will face us even more starkly when, as seems likely, we have the technology to design babies according to ideal genetic blueprints. What would that say about our attitudes to disability and difference, and about what we really value in life? It would surely be the ultimate commodification of human life, an attempt to suppress its ultimate mystery and gratuitousness, and to constrain its freedom and creativity, and for that reason repugnant; but it is hard to object to so long as we stay within the perspective afforded us by science and the market.

Much of the argument of this book has been to suggest that when man relies wholly on his own resources, when he treats himself as a purely natural, material object, and when he sees happiness just in terms of psychological satisfaction, human life is inevitably degraded. But all is not lost – yet. The degradation of life and the account of our higher faculties and aspirations as mere by-products of our genes struggling to survive and reproduce are not true to experience.

Through art, particularly the great masterpieces of the past, we do have intimations of beauty, of order, of divinity, even, way beyond the biological. In our moral experience we know that we are bound by obligations and duties, which are rather more than merely co-operating with those who may be able to help us or benefiting our blood relations (which is all that we are given on the Darwinian account of morality). And in our search for knowledge and understanding, we aim for truth for its own sake, as if the secrets of the Big Bang or of number theory or of the structure of distant galaxies or of ancient Egypt were worth discovering, quite irrespective of any practical benefits they might bring. In most such cases, there will be none, and we know there will be none; there may be harm even, as in research into nuclear physics, and certainly the expenditure of effort and intelligence cannot be justified on practical grounds, but we pursue these things none the less, rather as in the moral sphere we forgo the practical benefits of cheating or lying even when we know we will not be found out.

It is as if in our pursuit of serious knowledge for its own sake we are fulfilling a deep impulse that does not originate in us, to make articulate and intelligible what would otherwise be brute, dumb fact. It is as if in our moral behaviour we are subject to a law of personal integrity that must be obeyed – though, in the words of the poet Horace, the heaven fall. It is our sense of being bound by such a law which grounds our intuitive sense that human life is sacred. It explains our unease when utilitarian philosophers tell us that there is nothing wrong with human cloning, genetic engineering, freezing embryos, growing spare parts and the recycling of the body parts of the dead, or even of the living.

To be sure, if we were no different from animals and human life were no sacred thing but a commodity to be distributed and used simply to increase the sum total of pleasure in the world, there would be nothing wrong with any of these practices. They might indeed be enjoined on us, if the only moral considerations were quantities of pleasure and pain. The philosophers would be right. It would indeed be hard to see what might be wrong with snatching some feckless vagrant off the street and distributing his vital organs among half a dozen more useful and deserving individuals (brain surgeons and the like) who would die without organ transplants. This and similar examples are much discussed by moral philosophers and their students, but rarely simply dismissed out of hand as utterly abhorrent, as they surely should be.

But human life is not just a commodity to be used and exploited in any way we see fit. For one thing we are conscious. This is a property we share with animals, and which ought to limit what we do to them. Their being conscious explains Bentham's quite correct insight that it is wrong for us to torture animals or to cause them unjustifiable misery. Emphasizing the differences between humans and animals does not mean that it is right to treat live meat as dead meat, a practice in which most of us collude in one way or another, even as we condemn the far more benign practice of fox-hunting. (Unlike the battery-reared chicken or pig, the fox at least has a life when alive, and takes his chances as do all other creatures in the wild.)

But consciousness, whether human or animal, remains an imponderable mystery to science. We can identify the physical conditions in which creatures and their brains have to be to produce consciousness, but this does nothing to explain what consciousness is, or how electrochemical processes in the brain can bring it about.

If, to use Leibniz's telling image, we were able to walk round a brain, we would see all kinds of physical activity: we would see neurons firing, parts of the brain becoming excited, signals being transmitted, perhaps, but we would not see the experiences the owner of the brain was having. How is it that some bits of matter can both react in physical ways and experience, from the inside as it were, what is going on? It cannot just be a matter of one bit of the brain monitoring or controlling other bits, like a thermostat in a heating system, for the thermostat, though certainly part of the system and reacting to other parts, is not itself consciously aware of anything.

Maybe this potentiality of matter to become aware, to feel as well as to react and send out instructions, is something deep within the fabric of the universe in ways in which our science and our empirical knowledge cannot even begin to understand or explain. The terms in which our science is set up leave no room for experience, except as a by-product of unfeeling physical processes. But we know that experience is not just a by-product, that it is central to the world in which we live and to our lives. We know that experience causes physical things in the world, as when a pain or a thought induces us to perform bodily actions; experience is not just a matter of being acted on. A science that treats it as merely a by-product or epipheno-menon is bound to be incomplete. Maybe beings like us, or the higher animals, who are fully conscious, are at some privileged stage in the cosmic process by which the universe comes to develop superior powers of feeling and thought which were latent within it from the very beginning, but which our physical sciences have not the theoretical basis to acknowledge or explain.

But we are not just conscious in the ways higher animals are, remarkable as that is from a scientific point of view. We are also unified selves, capable of reflecting on what we feel and do and say and think, and of reasoning about it. It is possession of unified selfhood that takes human beings beyond anything in the animal kingdom.

It is because we are selves in this sense, living in community with other selves of the same sort, that we are able to develop theories about the world and to reason about them. As selves we are also free agents, capable of initiating action not just on feeling and immediate impulse, as animals do, but in the light of reason and what is good. It is from this that our sense of moral obligation arises, as well as our need for personal integrity. We are, as it were, forced into asking ourselves about the value and coherence of what we do. And as reflective selves we are capable of aesthetic experience: that is, of contemplating things around us for their own sake, as beautiful (or not), and not just as tools for other purposes.

Like consciousness, selfhood and its meaning eludes scientific explanation: there is, for example, no 'self' in the brain, no one bit of the brain unifying and governing the rest, even less any part capable of being influenced by notions of truth, goodness, beauty and the rest, as opposed to responding to electro-chemical impulses along causally determined lines. But that science cannot find a self does not mean there is no self. Selfhood is a property not of brains, but of people with brains, whose selfhood depends on the brain for its realization but which, once realized, takes on powers and perspectives not explicable in standard physical terms.

Further, given that science itself is a product of what I am calling the self – in its theoretical, enquiring mode – it is hard, if not impossible, to see how science could show that there is no such thing as the self. For without enquiring selves there would be no scientific theories in the first place, nor would there be beings to understand them, correct them and improve them in the light of truth and reason. Even if we were prepared to think of computers as producing documents and theories of various kinds, what the computer produces is to it meaningless. Meaning and understanding enter the picture only when there are conscious selves to turn otherwise meaningless marks and printouts into meaningful sentences and messages: science itself is intelligible only if we have powers and faculties beyond the power of science to explain or describe.

If, in order to make sense of our activity, we do have intimations of a level of reality beyond the narrowly material or the purely biological, we should look favourably on those systems of belief and practice which, over the centuries, have attempted to articulate those intimations and make sense of them, even though since the eighteenth century these systems have been routinely dismissed as obscurantist prejudice. I am thinking here of those religious systems that have been the fruit of long experience, thought and reflection, such as Christianity, Hinduism and Buddhism.

Saying this is not to advocate a straightforward commitment to any traditional religion. Each is at best a partial revelation. None has a monopoly of truth or of sanctity. Each is fatally mired in outdated metaphysics. But, given the way their message has been verified in the lives of creative, reflective and holy people over many centuries, it is more than possible that each contains important truths and, more important perhaps, important pointers to truth. It is possible that each could give us important pointers to the way we should lead our lives today.

Take, for instance, the Christian sequence of fall and original sin – incarnation – redemption. The notions of fall and original sin are distinctly unmodern, distinctly unenlightened. For all that, they contain a truth also articulated in the Platonic myth of human beings as fallen from a perfect world into this imperfect material one, and in the Indian notion of karma, the system whereby present existence is conditioned by failings in the past. Desperately unfashionable as this last idea is, as we saw in the embarrassing incident of the Prime Minister, the football coach and the faith healer, it is simply not true that we come to infancy unburdened with a sinful nature; we come burdened with a complex of aggressive, selfish and even violent tendencies. So, where do they come from?

After two centuries of Rousseauan romanticism and Enlightenment progressivism, we find infant malice almost impossible to accept. Childhood aggression – and worse – must, we feel, be due to the environment. It cannot come from within. So we just do not know what to do when confronted with the likes of

Mary Bell, the ten-year-old murderers of the toddler Jamie Bulger, or even the teenage killers of Stephen Lawrence, let alone the gun-toting adolescents prominent in American colleges, ethnic struggles and civil wars around the world today.

The strange thing is that, while the concept of original sin is unmodern, unenlightened, Darwinian biology would actually endorse the negative picture. There is a real and unresolved tension here, between Enlightenment environmentalism and what its most admired theory of human nature has to tell us about ourselves, that is, that we are survival and reproduction machines, and that all our moral airs and ethical graces are but devices in the ceaseless war of our genes against other genes.

But if this picture, the Darwinian picture, is realistic at the level at which most of us would opt for an easy sentimentality especially over childhood, at another level it is severely limited. Although burdened with original sin, human nature is redeemable. More: in the Christian myth God became man, in order, as the Greek fathers put it, that man might become God. Or, as the ancient Greeks and Romans envisaged, if the gods existed in human form, there must be something potentially divine in human nature. And in the Hindu–Buddhist tradition, initially illusion-ridden existence in the present life is supposed to give way to more spiritually enlightened forms of life once we rid ourselves of illusion and attachment to earthly things and desires. We are all ultimately sprung from an original divine source, into which, after many cycles of earthly existence, we are eventually destined once more to dissolve.

We have explored secular-cum-philosophical analogues of these images: human freedom and rationality, even in a physically determined material world; our possibilities of dignity and grace, and of lives freed from corruption and cruelty; our deeply embedded intuition of conscience; our yearning for beauty, for excellence, for knowledge and for ultimate peace; and our consciousness and self-consciousness themselves, as pointers to a more than material underpinning of matter itself.

In the Christian myth, redemption from sin, original and personal, comes through God's incarnation in Christ, through Christ's passion, death and resurrection, and through our dying to sin and rising up with him with the assistance of divine grace. All these notions point to key aspects of our situation. God, if there is a God, is not the remote architect of the world process envisaged in traditional philosophy. God is intimately involved in the world and in matter. The world itself is a creative process, tending towards the the efflorescence of life and the development of consciousness and thought. In this process, God suffers and understands suffering (also a key feature of Indian religious thought). And redemption depends on a power beyond human ambition and work.

It is the recognition of human inadequacy that most divides ancient wisdom from the brashness of modern times; ancient wisdom, whether it be the Olympian gods wreaking unbearable punishment on the hubris of humans who think themselves the equal of the gods, or the Hindu–Buddhist notion that salvation comes only through the dissolution of self in the greater process of which we are but a part, or the Christian view that pride is the ultimate sin against the Holy Ghost.

Human inadequacy is not only that we are subject to original sin, though it is that. More, it is that good works are not enough, that we cannot redeem ourselves on our own. This may be the hardest lesson for us to accept, because it goes so much against the grain of our age. It goes against the activist grain, the heresy attributed to Pelagius and condemned by Augustine in patristic times, that salvation lies primarily in doing. And it goes against our secularist grain: the sense that by our own efforts we can create paradise on earth.

It might be said that in the year 1999 we are thoroughly inoculated against this illusion. How many attempts have we seen in the twentieth century to create heaven on earth, only to see hells unimaginable in any previous age? And yet the illusions persist: too often and too easy are the evasions, the forgetfulness. What have Nazi Germany or Soviet Russia or Pol Pot's Cambodia or Mao's China or Castro's Cuba to do with us? We don't believe in that sort of thing (any more). We are not like that. We will not make those mistakes.

No, we will not. We will make our own mistakes, in our own way, but in one respect our way will not be so different. At bottom our mentality is not so very unlike those that enabled the great tyrannies of the twentieth century. Since the eighteenth century we have all shared the same beliefs about science, about humanity and about the past: we have our salvation in our own hands; science and reason hold the key to progress (we believe that even when, as with so much en- vironmentalism, we use science to attack science); human fulfilment consists in the production of pleasure and the avoidance of pain; the way forward (itself a telling, unconscious metaphor) is forgetfulness of the past, of ancient prejudice and outdated repression.

The difference beween our state and the totalitarian tyr- annies of the twentieth century is that we represent the liberal- democratic version of the same mixture of Enlightenment and Counter-Enlightenment thought and practice. In contrast to those who lived and who continue to live under tyrannies, we do not suffer either from political oppression or from material scarcity. For that we can only be thankful.

But in some ways our predicament, though less dramatic, is more stark. We are unable to draw on those reserves of human courage and freedom and integrity that so often come into play when people are faced with real tyranny or real hardship. Certain possibilities of hope and of greatness are closed off for us.

Thrown entirely, if undramatically, on our own resources,

we realize, at least implicitly, how ill-equipped we are as a society to confront the fundamental enigmas of the human condition: not just the death, sickness and unhappiness that are the lot of us all, but even more fundamentally what it is that elevates human life above the material and the animal, and gives life its worth, its dignity and its point. The worry is that without a sense of what this might be, human life will barely rise above the material and the animal, and what biology tells us about ourselves will become the truth about our condition.

If any attitude is appropriate at the turn of the millennium it is humility. We should cultivate a realization of what has been lost in getting to where we are today, a realization of the parlousness of our situation, humanly and spiritually.

Our worries over genetic, medical and other scientific advances are telling symptoms of our condition: that as a society we haven't a clue how to combine a sense of human dignity and of the sacredness of life with the technologies we now have available, and which, as things stand, are bound to be used to transform our lives, further eroding any sense we have of life as sacred. Our politics and our mass media are given only to the satisfaction of desire at the lowest and grossest level, and to the nurturing of lying discourses of equality. We look in vain for guidance from orthodox religions. The arts seem for once really to do no more than reflect what we are; in this case they reflect our degradation, and offer no enlivening or elevating vision. Education and psychology turn increasingly inwards, in vain attempts to build up the self-esteem of people who, apart from the sacred cow of egalitarianism, have been given no reason collectively or individually to think that they have any basis for being esteemed; at the same time, we dismantle the structures that might elevate selves by getting us to turn our minds to things which are really worth pursuing.

If redemption is to come, it has to come from outside the things that science and contemporary politics have to offer. It has to come from outside us altogether, from a recognition that our efforts on their own are not enough. We have to see ourselves as part of a larger process, whose end is not just that human beings should breed and swarm, but which is addressed to higher ends. We exist neither to serve nature's blind reproductive ends, nor to manipulate nature for our own purposes.

What we can do and uniquely do is to draw out aspects of agency and meaning that are potentially in the universe, but which need us to actualize. Doing this requires that we see ourselves as subject to that higher purpose. Focusing entirely on the world as material or on our own individual happiness will have the effect of blinding us to other potentialities that we and the universe have.

It is for this reason that our sense of beauty and our moral feelings are so significant. Morality is important because in morality we cease to see our selves as the centre of the world, but rather as part of a wider community of selves, to whom we owe duties and obligations that should not be ignored or broken, and that are as much part of the fabric of the universe as its atomic structure. Beauty is important because it alerts us to structures other than the atomic and to goals other than the utilitarian. Further, in appreciating the beauty of the world and of things in the world, we are seeing the world as endowed with value and meaning. And in contemplating the beauty of things we are letting them be, for their own sakes, as they are in themselves, and not as consumables, as no more than means to other ends in which they will be used and destroyed.

In responding to our experience of the world in moral and aesthetic ways, we are implying that there is something to be responded to. We are taking the world and its processes as more valuable and meaningful than the brute facts and regularities revealed by science. We are seeing the world and our own existence as created, guided and measured by what the religions have referred to variously as God or Brahman or the One. We are also seeing our own lives as having goals higher than those dictated by the twin masters of pleasure and pain, and as being achievable only through acceptance of the suffering necessary to break down our own egoisms, suffering which we all, ultimately, have to bear. We are seeing the world as animated by some higher quasi-personal purpose, operating through and behind the material processes revealed and studied by natural science.

And salvation, if it is to come, will have to come through that higher power. Pascal, whose spirit has animated much of my Conclusion, wrote this: 'Be comforted: it is not from yourself that you must expect it, but on the contrary, you must expect it by expecting nothing from yourself.' (*Pensée*, no. 517) The lesson, the hard lesson, we have to learn at the end of the twentieth century is that our own resources, scientific, political and personal, are not enough. Enlightenment must give way to humility: *sapere aude*, dare to know, has to cede to silence and to waiting.

We should end with a wisdom older and more profound than that of the Enlightenment or of our own time. It is that of the ancient Greeks, as articulated by Aeschylus, the oldest of the great tragedians, regarded as old-fashioned even in his own day, but who comes closer than anyone since to expressing our predicament in 1999:

Zeus, whoever he may be, if by this name it pleases him to be invoked.

By this name I call him.

Nothing is left that I can compare him with, having weighed all things

Except Zeus.

If I am to cast this vain burden of anxiety from me . . .

He has opened the way of wisdom to mortals, proclaiming as sovereign law:

CONCLUSION

By suffering comes understanding,
So accrues to the heart, drop by drop, during sleep.
The wages of dolorous memory:
And even without willing it, wisdom comes,
From the gods who sit at the celestial helm,
Grace comes violently.

Bibliography and Sources

In this section, I indicate the sources both of the ideas and of the quotations in the text. Most of the quotations are from classic texts, now available in many editions. In these cases, where appropriate, I refer to the place in the text (chapter, section) rather than to the page of a particular edition or translation. This bibliography is designed to be used as a source for further reading, and as a guide for the non-specialist reader's own further investigations.

1: Images of Enlightenment

Francis Bacon. Bacon's philosophy of science is laid out in his *Novum Organum* of 1620. The first three quotations in the text are from aphorisms 60, 36 and 31 of Book One. The remark about a pattern of the world is from the 'Plan of the Work' of the *Magna Instauratio* (1620), while the quotation from *The New Atlantis* (1627) is from the preface 'To the Reader'. Bacon's ideas on education and the quotation about the joys of the river Lethe are discussed by Michael Oakeshott in his important essay 'Education: The Engagement and its Frustration' of 1972 (reprinted in *The Voice of Liberal Learning*, a collection of Oakeshott's writings on education, edited by Timothy Fuller, Yale, 1989).

Isaac Newton. His *magnum opus*, in which he lays bare his theory of motion and basic laws is the *Mathematical Principles of Natural Philosophy* (the *Principia*) of 1687. His account of secondary qualities is in the *Opticks* of 1704. Pierre-Simon de Laplace's

253

demonic intelligence is to be found in the opening section of his *Philosophical Essay on Probabilities* of 1814.

Enlightenment Optimism. This section draws extensively, though not exclusively, on Charles Taylor's *Sources of the Self* (Cambridge, 1989), especially chapter 19. Voltaire's praise of Locke is from his *Philosophical Letters* of 1734. Diderot's *Encyclopaedia* was completed in 1772. The quotations from Condorcet are from his *Sketch for a Historical Picture of the Progress of the Human Mind* of 1795. The first quotation from La Mettrie is from his *Anti-Seneca* or *Discourse on Happiness* of 1775. That from Holbach is from his *System of Nature* of 1770, the second quotation from La Mettrie is from *The Man Machine* of 1748, and that from de Sade from his novel *Juliette*.

2: The Counter-Enlightenment

Rousseau. Émile (of 1762) is Rousseau's major work on education and psychology. The *Discourses on the Origins of Inequality* (1755) and *The Social Contract* (1762) are the main sources of his political thought. 'Man was born free' is the opening of *The Social Contract*; 'God makes all things good' and 'The first impulses of nature' are from *Émile*; 'The fruits of the earth' is from the *Discourses*, opening of part 11; 'The world of reality has its bounds' and 'mediocrity' are from *Émile*.

Herder. An excellent discussion of Herder is in the relevant part of Isaiah Berlin's *Vico and Herder* (London, 1976). Goethe's essay 'On German Architecture' is translated in *Goethe on Art*, edited by John Gage (London, 1980).

Burke and de Maistre. The quotations from Burke are from his *Reflections on the Revolution in France* (1790), from de Maistre from his *Considerations on France* (1796). The Cambridge University Press is issuing the main classics of political philosophy, including those of Burke, Herder, Fichte and de Maistre in attractive modern editions; the translation of de Maistre's *Considerations* has a useful introduction by Berlin. Hobbes's social contract is in his *Leviathan* (1651), Locke's in his *Two Treatises of Government* (1690), Rawls's in his *A Theory of Justice* (Cambridge, Massachusetts, 1971).

3: Two Hundred Years
of the Progress of Reason

Kant is an immensely difficult thinker, the only one of those so far referred to who could not be read reasonably easily by a patient non-philosopher. (Nietzsche called him the catastrophic spider for the way he transformed philosophy from a pursuit for any intelligent, educated person into something for university specialists, with the complexity and verbiage of natural science, but without science's empirical backing. Kant was a genius, one of the four or five most important philosophers in history; but his dire stylistic influence lingers today in virtually all academic studies in the humanities and social sciences.) His most accessible work of moral philosophy is the *Groundwork of the Metaphysic of Morals* of 1775. He develops his thoughts on politics and internationalism in a short work entitled *Perpetual Peace* (1795).

Utilitarianism. 'Two sovereign masters' is the first sentence from Jeremy Bentham's *An Introduction to the Principles of Morals and Legislation* (1789). He wrote pamphlets on the Panopticon in 1791 and 1812. John Stuart Mill's *Utilitarianism* appeared in 1863. Socrates, the fool and the pig are in chapter 2. Mill's distinction between public and private actions is expounded in chapter 4 of his *On Liberty* (1859).

Darwin. The key works are *The Origin of Species* (1859) and *The Descent of Man* (1871). The 'law of natural selection' is in chapter 4 of *The Origin.* Neo-Darwinism: see Richard Dawkins, *The Selfish Gene* (London, 1978), Helena Cronin, *The Ant and the Peacock* (Cambridge, 1993), and my own *Beyond Evolution* (Oxford, 1997). Dawkins is Oxford University's Professor of the Public Understanding of Science. He refused nevertheless to discuss evolution and the mind with me on BBC Radio 3. (Why?)

Marx's most direct writing is *The Communist Manifesto*, which he wrote with Friedrich Engels in 1848. In *Capital*, vol. 1 (1867) alienation becomes 'commodity fetishism'. The point about hunting, fishing, etc., is in *The German Ideology* (1846), also co-authored with Engels.

Freud. The notion of repression is one of the key concepts in Freudian theory. See Freud's *New Introductory Lectures on Psycho-Analysis* (1933).

Constructive Rationalism. The phrase and much of the argument I owe to F. A. von Hayek, especially in *The Fatal Conceit* (London, 1988), chapter 4 and 5. The quotations from Needham and Monod are taken from Hayek (pp. 56–7). The first quotation from Russell is from 'Free Thought and Propaganda', a lecture given in 1922, and reprinted in his *Sceptical Essays* (London, 1928, p. 168); the second is from *The Scientific Outlook* (London, 1931, p. 203). The quotations from Wells are from *Travels of a Republican Radical in Search of Hot Water* (Harmondsworth, 1939, p. 99) and *After Democracy* (London, 1932, pp. 202–3). The reactions of Western utopians to Stalin's Russia are culled from Paul Johnson's *Modern Times* (London, 1996, pp. 275–6). Russell's remarks on the sterilization of the feeble-minded are from his *Marriage and Morals* (London, 1929, p. 203).

Faith in Science. George Orwell: 'the *Tatler* and the *Bystander*' is at the end of 'The Lion and the Unicorn'; 'What kept England on its feet?' is in 'Wells, Hitler and the World State', both in *The Penguin Essays of George Orwell* (Harmondsworth, 1984).

4: The Uncertainty of Progress

Whig History. The phrase is Herbert Butterfield's. See his *The Whig Interpretation of History* (London, 1931). Stephen Hawking on the end of science: see the end of his *A Brief History of Time* (London, 1988). On Niels Bohr, see K. R. Popper, *Quantum Theory and the Schism in Physics* (London, 1982). Francis Fukuyama, see his *The End of History and The Last Man* (Harmondsworth, 1992) especially parts 1 and 2. The chart referred to is on p. 49.

Putting the Clock Back. Bellow on Lenin, in 'Writers, Intellectuals, Politics, Mainly Reminiscence', in *It All Adds Up* (London, 1994, pp. 103–4). The phrase 'the Great Headmaster' is apparently Edmund Wilson's.

Rhetorical History. The argument about our knowledge of future technology is taken from the preface to later editions of Popper's

The Poverty of Historicism (London, 1957). The point about unintended consequences of actions and policies is elaborated at length by Popper in *The Open Society and its Enemies* (London, 1945, and subsequent editions).

History and Evolution. The quotations from Darwin are from the final chapter of *The Origin of Species.*

5: Thinkers of Loss

Plato. *The Republic* is the main source for the political and educational views here expounded. The cave is in Book 7, the parts of the soul and the state in Book 4, the analysis of democracy in Book 8. On Plato on science, see *Phaedo.* On sexual attraction and true beauty, see *Phaedrus.* Of the vast literature on Plato. I will single out only Iris Murdoch's *The Fire and the Sun* (Oxford, 1978).

Aristotle. Aristotle's views on rulers, slaves and women are in Book 1 of his *Politics.* On happiness, practical wisdom, moral education and the good life generally, see his *Nicomachean Ethics.*

Augustine. The vision of Augustine and Monica is in section 10 of Book IX of his *Confessions* (AD 397–8). On the distinction between the two cities, see the second half of *The City of God* (AD 426), especially Books 14, 15, 18 and 19. The quotations from Voltaire are from his articles on Original Sin and Wickedness in his *Philosophical Dictionary* (1767). Augustine's words on infants are from Book 1 of the *Confessions,* those on sexual ecstasy from his *Contra Julianum Pelagianum,* chapter 4.

De Tocqueville. The source here is *Democracy in America* (vol. 1, 1835; vol. 2, 1848). The quotations are all from vol. 2; charitable establishments and education, both from chapter 5 of Part IV; the immense protective power from chapter 6 of Part IV; social conditions being equal from chapter 21 of Part III. Democratic pantheism is discussed in chapter 7 of Part I. Mill writes against state education in chapter 5 of *On Liberty.*

Nietzsche. *The Birth of Tragedy* (1872); Socrates is discussed in sections 13–5. Aristotle on cleverness and practical wisdom, *Nicolomachean Ethics,* VI.12. Nietzsche on slave morality and its opposites, *Beyond*

257

Good and Evil (1886), section 9, *The Genealogy of Morals* (1887), essay 1; on suffering and pity, *The Gay Science*, Book 4, section 338; on the discipline of great suffering, *Beyond Good and Evil*, section 225; on men without chests, *Thus Spake Zarathustra* (1884), Book II, 'Of the land of culture'.

The Pessimism of the Nineteenth Century. John Ruskin on the division of labour, in *Stones of Venice* (1853), vol. II, chapter 6; Augustus Pugin, *An Apology for the Revival of Christian Architecture in England* (1843); C. S. Peirce quotation from his 'Review of Clark University, 1889–99 in *Science*, 1900, pp. 620–22.

Spengler. Oswald Spengler, *The Decline of the West* (1917), English translation, 1926. The distinction between culture and civilization is elaborated in the Introduction to volume 1, from which all the quotations are taken.

6: The Twentieth Century

Profit and Loss. Larkin's line is from his poem 'Churchgoing' in *The Less Deceived* (London, 1955); R. S. Thomas's lines are from 'In Church' in his *Selected Poems 1946–68* (Newcastle-upon-Tyne, 1986).

Religion. A useful introduction to Barth is *The Theology of Karl Barth: An Introduction* by Herbert Hartwell (London, 1964). The quotations from Barth are from *The Epistle to the Romans* (1919), pp. 97–9 of the English translation. G. K. Chesterton: the remark is indeed famous, but no one seems able to locate it. Is it apocryphal?

Philosophy. For an overview, see David E. Cooper, *World Philosophies*, (Oxford, 1996), Part III, sections 1 and 3. See also Roger Scruton, *Modern Philosophy* (London, 1994), particularly chapter 30 ('The Devil'). Wittgenstein's later philosophy: see his *Philosophical Investigations* (Oxford, 1953) and *On Certainty* (Oxford, 1969). Heidegger's *magnum opus* is *Being and Time* (1927). Useful pointers to his later thought are given in his lectures of 1935–6 entitled 'On the Origin of a Work of Art' (published in 1950). On the connection of his philosophy with Nazism, his tactical affectation of obscurity and his 'stratagem of the elect' (who alone would understand him, and who would not subject his oracular sayings to

the normal processes of interpretation and discussion), see Herman
Philipse's *Heidegger's Philosophy of Being* (Princeton, 1998), especially pp. 172–278.

Art. On epiphanic art and also on early modernism, see Charles
Taylor's *The Sources of the Self*, chapter 23 and 24. Thomas Mann's
writings on Wagner are usefully collected in *Thomas Mann: Pro and
Contra Wagner* (London, 1985). Nikolaus Pevsner's *An Outline of
European Architecture* (Harmondsworth, 1943) illustrates and dis-
cusses Arnos Grove tube station on its penultimate page and holds
forth on more exacting amenities in its penultimate paragraph. Jean
Baudrillard's words are from an interview, 'Games with Vestiges', in
On the Beach, vol 5, pp 19–25, 1984. Peter Fuller's *Theoria* (London,
1988) is a fascinating discussion of art and spirituality over the last
two centuries from a Ruskinian perspective. Now that Fuller is
dead, I can recommend nothing on recent art. I would suggest that
readers avoid critics and art historians, and simply look, listen and
think. After all, art should be able to speak direct to the well-
disposed, well-educated public without verbal intermediaries and
theoretical baggage. It has done so in every century but ours, and on
the whole the results have not been too bad.

Education and Psychology. Rousseau: once again, *Émile* is the primary
source. John Dewey's main treatise on education is *Democracy and
Education* (1916). A later work, *Experience and Education* (1938), is
supposed to moderate some of earlier progressiveness – though it is
there that Dewey rails against the teacher as external boss or
dictator. Also important are a number of short works Dewey wrote
on education in the 1890s while involved in experimental schools
in Chicago. The 'highly influential textbook' is Edgar Stones's *An
Introduction to Education Psychology* (London, 1966). The W. H.
Kilpatrick quotation is from his *Education for a Changing Civilisation*
(New York, 1929, pp. 49–50). For sub-Marxist theorizing about
education, see the immensely influential collection *Knowledge and
Control* (London, 1971), edited by M. F. D. Young, nearly thirty
years old now, but almost any educational text of the 1990s still
follows suit to a greater or lesser degree. Two recent books on
education that do buck the trend and recognize that we have a

deep cultural problem in education are Melanie Phillips, *All Must Have Prizes* (London, 1996) and George Walden, *We Should Know Better* (London 1996). Significantly neither author is an education professional. Also interesting as a counter to the received idea of the late twentieth century, that the state and only the state should run education is Andrew J. Coulson's *Market Education: The Unknown History* (New Brunswick, 1999).

On psychology I have drawn on a useful article entitled 'OBE: Outcome Based Education' by W. R. Coulson (a former research associate of both Rogers and Maslow), published by the Research Council on Ethnopsychology (1994). The quotation from Rogers is from 'Interpersonal Relationships: USA 2000', in the *Journal of Applied Behavioral Science* (1968), vol. 4, no. 3; those from Maslow are from of *The Journals of A. H. Maslow*, entries of 14 and 15 April 1969.

Politics. Nozick on taxation as a form of slavery, see his *Anarchy, State and Utopia* (Oxford, 1974). On rationalism in politics, see Michael Oakeshott's collection of that title (Indianapolis, 1992).

Media. On the early history of broadcasting in Britain in general and on the Third Programme in particular, see vol. 9 of *The Cambridge Guide to the Arts in Britain*, ed. Boris Ford (Cambridge, 1988), pp. 11–17 and 160–67. The quotation from Kenneth Clark is from his *Civilization* (London, 1971), p. 2. Pascal and staying quietly in one's room, see his *Pensées* (1662), no. 139.

Sport. Orwell, 'The Sporting Spirit' in *The Penguin Essays of George Orwell.*

Conclusion

Aeschylus, from the Chorus in *Agamemnon*, lines 161–84, as translated and interpreted by Simone Weil in her *Intimations of Christianity Among the Greeks* (London, 1987), pp. 56–9.

Index

A NOTE ON THE AUTHOR

Anthony O'Hear is Professor of Philosophy at the University of Bradford and Director of the Royal Institute of Philosophy. He has contributed many national publications, notably the *Daily Telegraph*, the *Daily Mail* and the *Daily Express*, and is the author of a number of books on philosophy, including *What Philosophy Is* and *Beyond Evolution*.

A NOTE ON THE TYPE

The text of this book is set in Bembo. The original types for which were cut by Francesco Griffo for the Venetian printer Aldus Manutius, and were first used in 1495 for Cardinal Bembo's *De Aetna*. Claude Garamond (1480–1561) used Bembo as a model and so it became the forerunner of standard European type for the following two centuries. Its modern form was designed, following the original, for Monotype in 1929 and is widely in use today.